THE MULTINATIONAL CORPORATION

FOREIGN PRIVATE MANUFACTURING INVESTMENT AND MULTINATIONAL CORPORATIONS: AN ANNOTATED BIBLIOGRAPHY

FOREIGN INVESTMENT, TRANSNATIONALS AND DEVELOPING COUNTRIES (with Paul Streeten)

THE GROWTH OF THE PHARMACEUTICAL INDUSTRY IN DEVELOPING COUNTRIES

DEVELOPING COUNTRIES IN THE INTERNATIONAL ECONOMY

DEVELOPING COUNTRIES AS EXPORTERS OF TECHNOLOGY

THE MULTINATIONAL CORPORATION

Nine Essays

Sanjaya Lall

© Sanjaya Lall 1980

All rights reserved. No part of this publication may be reproduced or transmitted, in any form or by any means, without permission

First edition (hardcover) 1980
Reprinted (paperback) 1983

Published by
THE MACMILLAN PRESS LTD
London and Basingstoke
Associated companies in Delhi
Dublin Hong Kong Johannesburg Lagos
Melbourne New York Singapore Tokyo

ISBN 978-0-333-28170-3 ISBN 978-1-349-05228-8 (eBook)
DOI 10.1007/978-1-349-05228-8

TO RANI

Contents

Preface	ix
Acknowledgements	xi

PART ONE: FOREIGN INVOLVEMENT AND STRUCTURE — 1

1 Monopolistic Advantages and Foreign Involvement by US Manufacturing Industry — 3
2 Transnationals, Domestic Enterprises and Industrial Structure in Host LDCs: A Survey — 29
3 Multinationals and Market Structure in an Open Developing Economy: The Case of Malaysia — 65

PART TWO: INTRA-FIRM TRADE AND TRANSFER-PRICES — 91

4 The Pattern of Intra-Firm Exports by US Multinationals — 93
5 Transfer-Pricing by Multinational Manufacturing Firms — 110
6 Transfer-Pricing and LDCs: Some Problems of Investigation — 137

PART THREE: THE INTERNATIONAL PHARMACEUTICAL INDUSTRY — 159

7 The International Pharmaceutical Industry and Less-Developed Countries — 161
8 Price Competition and the International Pharmaceutical Industry — 199
9 The Political Economy of Controlling Transnationals: The Pharmaceutical Industry in Sri Lanka — 216

Author Index	257
Subject Index	261

Preface

The nine essays presented in this book have been published in various journals over the past six years. I have brought them together mainly for the readers' convenience. Some of the original articles have not been easily accessible. Several of the essays complement each other and so are more useful placed together. And the subject, the multinational corporation, continues to exercise the popular and the academic mind.

No attempt was made to rewrite the papers or to link them into a continuous argument. Apart from making the obvious reference amendments, I left the essays as they stood. In part this was done because it was felt that the pieces retained sufficient interest in the original; partly because the essays ranged over a rather broad field, and to change and combine them would have required a massive effort not commensurate with the possible improvement in the product. Thus, the reader may find some changes in perspective and emphasis between the essays: this is only natural over the course of time and needs little explanation. He will also find terminological shifts: 'multinational' and 'transnational' are used interchangeably.

The essays have been divided into three parts. The first part, on foreign involvement and structure, starts with an analysis of the determinants of overseas expansion by US firms and of their choice between exports and foreign investment as the mode of expansion. The second essay surveys the literature on multinationals and their effects on domestic enterprises, industrial structure, industrial conduct and certain kinds of performance, in less-developed countries. The third presents a case study of the impact of MNCs on market structure, applying an econometric model of market-structure determination to Malaysia.

The second part deals with intra-firm trade and transfer prices. The first paper in this set uses the concepts of vertical integration theory to analyse the influences on intra-firm exports by US industries in 1970. The second discusses the possible motives for MNCs to manipulate the prices attached to intra-firm trade, and presents some data from Colombia. The third, aimed at policy makers in less-developed countries, goes into the various problems faced by host governments in investigating and assigning transfer-prices.

The third part presents three papers on one particular multinational industry – pharmaceuticals. The first of these argues that the normal method of operation of pharmaceutical multinationals entails several social and economic costs for less-developed host countries, and presents some information on the industry in India. The second debates whether price competition in the industry can be taken to be fully effective, and concludes that such competition, while it does exist, is unable to eliminate the market power of leading firms over the long run. The final essay, written jointly with (the late) Professor Bibile, presents a political-economic analysis of Sri Lanka's attempts to reform the pharmaceutical industry: this experience provides insights, not only into the realities of multinational operations, but also into the intricacies of providing medicines economically to poor countries.

My grateful thanks are due to all those who commented on the various drafts – specific acknowledgements are mentioned in each essay. I also wish to record my immense debt to, and great personal regard for, Senaka Bibile, my co-author for the last essay, whose untimely death deprived the Third World of a great champion of its right to adequate medication. The Oxford University Institute of Economics and Statistics provided the ideal *ambiance* for research: to its Director and Librarian, therefore, I owe thanks, and to all those who so efficiently typed various drafts of various manuscripts.

Acknowledgements

I would like to thank these journals for permission to reprint the following papers:

Chapter 1: 'Monopolistic Advantages and Foreign Involvement by US Manufacturing Industry', *Oxford Economic Papers*, vol. 32, no. 1 (Oxford: The University Press, Mar. 1980).

Chapter 2: 'Transnationals, Domestic Enterprises and Industrial Structure in Host LDCs: A Survey', *Oxford Economic Papers*, vol. 30, no. 2 (Oxford: The University Press, July 1978) pp. 217–48.

Chapter 3: 'Multinationals and Market Structure in an Open Developing Economy: The Case of Malaysia', *Weltwirtschaftliches Archiv*, Band 115 (Tübingen: J. C. B. Mohr, June 1979) pp. 325–50.

Chapter 4: 'The Pattern of Intra-Firm Exports by US Multinationals', *Oxford Bulletin of Economics and Statistics*, vol. 40, no. 3 (Oxford: Basil Blackwell, Aug. 1978) pp. 209–22.

Chapter 5: 'Transfer-Pricing by Multinational Manufacturing Firms', *Oxford Bulletin of Economics and Statistics*, vol. 35, no. 3 (Oxford: Basil Blackwell, Aug. 1973) pp. 173–95.

Chapter 6: 'Transfer-Pricing and Developing Countries: Some Problems of Investigation', *World Development*, vol. 7, no. 1 (Oxford: Pergamon Press, Jan. 1979) pp. 59–71.

Chapter 7: 'The International Pharmaceutical Industry and Less-Developed Countries', *Oxford Bulletin of Economics and*

Statistics, vol. 56, no. 3 (Oxford: Basil Blackwell, Aug. 1974) pp. 143–72.

Chapter 8: 'Price Competition and the International Pharmaceutical Industry', *Oxford Bulletin of Economics and Statistics*, vol. 40, no. 1 (Oxford: Basil Blackwell, Feb. 1978) pp. 9–21.

Chapter 9: 'The Political Economy of Controlling Transnationals: The Pharmaceutical Industry in Sri Lanka (1972–76)', with Senaka Bibile, *World Development*, vol. 5, no. 8 (Oxford: Pergamon Press, Aug. 1977) pp. 677–97.

Part One

Foreign Involvement and Structure

1 Monopolistic Advantages and Foreign Involvement by US Manufacturing Industry[1]

I INTRODUCTION

Recent years have witnessed a growing overlap between empirical analyses in three different branches of economics: the determinants of market concentration in industrial economics; the determinants of comparative advantage in trade theory; and the determinants of the growth of multinational corporations (MNCs) in the study of international direct investment.[2] The factors which have been found to lead to the emergence of oligopolistic structures within the industrialised countries have, to a large extent, been used by 'new' trade theorists to explain the growth of manufactured exports and by MNC analysts to explain the 'internationalisation of production' by manufacturing industry. The factors which, in other words, have been observed to cause the growth of large firms internally also seem to cause them to get more 'involved abroad' by exporting commodities and by setting up production affiliates. The concurrence between these various relationships is not exact, as we shall see later, but it is strong enough to merit more explicit attention than it has received till now.

Casual empiricism suggests that there is a good deal of common ground between internal oligopoly, export performance and overseas production. In advanced economies like the US, it is the large firms that grow to dominate their domestic industries which are also the main investors abroad, and it is these multinationals which account for some three quarters of the country's total exports of manufactured products.[3] It seems reasonable, therefore, to view the growth of firms within countries and their 'involvement' abroad – by exports and foreign production[4] – as closely linked processes, and to attempt to explain foreign involvement with reference to the factors that cause the emergence of large firms and, at the industry level, more concentrated market structures.

This paper seeks to achieve two things. First, it tries to explicitly relate the total foreign 'involvement' (i.e. exports plus foreign production) of US manufacturing industries in 1970 to several determinants of concentration – the 'barriers to entry of new competition' which confer monopolistic advantages on the dominant firms in each industry. In this, it extends the existing body of literature which has either explained total foreign involvement with reference to one or two monopolistic advantages (mainly advanced technology) or else has used such advantages to explain one or the other forms of involvement (exports or foreign production) separately. Secondly, it tries to explain the choice between the two forms of foreign involvement with reference to the *nature* of the monopolistic advantages possessed by various industries in the US. This choice has generally been explained by such factors as labour costs, market size, tariffs, and so on in specific foreign countries relative to the US. The relationship between the nature of the factors which lead to firm growth and foreign involvement and the form of such involvement has remained empirically unexplored.[5]

Section II presents the background to the literature. Section III lays out the main argument of this paper and the hypotheses to be tested. Section IV describes the variables used and the results of the empirical work. Section V draws the main conclusions.

II FOREIGN INVOLVEMENT AND MONOPOLISTIC ADVANTAGES

The increasingly concentrated structure of many manufacturing industries in advanced economies like the US, and the growing dominance of their leading firms over foreign involvement (in both forms) by those industries has prompted different sorts of attempts to integrate traditional explanations of industrial market structure within countries with those of foreign investment, foreign trade, or both together.

(a) Perhaps the most advanced of these is the integration of industrial organisation theory with explanations of direct foreign investment. Following upon the seminal thesis of Hymer, several theoretical and empirical studies[6] have argued that the possession of 'monopolistic advantages' at home is required before industries launch production abroad. Such advantages are considered necessary to offset the extra costs of setting up and operating facilities across geographical, cultural and legal boundaries.

The 'monopolistic advantages' that promote overseas production are taken to arise from the barriers to entry of new competition that promote concentrated market structures within countries. While the role of some of these factors in raising concentration is disputed in the industrial organisation literature, the following have been shown to provide a competitive edge to foreign investors: superior technology, product differentiation, large minimum capital requirements, scale economies and superior skills.[7] These are all *industrial* characteristics leading to the emergence of large dominant firms. It is also possible that, at the firm level, large *size* itself cumulatively creates other advantages apart from those conferred by industrial characteristics.[8] This is a question into which we cannot enter here. This paper only deals with industry-level data, so we make the simplifying assumption that size by itself does not confer a distinct monopolistic advantage. Thus, the behaviour of the leading firms in each industry is taken to be explicable only by the characteristics of the sectors to which they belong. By this assumption, we can talk interchangeably about industries and their dominant firms.

The studies that have demonstrated that the possession of monopolistic advantages in the US is positively associated with the propensity to produce abroad have assumed, implicitly or otherwise, that such advantages are great enough to overcome similar advantages presumably accruing to their counterparts abroad. If barriers to entry derive from inherent industrial characteristics, then the same barriers should exist in all locations, and the possession of monopolistic advantages in any one of them may not provide its firms with a sufficient competitive edge to break into foreign markets, unless the home economy is so large, technologically advanced or sophisticated in its consumption, that an advantage there also entails a differential advantage abroad.[9] This is, in fact, plausible as far as the US is concerned *vis à vis* other countries, and will be taken for granted here. However, it is not clear whether hypotheses tested on US evidence can be generalised to other countries, especially to small European countries (Holland and Switzerland) which have produced some large multinationals. This paper must, therefore, be taken to describe US industrial propensities and not necessarily those of other countries.

(b) The integration of industrial organisation with trade theory has not progressed as far as that of direct investment. The determinants of comparative advantage in the 'neo-Heckscher Ohlin' theorems (human capital or skills as well as physical capital) and 'neo-technology' theorems (technological leads, scale economies, product differentiation)[10] are practically identical with the entry barriers that account for internal concentration and for international investment. However, since the trade literature is concerned with country-level rather than industry- or firm-level characteristics, it does not distinguish between endowments possessed by a country in general (and so available to all firms equally) and those possessed by specific firms or industries (and so acting as monopolistic advantages).[11] It is obvious that many endowments would, given normal market imperfections, take the form of monopolistic advantages accruing to firms dominating particular industries. With only a slight shift of perspective, therefore, new trade theories could easily serve to explain how barriers to entry at home determine international competitiveness. As with direct investment, the assumption would have to be made that advantages that are manifested at home are large enough to provide an edge over counterparts in the same industries overseas.

The empirical tests conducted for both sets of trade theories suggest strongly that skill, technological and scale advantages promote international export competitiveness.[12] Since the same factors, with the important addition of product differentiation, also promote foreign production, they must also promote *total foreign involvement* by concentrated industries. Furthermore, to the extent that foreign production and exporting are alternative ways of serving foreign markets, these factors must (as Horst (1972b) notes) promote total involvement to a *greater extent* than they promote either component of such involvement.

No attempt has yet been made to relate total foreign involvement to the whole set of entry barriers that one normally associated with oligopolistic market structures. Three more limited tests have, however, been made: Horst (1972b) has tried to explain US involvement in Canada with reference to only one monopolistic advantage, technological superiority, finding that it does promote such involvement more than either component; Wolf (1977) also uses technology to explain US involvement abroad in general, and comes to the same result (he also uses firm size as an independent variable, but this does not help in the identification of which industrial advantage is at work); Dunning and Buckley (1977) add skill and scale variables to technology to explain the *relative* foreign involvement of US as compared to UK industries, but get poor statistical results. It seems appropriate, therefore, to try and explain total foreign involvement by US industry, as well as both its component forms, by using a comprehensive set of monopolistic advantages in order to clarify which advantages promote foreign involvement, and in what form. This then is the first aim of this essay.

(c) The integration of foreign investment and trade theory has been rigorously achieved in 'pure' trade theory, assuming perfect competition and capital mobility in a two-factor model (and treating the two as alternative means of serving foreign markets).[13] In a more realistic setting, however, with imperfect markets, many factors, and different production functions between countries, the integration has taken a more intuitive empirical form.[14] The choice between producing abroad and exporting to some given foreign market depends on two sets of factors – the mobility of the various factors of production and the costs of production at home and abroad – and both are difficult to determine with precision.

As far as factor mobility is concerned, the classical procedure in pure theory is to take labour as completely fixed in location and capital as fully mobile. Once production and transport costs are given and production functions in different locations specified, it is fairly straightforward to derive precise conclusions about exporting and foreign production. However, the introduction of other factors (the monopolistic advantages of MNCs) raises complications. Skilled labour, managerial and marketing knowhow, or process and product technology may be mobile but imperfectly so; moreover, their mobility may change over time as they become better diffused or standardised. In this case, while theoretically it is possible to derive rigorous conclusions about location once the nature of factor mobility is known[15] in practice this is extremely difficult to assess.

Empirical work on factor mobility as a realistic determinant of location has generally concentrated on one factor – new product technology – given labour immobility and capital mobility: this is the familiar 'product cycle' model, based on the pathbreaking work of Vernon (1966) and Hirsch (1969). The mobility of other factors which affect foreign involvement (skills, scale, product differentiation) has not been separately examined in order to discover how location decisions are made, but the product cycle model itself has been formulated in such a general way that it may cover all these factors. Perhaps because of this vagueness, and certainly because of its dynamic properties, it has not been properly tested.[16] The importance of technology in promoting exports and direct investment is well known,[17] and there is plenty of anecdotal evidence about life 'cycles' for particular technologies, but as an explanation of trade patterns the product cycle remains a general (and powerful) hypothesis rather than an established theory.[18]

As far as differences in production costs are concerned, the main difficulties in empirical work arise from comparing efficiency wages, minimum efficient sizes, import costs for traded goods (where important costs may be affected by arbitrary transfer prices) and the costs of non-traded goods, and the like, across countries: general and well-recognised problems which need not concern us here. What is more important is that the attempts that have been made to assess the effect of location-specific costs on the export/foreign production decision of MNCs[19] have abstracted from the effect of imperfect mobility of the production factors used by these firms in affecting their location. They have assumed that these factors are perfectly mobile: that the possession by MNCs of skill, technological or other advantages enables them to capture foreign markets, and that the choice of where to produce to serve those markets depends only on relative production (and physical transport) costs.

The possibility that the *imperfect transferability of monopolistic advantages across countries may influence the location of MNCs' production* has therefore escaped empirical examination (with the exception of the analysis of technology cycles), though the theoretical basis for such an influence is quite obvious. It is, in other words, possible that the factors which give rise to internal oligopolies not only provide the advantage necessary for particular industries to enter into foreign markets but also affect the location of production to serve these markets. This is not to deny the role of location-specific cost factors, only to stress the part played by industry-specific monopolistic advantages.[20] The second aim of this paper is, then, to demonstrate that the transferability of particular monopolistic advantages does affect the choice of how to serve foreign markets.

III TRANSFERABILITY OF MONOPOLISTIC ADVANTAGES

Each manufacturing industry in the US possesses a combination of skill, technology, marketing, scale and other advantages which enables it to penetrate foreign markets, to a greater or lesser extent, by exporting, producing abroad or both.[21] Each industry produces several products of different degrees of technological novelty, requiring different levels of skill and different intensities of promotion. It is assumed that tastes abroad are broadly similar to the US, or are slightly 'behind' it because incomes are somewhat lower. Production labour costs abroad are assumed to be lower, and raw materials and non-traded inputs are taken to be available at the same price as in the US.[22] Transport costs are assumed absent, and government measures such as tariffs or subsidies are assumed not to influence the overall choice of industries between exporting from the US and producing abroad. Finally, it is assumed that exports and foreign production are alternative methods of serving given foreign markets, that, in other words, the choice of method does not affect the size of the foreign market.

Under these simplifying assumptions, the *extent* of foreign involvement of each industry depends on its particular combination of monopolistic advantages, and the *form* of foreign involvement (by exports or foreign production) depends, given lower direct production costs abroad, on the transferability of those advantages from the US. The easier are an industry's advantages to shift abroad, the more will that industry choose to produce abroad, and the more 'tied' are the advantages to the US, the more will it choose to export. The deliberate exclusion of location-specific and transport costs thus enables us to see how far this particular explanation will take us.

Monopolistic advantages may be 'tied' to the US for two sorts of reasons: first, they are difficult, for institutional or cultural reasons, to shift abroad; and, second, they are tied to the head office, the technological infrastructure, the main market or the main production base because, for some time, they have to be exploited near one or both of these. The first renders an advantage permanently non-transferable. The second renders it temporarily non-transferable, imparting a 'cycle' effect: factors which exhibit such cycles will, at any time, possess advantages which are both non-transferable (and so promote exports) and fully transferable (and so promote foreign production). Depending on the significance of these two elements in the advantage as a whole, of course, there will be a net effect in favour of one or the other form of involvement.

Let us now examine the main monopolistic advantages used below to see whether *a priori* considerations enable us to set up hypotheses about their likely effects on foreign involvement.

TECHNOLOGY

The product cycle literature provides a convincing explanation of why new technology should experience a 'cycle' effect and why it has generally been found to promote both exports and foreign production.[23] In the early stages of innovation, there are both country-specific (large markets, technological infrastructure) and firm-specific (coordination required between scientific, engineering, production and marketing units) reasons for keeping production at home. In later stages, as techniques, skills and products become standardised, foreign demand grows and competition arises, it becomes an advantage which is easy and profitable to transfer abroad. We expect to find, therefore, that high-technology industries have a greater overall foreign involvement than others, and that they are also more prone to both export and produce abroad. The evidence does not, however, enable us to predict, given the size of total foreign markets served, which form of involvement is more important for technology intensive industries, and we must await the results of our tests.

PRODUCT DIFFERENTIATION

Though a controversial barrier to entry within countries,[24] product differentiation (generally, though perhaps not very accurately, represented by advertising intensity) has been found to lead to greater foreign production (Caves (1974), Horst (1975)), and in one study (Goodman and Ceyhun (1976)) also to higher export propensities. This suggests a 'cycle' effect, which runs counter to expectation. The ability to differentiate products successfully should be a highly transferable factor. Not only does it not require the close coordination of scientific, engineering, production and management functions that the introduction of new technology does, but its successful implementation necessitates that differentiation activity (packaging, colouring, appearance, performance, advertising) be carried out near the final markets. Given the basic design of the product, and given perhaps even the basic strategy of selling, we expect that high product differentiation propensities lead to foreign production and not to exports.

CAPITAL INTENSITY

High capital intensity is commonly regarded as a concentration-promoting factor because it requires large minimum investments, and given imperfections in capital markets, large firms can raise most easily the sums needed to establish efficient facilities. Since this is an advantage which MNCs can exercise anywhere, we expect it to promote foreign production rather than exports. As Jones (1970) has noted, the role of capital abundance in promoting exports of capital-intensive products becomes irrelevant once the operations of multinationals render it mobile across countries.

SCALE ECONOMIES

The existence of scale economies has been found to promote industrial concentration and higher exports as well as foreign production.[25] There is clearly a cycle-effect in operation here. New facilities are set up in the US and the benefits of scale are first reaped there; there is thus an initial non-transferability, which ends when the domestic facilities reach a certain size and foreign markets grow large enough to permit the transfer of capital for economic operations abroad. We expect to find, therefore, that scale economies promote both forms of foreign involvement; the balance of choice between them cannot (as with technology) be predicted.

SKILLS

This covers a variety of advantages exploited in foreign markets by firms, which fall into each of three groups: non-transferable, partially transferable and fully transferable. Non-transferable skill advantages are not, for institutional and cultural reasons, rendered mobile by the international activity of large firms: production-labour skills are the main example. Partially transferable skills are those which are introduced by particular industries or firms, and which are 'tied' to the US because skills related to new products, processes, organisational techniques, management practices, etc. necessarily take time to become standardised and get diffused from the head office to affiliates. In this, new skills follow the same 'cycle' as new technology. Fully transferable skills are 'standard' managerial and technical skills which can easily be deployed abroad by MNCs by shifting high-level manpower or by setting up training programmes and integrated managerial structures. Insofar as we can distinguish in practice between these different types of skills, therefore, we expect to find a mixture of effects for the skill factor.

In this model, therefore, both the extent and form of foreign involvement of US industries depend on the nature of the monopolistic advantages possessed by them: the product cycle sequence appears as a part of a larger complex of forces determining how and where they serve foreign markets. It may be worth repeating that our deliberate

12   *The Multinational Corporation*

abstraction from transportation and location-specific cost factors is not intended to deny their importance, but to see how far our own explanation can take us in understanding the export/foreign production propensities of US manufacturers.

IV THE EMPIRICAL TESTS

The US Tariff Commission's (1973) study of US MNCs provides the basic data on US and foreign production and exports in 1970 which are used here. A sample of 25 industries was extracted from data provided at the two and three digit levels;[26] an appendix to this paper shows the foreign involvement propensities of the sample and gives other sources of data.

THE DEPENDENT VARIABLES ARE:

USINVOL The total involvement of US industries in foreign markets, measured by total affiliate sales abroad plus total exports from the US,[27] expressed as a percentage of total US production (domestic sales plus exports) in each industry.

FP Foreign sales by US affiliates (excluding sales to the US) as a percentage of total US production in each industry, a measure of foreign production propensity.

USX Total exports (by MNCs and other firms) as a percentage of total US production in each industry, a measure of export propensity. FP and USX sum to USINVOL.

MNCX Exports by MNCs only as a percentage of total US production in each industry (data on domestic production by MNCs only are not available), a measure of MNCs' export propensity.

XCHOICE Exports by MNCs as a percentage of MNC exports plus affiliate sales abroad, an indicator of the choice of MNCs to use exports as the means to supply foreign markets.

The variable MNCX is very similar to USX, since MNCs account for such a large proportion of the country's exports (the simple correlation

Foreign Involvement by US Manufacturing Industry 13

coefficient between them is 0.825); however, it is useful to examine MNCX separately to see how its determinants differ from those of USX.

THE INDEPENDENT VARIABLES ARE:

RD Total research and development expenditures in each industry as a percentage of sales, the standard measure of technological intensity.

AD Advertising expenditures as a percentage of industry sales as a measure of product-differentiation propensity. There are some well-known problems with this measure, but at this level of aggregation it is impossible to find a better one.

KL Total net fixed assets in each industry divided by the total number of employees as a measure of capital intensity.

SCALE Value-added per establishment in each industry as a measure of scale economies. This measure, used, among others, by Hirsch (1977), suffers from the risk that large establishment size may capture other factors (such as market power based on advertising) besides production economies of scale. However, most scale-economy measures suffer from this problem,[28] especially at this level of aggregation, and this one at least has the advantage of ease of calculation.

SAL Salaried employees as a percentage of the total workforce in each industry. This measure is commonly used (e.g. Caves (1974)) to capture the availability of entrepreneurial resources in general. Since it is calculated from the *numbers* of salaried employees, it can be used to proxy the 'physical availability' (rather than skill levels) of managerial, marketing, technical and similar (non-production) personnel.

PW Average wage per production worker as a measure of the level of production skills (on our reasoning a non-transferable component of skill advantages) in each industry.

AW Average wage per employee, as a measure of the general level of skills (production and other) in each industry. This is similar to, but not identical with, SAL, since SAL captures 'spare capacity' in management. The use of AW as a skill measure involves assuming that market remunerations are commensurate to skill levels, i.e. that labour markets function more or less competitively.

No variables were employed to denote the size of firms or levels of industry concentration, since these are regarded more as the *result* of the various monopolistic advantages than a cause of such advantages, and we are interested in relating the advantages themselves to performance abroad. The statistical technique used is OLS multiple regression, with all the variables expressed in natural logarithms. Linear formulations were also tried; they yielded similar but less significant results.

Numerous studies using variables of the sort employed here have remarked on the incidence of multicollinearity between the independent variables. Indeed, given the nature of the variables it would be suspicious if they were *not* inter-related: innovative activity requires, and gives rise to, high skill levels and large establishments; capital-intensity leads to higher productivity and wages, and its 'lumpiness' gives rise to scale economies; establishments enjoying scale economies may require higher skills if their technical sophistication rises with size; and so on. Table 1.1 gives the simple correlation coefficients of the independent variable, and shows the expected inter-relations between the variables. Some coefficients are somewhat difficult to explain: why, for instance, should AD and SAL be so highly correlated, when SAL captures the availability of many other skilled personnel besides those engaged in marketing? The negative (but low) correlation between RD and KL is interesting: innovation is clearly not related to capital intensity, though it requires high skill levels. These collinearity problems force us to use the variables selectively, and call for very careful interpretations of the results.

Table 1.2 sets out the main findings for the first three dependent variables, which measure total US involvement abroad and its two components for all US firms (results for the export propensities and export choice of MNCs are described later). Each dependent is tried with the same independent variable (or set of variables), and we present the results in sets of three for ease of comparison.

The results serve to confirm many of the expectations advanced above. RD has a strong positive effect on the total foreign involvement of US industry and on both foreign production and export propensities,

TABLE 1.1 Simple correlation coefficients for independent variables

RD	1.00						
AD	0.268	1.00					
KL	−0.121	0.015	1.00				
SCALE	0.499	0.334	0.519	1.00			
SAL	0.400	0.696	0.198	0.404	1.00		
PW	0.164	0.130	0.543	0.456	0.472	1.00	
AW	0.535	0.257	0.449	0.610	0.638	0.838	1.00
	RD	AD	KL	SCALE	SAL	PW	AW

and the equations are all significant at 99 per cent. It explains more of the variation in total involvement than in either component, reinforcing the results obtained by Horst (1972b) and Wolf (1977). Unlike Horst, however, and in line with Wolf, we find that the significance and coefficients of RD are higher for export than for foreign production: the technological prowess of US manufacturing is more exploited by production for export than production abroad.

SCALE and AW have similar but less significant effects: they promote foreign involvement overall and in both its component forms, and 'explain' total involvement better than either of the components. However, SCALE is more significantly related to FP than to USX, while the opposite is the case for AW. Scale economies thus lend a significant competitive advantage to US industries, and seem to promote foreign production more than exports when tried on their own. When SCALE is tried with other variables, however, the emphasis changes, and the coefficients of export exceed those of foreign production.

For AW, the coefficients for export are always larger than those for FP (other regressions not shown here). Since AW covers the whole range of skills, it is difficult to decipher its effects clearly. The results are compatible with the hypothesis that some skills promote exports because they are non-transferable (production skills, which remain country specific, and new 'high level' skills, which are initially difficult to transfer abroad) and others promote direct investment because they are easily transferable. The results for PW (equation 8) weakly support this

16 The Multinational Corporation

TABLE 1.2 Determinants of foreign involvement, foreign production and export propensities

Equation		RD	AD	KL	SCALE	SAL	PW	AW	Const.	R^2
(1)	USINVOLV	0.510[a] (5.13)							−3.15	0.513[a]
	FP	0.489[a] (4.20)							−3.41	0.409[a]
	USX	0.618[a] (4.89)							−4.96	0.488[a]
(2)	USINVOLV				0.482[a] (3.23)				−4.18	0.282[a]
	FP				0.489[a] (3.01)				−4.53	0.251[a]
	USX				0.447[a] (2.20)				−5.50	0.138[b]
(3)	USINVOLV							2.559[a] (2.77)	−17.32	0.217[b]
	FP							2.263[b] (2.19)	−15.83	0.137[b]
	USX							2.988[a] (2.56)	−21.45	0.188[b]
(4)	USINVOLV	0.464[a] (4.69)	0.204[c] (1.71)						−3.57	0.551[a]
	FP	0.413[a] (3.84)	0.345[a] (2.67)						−4.11	0.533[a]
	USX	0.692[a] (5.76)	−0.335[b] (−2.32)						−4.27	0.570[a]

Eq.	Dep. Var.								const.	R^2
(5)	USINVOLV	0.500[a] (4.43)		0.222[c] (1.48)		0.406[a] (2.62)			−4.38	0.316[a]
	FP	0.449[a] (3.41)		0.359[b] (2.34)		0.365[b] (2.32)			−4.85	0.374[a]
	USX	0.719[a] (0.16)		−0.289[c] (−1.41)		0.546[a] (2.59)			−5.23	0.174[b]
(6)	USINVOLV				0.158 (0.901)		0.152 (0.474)		−4.43	0.500[a]
	FP				0.117 (0.571)		0.344 (0.918)		−5.04	0.398[a]
	USX				0.211 (0.972)		−0.603 (−1.52)		−4.28	0.502[a]
(7)	USINVOLV					0.413[a] (2.53)	0.388 (1.05)		−5.13	0.285[a]
	FP					0.395[b] (2.26)	0.526[c] (1.33)		−5.81	0.275[b]
	USX					0.475[b] (2.10)	−0.160 (−0.31)		−5.11	0.103
(8)	USINVOLV	0.463[a] (4.52)		0.203[c] (1.65)				0.094 (0.127)	−4.12	0.530[a]
	FP	0.417[a] (3.75)		0.348[a] (2.62)				−0.209 (−0.26)	−2.89	0.512[a]
	USX	0.689[a] (5.55)		−0.338[b] (−2.28)				0.202 (0.225)	−5.45	0.551[a]

NOTES

R^2 corrected for degrees of freedom; t value in parentheses. Levels of significance (one tail test) denoted: [a] significant at 99 %; [b] significant at 95 %; [c] significant at 90 %.

argument, in that production skills appear non-transferable, though they are far from reaching significance (to anticipate later results, however, it seems that PW does significantly promote exports rather than foreign production as far as MNCs, on their own, are concerned). So do the results for SAL (equations 6 and 7): the existence of relatively large numbers of salaried, and potentially mobile, personnel seems to promote foreign production rather than exports. While again the signs are not always statistically significant, the existence of 'spare capacity' in skilled personnel seems to provide a transferable advantage which outweighs the centralising pressure created by the introduction of new skills. There appears to be, as expected, a complex of different forces at work as far as skill advantages are concerned, but more refined tests are needed to test these findings, especially about the 'cycle' effect in introducing new skills.

AD has the expected positive effects on foreign involvement as a whole and on foreign production. As Horst (1975) found in his tests, the ability to differentiate products provides a significant advantage to US industries in undertaking investments abroad. Moreover, the results show clearly that this is a highly transferable advantage: AD has negative (and statistically significant) effects on the export propensities of US industries, contrary to the findings of Goodman and Ceyhun (1976). Equation 4, with RD and AD as the independent variables, 'explains' the maximum amount of variation in all three dependents; the addition of others reduces the explanatory power of the equation. It shows, moreover, that the inclusion of AD improves the performance of RD in explaining export performance: once the negative effect of product differentiation is taken into account, the advantage to exporting offered by technological factors appears even stronger than in equation 1, and the explanatory power of the USX regression exceeds that of the regressions for foreign involvement or foreign production. RD remains the stronger influence of the two in every equation.

KL fails to reach significance in any of the regressions; furthermore, in other tests not reported here, its sign changes erratically. It seems that it is not a factor which is important in influencing the foreign involvement propensities of US industries. In this, we concur with those studies which have cast doubts on the validity of simple Heckscher-Ohlin theories of comparative advantage. We further infer that capital intensity is not a significant source of monopolistic advantage for foreign production.

In sum, therefore, the findings of our tests so far suggest that there is a good deal of mileage in explanations of foreign involvement based only on the nature of monopolistic advantages. The factors that make for concentrated structures in industries within countries (in particular, technological and product-differentiation intensities), also influence, to a greater or lesser extent, the extent and form of their foreign involvement. The presence of firms producing internationally means that the possession of advantages which are easily transferred from the home country promotes direct investment, while the possession of advantages which are, temporarily or permanently, 'tied' to the home country promotes exports.

Let us now briefly consider the results for the dependent MNCX, the exports of MNCs as a percentage of total US production. This variable was used to see if there were differences between the influences on export propensities of all US firms and of MNCs separately. A markedly different pattern was not anticipated, of course, since MNCs account for nearly three-fourths of US exports, but it was expected that the strength of the various influences would differ. As MNCs are acknowledged leaders in innovation, skill creation as well as product differentiation, these were expected to have a greater influence on their export performance. Table 1.3 sets out the most interesting results. It may be noted that KL and SAL have been dropped from the independent variables because they failed to reach significance (SAL maintained its negative sign throughout).

A comparison with the results for USX in the previous table shows the following:

(a) The technological variable RD has a stronger and more significant positive effect on MNCX than on total US exports;
(b) the negative effect of AD persists, but is slightly weaker and less significant;
(c) SCALE has a stronger and more significant positive effect;
(d) PW is positive and achieves significance for MNCs; and
(e) AW has a much stronger and more significant positive effect.

In general the regressions 'explain' more for MNCs than for all US firms. Most of the results are expected; only two require further comment: the reduced significance and strength of AD, and the increased significance and strength of PW.[29] The product differentiation advantage, while still negatively related to export performance, has somewhat less of a retarding influence for MNCs than for all US firms, suggesting that the transfer of this advantage abroad also takes place through the activities of *non-US* firms, and poses more of a threat to the foreign involvement of non-multinationals than to MNCs (this

TABLE 1.3 Determinants of MNC export propensities

Equation	RD	AD	SCALE	PW	AW	Const.	R^2
(1)	0.675[a] (6.32)					−5.55	0.618[a]
(2)	0.727[a] (6.88)	−0.232[b] (−1.83)				−5.08	0.653[a]
(3)			0.553[a] (2.98)			−6.47	0.246[b]
(4)	0.703[a] (6.87)	−0.251[b] (−2.05)		1.257[c] (1.70)		−12.43	0.681[a]
(5)	0.610[a] (5.34)	−0.266[b] (−2.22)			1.702[b] (2.04)	−15.05	0.697[a]
(6)					3.68[a] (3.53)	−26.10	0.323[a]

NOTE
See Table 1.2.

does not, of course, reduce the positive role of AD in promoting foreign production by US multinationals). As far as PW is concerned, its increased importance for MNC rather than all US exports suggests that this is a significant non-transferable factor for firms which are able to shift other advantages abroad, and that production skills are a real country specific advantage to the international competitive position of the US.

So far we have drawn inferences about the transferability of advantages from total export and foreign production propensities. We can now tackle the question of how MNCs choose to exploit their advantages more directly, by taking the share of their exports in their total foreign sales as the dependent variable. This variable, XCHOICE, shows, for a *given foreign market*, which monopolistic advantages are transferred abroad by MNCs, and which tend to be exploited within the US.

Table 1.4 sets out the main results. KL has been excluded again for its failure to approach acceptable levels of significance, but SAL is included. We are particularly interested in the signs of the variables which exercised positive effects on both exports and foreign production: a positive sign in respect of XCHOICE indicates that, *on balance*, the variable promotes domestic rather than foreign production to serve foreign markets (by definition, it has a negative effect on the share served by foreign affiliates).

The most striking result in Table 1.4 is the powerful negative effect of AD on export choice; this variable 'explains', by itself, over a third of the variation in the dependent. Clearly, product differentiation is an advantage which strongly propels US MNCs to invest abroad rather than export from the US. RD serves, on the other hand, to promote exports, especially when AD is taken into account: given the extent of foreign involvement, therefore, technological advance tends to be exploited more at home than abroad.[30] Despite some recent criticisms of the product cycle theory, based on the observation that some internationally integrated MNCs are able to launch new products or processes in any country,[31] this finding supports the hypothesis that innovations are still strongly 'tied' to the home country. Economies of scale, production skills and general skills all seem to strengthen the propensities of US firms to use exports to serve given overseas markets, though the coefficients do not achieve high levels of significance. The possession of 'spare capacity' in the salaried workforce, however, promotes foreign production; once again, we find evidence of the tendency of the different skill measures to go in opposite directions.

TABLE 1.4 Determinants of MNC choice of exports to serve foreign markets

Equation	RD	AD	SCALE	SAL	PW	AW	Const.	R^2
(1)	0.155[c] (1.42)						−2.27	0.04
(2)		−0.395[a] (−3.63)					−0.774	0.34[a]
(3)	0.262[a] (3.35)	−0.479[a] (−5.11)					−1.29	0.54[a]
(4)						1.09[c] (1.37)	−8.50	0.04
(5)		−0.461[a] (−4.18)	0.202[b] (1.78)				−1.64	0.39[a]
(6)			0.014 (0.090)	−0.528[c] (−1.47)	1.620[c] (1.66)		−9.75	0.03
(7)		−0.456[a] (−4.25)	0.122 (0.99)			1.03[c] (1.47)	−7.37	0.43[a]

NOTE
See Table 1.2.

The signs of these variables are plausible, but they are not, apart from AD and RD, able to explain much of the variation in XCHOICE. Clearly, the location-specific factors (tariffs, transport costs, marketing factors, material costs, and so on) which have been excluded from this analysis play an important role in this choice. Indeed, it would be surprising if it were otherwise. What is interesting is that the 'transferability' explanation does take us as far as it does. It manages, despite its simplifications, to throw light on some neglected aspects of international involvement, and especially on the powerful joint influence of technology and product differentiation.

V CONCLUSIONS

This paper has sought to extend the common ground between empirical analyses of industrial concentration within countries, export performance and direct foreign investment, by using the determinants of concentration to analyse the 'foreign involvement' of US industries. The hypothesis, drawing upon (generally unrelated) work on trade and MNCs, is that the same factors that lead to greater internal concentration also lead, by affording the dominant firms certain 'monopolistic advantages', to greater success in foreign markets. However, since the existence of multinational companies enables certain advantages to be moved across countries, the nature of the advantages themselves is expected to influence the form of foreign involvement. Transferable advantages are expected to promote overseas production and non-transferable ones to promote exports.

Using a simple model which abstracts from location-specific costs of production abroad, it has been shown that there are significant associations between internal barriers to entry and foreign involvement, and that the 'transferability' of monopolistic advantage does influence the export-foreign production choice. Technological intensity serves, at different stages of the product cycle, to promote both exports and foreign production, but on balance it favours exports as a means of serving foreign markets. The product differentiation advantage appears to be highly transferable, and to promote foreign production instead of exports. Capital intensity does not show any statistically significant influence on either form of foreign involvement. Scale economies and the possession of production and other skill advantages have similar effects to technological intensity, though their influence is statistically somewhat weaker. The possession of large numbers of salaried personnel serves to promote foreign production rather than exports. The combination of technological and product-differentiation factors exercises the largest effects on foreign involvement in all its forms: they seem to be the main 'engines of growth' behind the overseas expansion of US industries.

In general, therefore, it seems that the use of an approach linking these different disciplines is a fruitful one. It confirms the interrelationships between different forms of entry into foreign markets, and it takes account of the observed fact that both exports and foreign investment are largely accounted for by the same firms, which are also dominant in their home countries. Despite its obvious simplifications, it suggests strongly that any study of international involvement which leaves one or the other of these aspects out of account may be rather unrealistic.

APPENDIX

TABLE A.1.1 International involvement of US industries (1970) (percentage)

Industry	FP	USX	MNCX	XCHOICE	USINVOLV
1. Grain Mill Products[1]	11.7	2.0	2.0	14.9	13.7
2. Beverages[1]	8.3	0.4	0.4	5.3	8.7
3. Other Food Products[1]	7.4	1.0	1.0	13.8	8.4
4. Paper	9.1	4.3	2.3	20.5	13.4
5. Pharmaccuticals	39.0	5.8	5.0	11.3	44.8
6. Soaps, Cosmetics[1]	30.9	1.5	1.5	5.0	32.4
7. Industrial Chemicals	14.9	9.5	7.1	32.4	24.4
8. Plastics	29.5	6.9	3.3	10.2	36.4
9. Other Chemicals	20.6	9.7	3.1	13.2	30.3
10. Rubber	17.1	3.0	2.4	12.3	20.1
11. Primary Metals	3.3	3.7	2.3	41.5	7.0
12. Fabricated Metals	13.4	2.8	2.4	15.6	16.2
13. Farm Machinery	17.6	12.5	7.8	30.7	30.1
14. Other Machinery & Electronic Components	54.3	17.0	10.7	16.5	71.3
15. Industrial, 'Other' Machinery	11.4	12.3	4.8	29.7	23.7
16. Household, 'Other' Electrical Equipment	29.3	7.2	2.2	7.2	36.5

TABLE A.1.1 (continued)

Industry	FP	USX	MNCX	XCHOICE	USINVOLV
17. Electrical Equipment[1]	20.0	6.6	6.6	31.7	26.6
18. Electronic, T.V., Radio	9.6	4.6	2.8	22.8	14.2
19. Transport equipment[1]	20.0	8.6	8.6	30.1	28.6
20. Textiles	3.6	1.9	0.5	12.4	5.5
21. Lumber, Wood, Furniture	5.1	1.6	1.5	23.5	6.7
22. Printing, and Publishing	2.6	1.2	0.5	17.4	3.8
23. Stone, Clay, Glass	11.0	2.0	1.5	12.3	13.0
24. Instruments	21.7	8.7	6.5	23.3	30.4
25. Other Manufacturing	22.5	5.6	2.0	8.3	28.1

NOTES
For explanation of variables see main text.
1. Total US exports in these six sectors were shown as less than reported US MNC exports in Table A-21 of US Tariff Commission (1973); to reconcile the two figures we assumed that US exports equalled the value of MNC exports.

SOURCE
Data on production, sales, wages, assets and exports were taken from the US Tariff Commission (1973). R & D data were taken from the National Science Foundation, *Research and Development in Industry 1973*, Washington, DC, 1975. Advertising data were taken from the *Statistical Abstract of the United States, 1972*, and Comanor and Wilson (1974); some of these data pertained to different years, but were left unchanged on the assumption that advertising propensities at broad industrial levels were fairly stable. A few interpolations had to be made to fill in gaps in advertising data from Bailey (1975). Since his figures are presented on a different basis, adjustments based on comparable items had to be made.

NOTES

1. The author is grateful to Dermot McAleese, Ajit Singh, Raymond Vernon and an anonymous referee of Oxford Economic Papers for comments, and particularly to Robert Bacon for extensive discussions and very helpful suggestions at various stages of preparing this paper.
2. For a recent survey see Dunning (1977a).
3. For data on the role of large firms in international investment and trade see the UN (1973); for a comprehensive analysis of US MNCs see the US Tariff Commission (1973). Bergsten, Horst and Moran (1978) and Goodman and Ceyhun (1976) comment on the role of large corporations in US exports and foreign investment.

Foreign Involvement by US Manufacturing Industry 25

4. The licensing of technology and sales of various services abroad are another form of foreign involvement, but, following most studies in this field, we abstract from it here.
5. For a theoretical analysis which links them, however, see Hirsch (1976). For a survey of empirical work on the choice between exports and foreign production see Dunning (1977b).
6. For theoretical explanations see Caves (1971), Dunning (1973) and Kindleberger (1969), and for empirical works see Horst (1972a), (1975), Dunning (1977b), Caves (1974), and Baumann (1975).
7. The role of product differentiation as a barrier to entry is particularly controversial (see Ornstein *et al.*, 1972), and it is possible, though we shall abstract from this, that the causation runs from concentration to differentiation rather than the other way around. Furthermore, skill advantages are not generally counted as an entry barrier, since skilled labour is taken to be equally available to all firms in a country. If, however, certain managerial, technical or marketing skills are created within particular organisations by their own activities, they become firm specific and so afford an advantage not possessed by others. For international operations, in particular, a highly developed organisational structure, with integrated communications across countries, can serve as a formidable entry barrier to potential competitors.
8. Large firm size may, for instance, provide underutilised managerial resources, privileged access to capital markets, special relations with governments, spare internal finance, and so on, which may enable them to expand in the same sector or to enter unrelated sectors by take-over. The diversification of large firms *across* industries within the home country is studied by Wolf (1977) but it has not, for lack of data, been studied for conglomerate activity across countries: we ignore it in this paper. For the influence of size on foreign expansion see Wolf (1977) and Horst (1975).
9. Furthermore, certain 'feedbacks' are possible from foreign expansion, which cannot be considered here: for instance, foreign spread may afford certain advantages of geographical diversification which strengthen entry barriers at home (Horst, 1975), and it may raise entry barriers in host countries so that the differential between foreign and local firms rises over time, especially in LDCs (see Chapter 3).
10. The literature on recent comparative advantage theory is too vast to describe here, but see Grubel and Lloyd (1975), Hufbauer (1970) and Hirsch (1977) for surveys.
11. See Dunning (1977a) for a longer discussion.
12. For recent comprehensive tests and reviews of findings see Goodman and Ceyhun (1976) and Hirsch (1977).
13. See Jones (1970) and Ferguson (1978) for the role of capital mobility in a neo-classical framework with technological differences between countries.
14. For a short but succinct analysis see Corden (1974). For an exposition of the determinants of location from the MNC's point of view see Hirsch (1976), Vernon (1974) and Dunning (1977a and b).
15. See Corden (1974) pp. 196–8.
16. Hirsch (1977). An even more general formulation by Magee (1977) applies

26 *The Multinational Corporation*

'life cycles' to entire industries: his theory is subjected to very simple, and unsatisfactory, empirical tests.
17. Gruber, Mehta and Vernon (1967).
18. Professor Vernon notes (in private correspondence) that the cycle effect has depended, not only on dynamic changes in the nature of the technology, but also on the historical evolution of factor costs and incomes abroad. 'The products innovated in the US found an easy export market abroad, partly because subsequent factor cost changes in foreign countries brought those countries closer to the pattern of the US economy; that is to say, labour costs increased relative to other costs, and per capita income rose.' Thus, the hypothesis has been advanced to explain particular historical developments (1950s and 60s) in particular countries (Europe & Canada), and not as a general trade theory: any criticisms based on its diffuse character are therefore somewhat misplaced.
19. See Horst (1972b) and Dunning (1977b). The factors used have been relative market size and growth, tariff rates and labour costs.
20. We assume that location decisions are not affected by oligopolistic, 'follow-the-leader' interaction between the leading firms; for a study of such interaction see Knickerbocker (1973).
21. An oligopolistic advantage in the US is taken to give a competitive edge over producers abroad, as discussed above.
22. Information about foreign markets is included in these inputs.
23. See Vernon (1966), (1974), and Gruber, Mehta and Vernon (1967).
24. See Ornstein *et al.* (1972) and Comanor and Wilson (1970).
25. See Hirsch (1977), Dunning (1973), Vernon (1974) and Caves (1974).
26. Where a three-digit industry (e.g. drugs) was used, the relevant two-digit industry (chemicals) was dropped. This mixture of different levels of aggregation is acceptable in this case because the 9 two-digit sectors seem homogeneous enough to permit meaningful comparison with the 16 three digit ones.
27. It is not clear whether the Tariff Commission's figures on affiliate sales include or exclude the resale of finished products exported from the US. However since that study does add total exports to affiliate sales to show total US 'penetration' of foreign markets (p. 374), we assume that there is no double-counting involved.
28. See Caves *et. al.* (1975), and Ornstein *et. al.* (1972).
29. To test the difference between USX and MNCX further, we constructed another dependent variable – the percentage of US exports accounted for by MNCs in each industry – and regressed this on all the independent variables. Most variables (including RD) failed to approach significance. However, AD came out with a positive sign, and almost achieved significance; PW was the only other variable to exert an influence and the equation was $1.143 PW^b - 7.22$, $R^2 = 0.10$, $F = 3.58$. The (1.89) coefficient was significant at 95 per cent. These results support the remarks made in the text.
30. Wolf (1977) tests the effect of firm size as the inverse of XCHOICE (i.e. on the choice to serve given foreign markets by overseas production) for US industries, and finds that large size tends to promote foreign production rather than exports. This result cannot, unfortunately, be compared to

ours, since we do not have a variable for firm size (SCALE measures average plant size); it may, however, be due to AD being strongly associated with firm size in Wolf's sample.
31. See, for instance, Leroy's (1976) examination of the behaviour of 5 US MNCs.

REFERENCES

Bailey, E. L. (1975), *Marketing Cost Ratios of U.S. Manufacturers* (New York: The Conference Board).
Baumann, H. G. (1975), 'Merger Theory, Property Rights and the Pattern of US Direct Investment in Canada', *Weltwirtschaftliches Archiv*, pp. 676–98.
Bergsten, C. F., Horst, T. O. and Moran, T. (1978), *American Multinationals and American Interests* (Washington, DC: Brookings Institution).
Caves, R. E. (1971), International Corporations: The Industrial Economics of Foreign Investment', *Economica*, pp. 1–27.
—— (1974), 'Causes of Direct Investment: Foreign Firms' Shares in Canadian and United Kingdom Manufacturing Industries', *Review of Economics and Statistics*, pp. 279–93.
Caves, R. E., Khalilzadez-Shirazi, J. and Porter, M. E. (1975), 'Scale Economies in Statistical Analyses of Market Power', *Review of Economics and Statistics*, pp. 133–40.
Comanor, W. A. and Wilson, T. A. (1970), *Advertising and Market Power* (Cambridge, Mass.: Harvard University Press).
Corden, W. M. (1974), 'The Theory of International Trade', in J. H. Dunning (ed.), *Economic analysis and the Multinational Enterprise* (London: Allen & Unwin).
Dunning, J. H. (1973), 'The Determinants of International Production', *Oxford Economic Papers*, pp. 289–336.
—— (1977a), 'Trade, Location of Economic Activity and the MNE: A Search for an Eclectic Approach', in B. Ohlin, *et al.* (ed.), *The International Allocation of Economic Activity* (London: Macmillan).
—— (1977b), 'Trade, Location of Economic Activity and the MNE: Some Empirical Evidence', University of Reading, Discussion Papers in International Investment and Business Studies, no. 37.
Dunning, J. H. and Buckley, P. J. (1977), 'International Production and Alternative Models of Trade', *The Manchester School*, pp. 392–403.
Ferguson, D. G. (1978), 'International Capital Mobility and Comparative Advantage: The Two Country, Two Factor Case', *Journal of International Economics*, pp. 373–96.
Goodman, B. and Ceyhun, F. (1976), 'US Export Performance in Manufacturing Industries: An Empirical Investigation', *Weltwirtschaftliches Archiv*, pp. 525–5.
Grubel, H. G. and Lloyd, P. J. (1975), *Intra-Industry Trade* (London: Macmillan).
Gruber, W. H., Mehta, D. and Vernon, R. (1967), 'The R & D Factor in International Trade and International Investment of US Industries', *Journal of Political Economy*, pp. 20–37.

Hirsch, S. (1969), *Location of Industry and International Competitiveness* (London: Oxford University Press).
—— (1976), 'An International Trade and Investment Theory of the Firm', *Oxford Economic Papers*, pp. 258–70.
—— (1977), *Rich Man's Poor Man's and Every Man's Goods* (Tübingen: J. C. B. Mohr).
Horst, T. (1972a), 'The Industrial Composition of US Exports and Subsidiary Sales to the Canadian Market', *American Economic Review*, pp. 37–45.
—— (1972b), 'Firm and Industry Determinants of the Decision to Invest Abroad: An Empirical Study', *Review of Economics and Statistics*, pp. 258–66.
—— (1975), 'American Investment Abroad and Domestic Market Power', (mimeo) (Brookings Institution). Subsequently published in Bergsten, Horst and Moran (1978) ch. 7.
Hufbauer, G. C. (1970), 'The Impact of National Characteristics and Technology on the Commodity Composition of Trade in Manufactured Goods', in R. Vernon (ed.), *The Technology Factor in International Trade* (New York: National Bureau of Economic Research).
—— (1975), 'The Multinational Corporation and Direct Investment', in P. B. Kenen (ed.), *International Trade and Finance* (London: Cambridge University Press).
Jones, R. W. (1970), 'The Role of Technology in the Theory of International Trade', in R. Vernon (ed.), *The Technology Factor in International Trade* (New York: National Bureau of Economic Research).
Kindleberger, C. P. (1969), *American Business Abroad* (New Haven: Yale University Press).
Knickerbocker, F. T. (1973), *Oligopolistic Reaction and Multinational Enterprise* (Harvard: Graduate School of Business Administration).
Leroy, G. (1976), *Multinational Product Strategy* (New York: Praeger).
Magee, S. P. (1977), 'Information and the Multinational Corporation: An Appropriability Theory of Direct Foreign Investment', in J. N. Bhagwati (ed.), *The New International Economic Order* (Cambridge, Mass.: MIT Press).
Ornstein, S. I. et al. (1972), 'Determinants of Market Structure', *Southern Economic Journal*, pp. 612–25.
United Nations (1973), *Multinational Corporations in World Development* (New York: UN).
US Tariff Commission (1973), *Implications of Multinational Firms for World Trade and Investment and for US Trade and Labor* (Washington, DC: GPO).
Vernon, R. (1966), 'International Investment and International Trade in the Product Cycle', *Quarterly Journal of Economics*, pp. 190–207.
—— (1974), 'The Location of Economic Activity', in J. H. Dunning (ed.), *Economic Analysis and the Multinational Enterprise*, (London: Allen and Unwin).
Wolf, B. M. (1977), 'Industrial Diversification and Internationalisation: Some Empirical Evidence', *Journal of Industrial Economics*, pp. 177–91.

2 Transnationals, Domestic Enterprises and Industrial Structure in Host LDCs: A Survey[1]

I INTRODUCTION

This paper reviews the literature on the relationships between transnational corporations (TNCs) in the manufacturing sector and domestic enterprises as well as industrial structures in host LDCs. There are two broad sets of relationships involved, both of which are of significance for understanding the effects of TNCs on host economies and to the formulation of policy. The 'direct' relationships that TNCs strike up with local suppliers or purchasers (backward and forward 'linkages' in the Hirschman sense) can constitute powerful mechanisms for stimulating (or retarding) economic, and particularly industrial, growth in LDCs. The 'indirect' effects that the entry and operations of TNCs may have on local industrial structure, conduct, and performance may be equally important: TNCs may change the nature and evolution of concentration; they may affect the profitability and growth of indigenous firms; they may alter financing, marketing, technological, or managerial practices of the sectors that they enter; they may, by predatory conduct, drive domestic firms out of business; and so on.

The continuing debate on the costs and benefits of TNCs for poor host countries[2] has touched upon several of these issues, but the outcome has, in the absence of sufficient empirical work of real value or relevance, remained unclear. Policy making has continued to rely on generalisations drawn from scanty evidence, or, more commonly, on *a priori* beliefs about the behaviour and impact of TNCs. It is hoped that the present survey will indicate how much is known about the direct and indirect effects of TNCs on domestic enterprises, and how much remains unknown. Section II deals with direct 'linkages'; section III

II DIRECT LINKAGES

Direct linkages may be defined to constitute those relationships between TNCs and domestic enterprises trading with them that have led the latter to respond, positively or otherwise, to technological, pecuniary, marketing, or entrepreneurial stimuli provided by the former.[3] A 'linkage' in this sense is clearly different from a normal transaction in a competitive market; it refers essentially to *externalities* created for domestic industry by the entry of TNC investment. The classic general discussion of the role of linkages in the development of LDCs is by Hirschman (1958), who proposes a deliberate strategy of creating imbalances to harness the forces of entrepreneurship and growth that lie latent in every economy. Particular investments are thus supposed to create such strong external economies in sectors that supply or buy from them that new investments are undertaken in order to exploit them; foreign investment is assigned a vital role, 'to enable and to embolden a country to set out on the path of unbalanced growth . . . [and] to take the first "unbalancing" steps in growth sequences'.[4]

While it is obvious that TNC investments can create strong local linkages in this sense, and indeed the policies of many host LDCs to compel TNCs to maximize their purchase of local inputs have aimed at exploiting these linkages, it is far from clear how the actual experience of TNCs in LDCs is to be evaluated. The normal procedure, of using the proportion of local to total purchases by TNCs as an indicator of backward linkages, is inadequate, since it does not take account of externalities and does not enable us to assess the 'efficiency' of linkage creation. Though it may serve as a crude approximation to the outer limits of the stimulus aprovided by TNCs to local enterprises, it does not, for instance, show (a) if the local enterprises would have been set up in the absence of TNC investments; (b) whether they gained or lost by having TNCs as major customers (where this is the case); (c) if the host economy could have created the same linkages at lesser cost, say by replacing the TNC by a local firm; (d) if the linked local enterprises are desirable from the social point of view (where the linkages are fostered behind heavy protective barriers); and (e) whether negative linkages were created by stifling potential local investment. The proper economic evaluation of linkages must be based on a case-by-case cost/benefit examination of actual situation and plausible alternatives, necessarily a difficult and impressionistic procedure; however, the existence and desirability of TNC linkages can only be judged by some such method. Let us now consider how the existing literature has treated the issue.

Our review is confined to *backward* linkages, since there appears to be hardly any emperical work on forward linkages created by TNCs: perhaps not a great omission, since forward linkages cannot be expected to be very strong. We may consider backward linkages for the two main forms of TNC investment—import-substituting and export-orientated—separately, as the issues raised are rather different.

IMPORT-SUBSTITUTING TNCs

The vast bulk of foreign manufacturing investment in LDCs has gone into protected import-substituting activities, where governments have been able, especially in the larger and more industrialised areas, to push firms into buying large proportions of their inputs from local sources. TNCs have, consequently, developed extensive and long-standing relationships with local enterprises in countries like India, Mexico, Brazil, Argentina, and so on. Despite the significance of the phenomenon, however, the existing work on TNCs has paid scant attention to examining the economic benefits and costs of the linkages created.

Most of the studies of foreign investment in LDCs have simply noted the extent of local purchasing by TNCs and sometimes remarked on the general difficulties of local procurement (due to technological backwardness, small scale, high cost, poor quality, or unreliability) without attempting to analyse the linkages created in any detail. Thus, a study of six developing countries commissioned by UNCTAD produced data on the import propensities of 159 firms, foreign and domestic, in Kenya, Jamaica, India, Iran, Colombia, and Malaysia, without going into the economics of domestic purchase.[5] Similarly, studies of US investment in LDCs in general,[6] Peru,[7] Iran,[8] South Korea,[9] Malaysia,[10] and some others,[11] have discussed the use of local inputs by TNCs. The general findings, that TNCs buy relatively few inputs within the less-industrialised host economies but may be forced or persuaded to increase local content by the more advanced ones, add little to our understanding of the significance or desirability of the externalities created in LDCs.

There are three other studies which may be mentioned separately because they tackle the issue of TNC linkages more directly. Reuber and associates (1973), using information provided by the head offices of

TNCs, noted that import-substituting investments created far more local linkages than export-orientated ones, and found, for sixty-four sample firms, that 45 per cent of inputs in 1970 came from local sources. Parent companies were asked whether their operations had given rise to local suppliers or distributors, and their answers indicated that some one-third of the investments had directly given rise to such local activity. Reuber made no attempt to assess the costs and benefits of such linkages, and also qualified the estimates by noting that 'such figures must be viewed with some suspicion both because of the many conceptual and practical difficulties in deriving estimates of this kind and because of the vested interest of respondents in presenting the spin-off effects of their activities in as favourable a light as possible' (p. 156).

Watanabe (1972a and 1974b), in his examination of subcontracting in LDCs, presents a general but useful analysis of this particular (and rather strong) form of linkage.[12] Though he is not concerned exclusively with TNCs, he cites examples of foreign firms (like Singer in South East Asia) which have used subcontracting successfully, and concludes that such activity, 'by stimulating entrepreneurship and encouraging industrial efficiency, can help to promote the industrialisation of the less-developed countries and thus create the additional employment opportunities they badly need'.[13] He analyses the conditions for success of such linkages (which he terms 'within-border industrial subcontracting'), briefly notes the contribution that TNCs may make by providing assistance with investment, technology and quality control, and recommends policies for increasing linkages; he does not, however, examine in detail any specific instances of subcontracting by foreign firms. In his 1974b paper he examines the problems of subcontracting in India (though without discussing the role of TNCs), and compares its experience to the highly successful one of Japan.

A more pessimistic view of the virtues of local purchasing emerges from Baranson's study of the Cummin's diesel-engine project in India and his analysis of the automotive industry in LDCs generally.[14] He comments at length on the problems raised by the high cost, poor quality, and unreliability of local suppliers in cases where the government has forced the pace of buying local inputs,[15] and discusses the reasons for this state of affairs (protection, technological and skill shortages, lack of experience, small scale, and the like). We must not, however, draw unfavourable general conclusions about the desirability of linkages or the capabilities of local enterprises from this experience: there are several other industries (see below) where domestic linkages have been economically viable, and even for India the recent boom in exports of medium-to-high technology goods (including transport equipment, chemicals, and engineering goods) indicates that some of the problems described by Baranson for the 1960s may have been the teething difficulties of launching new and complex industrial processes.

To return to TNCs, however, we find that we are left with very little empirical work on the process and value of creating linkages.[16] The general impression conveyed by the literature is that TNCs establish relatively few linkages in small or industrially backward economies; that in larger economies they may create extensive linkages, mostly because of government pressure; and that a substantial part of these linkages in import-substituting industries may be excessively costly and uneconomical.[17] This is all in line with *a priori* expectation, but it is sadly inadequate in explaining the specific nature of the linkages that have been created, and in providing the sort of evaluation of their social value that was described earlier.

EXPORT-ORIENTATED TNCs

The recent growth of manufactured exports from LDCs by foreign firms has attracted a great deal of attention, and the creation of linkages, especially by subcontracting, has often been mentioned in this context.[18] In contrast to the inefficiency usually associated with linkages in import-substituting industries, it may be expected that linkages created by firms competing in world markets will be more efficient and beneficial for the host economies (at least in a narrow technical sense, without referring to distributional, social, or political effects). It would be useful to start by distinguishing four types of export-orientated TNCs which have different implications for the creation of domestic linkages.

First, there are TNCs which started by substituting for imports and have grown internationally competitive enterprises with substantial export interests (VW in Brazil or Singer in Asia may be good examples). Such activities usually involve technologies which are stable and not very sophisticated, and they are based in areas with a cheap but relatively skilled labour force and an experienced indigenous sector. The use of the TNCs' marketing networks and established brandnames are important in such export activity. These TNCs may have established considerable domestic linkages in the early phases, though, of course, the extent and nature of these linkages may change as they gear themselves for world markets.

Second, there may be foreign firms which produce and export

'traditional' products like footwear, textiles, processed foods, or sports goods. For those industries (like textiles) where technology is easily available and product differentiation is insignificant, the foreign firms involved may be buying groups, retailers, or small manufacturers (sometimes from other LDCs, like Hong Kong firms in Malaysia) rather than TNCs proper. For those (like food processing) where product differentiation, marketing, or product innovation are important, however, large TNCs may predominate in production and export activity.[19] In both cases, there exists a vast potential for linkages with domestic producers, who may manufacture components or whole products for foreign firms.

Third, there are new TNC investments in 'modern' industries in LDCs undertaken specifically for export, transferring fairly complex technologies to LDCs to service established world markets. A constellation of factors (labour and transport costs, the nature of the technology, need for short production-runs, managerial requirements, and, of course, political stability)[20] influences the decision to locate such investments, good examples of which are the Philips and General Electric complexes in Singapore, or some 'border industries' in Mexico; the availability of local components is not, however, one of the important factors attracting them. In most cases, such investments are tightly controlled from abroad, the components and processes may be quite advanced, and there may not be much scope for local linkages. It is possible, nevertheless, that local enterprises may be able to provide some products at the right price and quality, and a few linkages may develop in the more advanced of the host economies.[21]

Fourth, there are 'sourcing' investments where only a particular (labour-intensive) process is transferred to LDCs, the more capital-intensive processes being retained in the home countries where the requisite equipment, skills, and R and D facilities exist. The best-known example of this is the electronics industry, especially the semiconductor sector, where the demanding specifications, the rapidly changing technology, and requirements of cost minimisation reduce the scope for domestic linkages to practically nothing.[22]

Of these four types of TNC investment, the first two are likely to create the most linkages, the third rather less, and the fourth least of all. The extent of linkages created in particular LDCs depends upon the stage of development of indigenous industry, the availability of local skills and technology, institutions and government policies, changes in demand and technology in world markets and their political attractiveness to TNCs.[23] The main benefits of such investment are generally supposed to be employment creation, export promotion (though net foreign exchange benefits may be very low for the third and fourth groups that depend heavily on imported components), skill and technology transfer (particularly in the first and second, sometimes the third, groups), and the stimulation of local linkages (see below). The main costs mentioned are the generous fiscal and infrastructural incentives that LDCs have to offer (especially for investments in the fourth category), the socio-political constraints of having to ensure a docile and low-cost labour force, the danger of losing 'footloose' TNCs when costs rise, the risk of getting poor terms from monopsonistic buyers, and the instability of demand for exports. Of these, the danger of 'footloose' behaviour does not seem to have been realised;[24] fiscal concessions certainly have been generous; TNCs have clearly shown a marked preference for stable regimes with little or no labour problems; the incidence of 'squeezing' local firms needs further investigation; and export market instability is not a particular feature of TNC exports. On the whole, the benefits seem to have outweighed the costs with LDCs, and many of them are now seeking to attract TNCs or foreign buying groups.[25]

Besides the general studies of this phenomenon mentioned above, a number of country studies have discussed export-orientated foreign investment (and subcontracting) for Mexico,[26] Hong Kong,[27] Singapore,[28] the Caribbean,[29] and Taiwan.[30] Nearly all of them – with the exceptions of Evers (1977) and Fernandez (1973) – have come to favourable conclusions about the net benefits of such activity to host LDCs, but their discussion of linkages as such has remained desultory and unsatisfactory. There are some impressionistic and anecdotal accounts[31] of the potential for creating beneficial linkages which confirm the general analysis given above, but none of these studies has attempted a systematic evaluation of the extent, costs, and benefits of linkages from the viewpoint of the host economy or the local enterprises. Of those which have touched on linkages, the following may be mentioned.

(a) Evers *et al.* (1977), on the textile and clothing industries in Hong Kong, discuss the role of trading companies in developed countries that subcontract to local manufacturers. They find that local linkages for clothing manufacture, in terms of the purchase of local cotton textiles, has weakened rather than strengthened in recent years with the growth of exports, for two reasons: discrimination in developed countries against cotton, and the demand for higher quality products, both leading to a greater dependence on imported textiles (often supplied by the buyers). The authors comment extensively on poor working conditions, use of child labour, excessive working hours (up to 105 hours per week for men), and low wages that support the success of the industry in Hong Kong, and draw unfavourable conclusions for the distribution of benefits resulting from such export-led growth. Conditions are apparently worse in small establishments, since large ones have themselves become multinational and gone to cheaper areas like Malaysia and Indonesia.

(b) Lim and Pang (1976), who survey the electronic industry in Singapore, note that European firms buy a fair amount of their inputs (40–50 per cent) locally, while US (under 10 per cent), and Japanese (about 20 per cent) buy much less. This is due to the fact that US firms are specialised in the semiconductor sector and Japanese firms in high-technology components, beyond the technological capabilities of domestic firms, while European firms manufacture mainly consumer electronics where the scope for local purchase is higher. However, local products tend to be rather costly, and are purchased chiefly in order to qualify for GSP privileges in selling to Europe (a minimum local content is required for these exports). Local firms face the usual problems of quality, technology, high costs, and so on, and are sometimes assisted by the local TNCs from whom they subcontract by free technology transfers. Firms which subcontract to foreign buying groups seem to face greater problems; their wage costs are higher than Hong Kong or Taiwan so that they are constantly threatened with losing their markets; they complain of little assistance from the government; and they are short of finance and new technology.

(c) UNCTAD (1975) reviews the electronics industry in LDCs generally, and reaches optimistic conclusions about the effects and prospects for subcontracting. It finds that several finished electronic products can be successfully manufactured by local enterprises in South East Asia, and subcontracting has led to 'a whole network of small manufacturers that were set up as a result of the backward linkages created' (p. 26).[32]

Clearly, much more evidence is needed on the experience of different industries in different LDCs before we can generalise about the impact of TNC linkages in export-based industries. It is obvious that substantial linkages have been created, and that in some sectors, like electricals, they have been beneficial to host countries; however, it is possible that in some other industries, like textiles, linkages have been weakening and have had undesirable effects on distribution and welfare. A related question which has been almost totally neglected is whether such exporting activity (perhaps excluding very high-technology products) could have been undertaken more economically by local firms in countries like India, where the bulk of 'modern' manufactured exports are not in fact accounted for by TNCs, and whether this would have created more beneficial linkages. This whole area is of vital importance to policy-making, and cries out for detailed empirical research.

III INDUSTRIAL STRUCTURE, CONDUCT, AND PERFORMANCE

What we have termed the 'indirect' effects of TNCs on domestic enterprises can be conveniently reviewed under the standard industrial economics format of structure, conduct, and performance. While there exists a multitude of issues of interest here, we shall only mention those which have aroused concern in the literature. Since much of the work has gone into *comparing* the conduct and performance of TNCs and domestic firms rather than evaluating the effects on one or the other (a much more difficult task), we shall also include these studies in this survey.

STRUCTURE

Before we come to the effects of TNCs on industrial structure in LDCs, let us note that there are relatively few systematic studies comparing the industrial structures of developing countries[33] or analysing the structures in particular LDCs. A forthcoming (as yet unobtainable) study[34] shows measures of concentration for ten Latin American countries (excluding Brazil) and finds that 'there exists a similar pattern of industrial concentration in Latin American countries... [Industries] with the highest levels of concentration are tobacco, rubber, basic metals, and the manufacture of paper. Latin American countries which have smaller market size have systematically higher levels of concentration than others.' Most country studies, which include those of Pakistan,[35] Chile,[36] India,[37] and Kenya,[38] are forced to rely on poor data, are often not comprehensive, and generally do not (with the exception of Ghosh, 1975) analyse the determinants of changes in structure over time.

It is notoriously difficult to trace the exact casual relationships between industrial structure, the conduct of firms, and their performance,[39] all of which seem to interact in complex ways. Given the nature of data in developing countries, moreover, it may be expected that studies of the impact of TNCs on the structures of host LDCs would face severe informational and methodological problems. The literature on TNCs in developed countries is not clear on the nature of their effect on industrial structures:[40] initially the entry of foreign competition may reduce the existing level of concentration, but in the longer run the oligopolistic nature and large size of TNCs may well increase it. The facts that industrial concentration has tended to increase in developed countries, and that the growth of TNCs has taken place mainly in sectors characterised by growing oligopoly, may suggest that TNCs have actually caused a rise in concentration in the sectors in which they are active. However, it is not clear to what extent TNCs have contributed *independently* to concentration (by, say, unwarranted takeovers or predatory behaviour based on advantages conferred by size or financial power), as distinct from simply embodying or transmitting changes caused by technological, marketing, financial, or organizational developments. Thus, efficient production and trade may, in some industries, require larger firms and increased concentration over time; financial or economic factors may cause takeovers or mergers independently of the nationality of firms; marketing and R and D economies may compel larger size; and so on—these factors must be disentangled from TNC presence before their separate effect is apparent.

Unfortunately, the few studies that exist for LDCs have not tried to grapple with these problems.[41] Most of them, concentrating on Latin America, have tried to show the extent of 'denationalisation' (the proportion of foreign ownership) in particular sectors or countries, and to relate TNC presence (but not other variables) to concentration levels. While the results have been useful and suggestive, they have not been able to answer the central question concerning the effect of TNC entry on structure. Let us quickly review the literature by country.

a. Mexico

Newfarmer and Mueller (1975) have used data on a sample of 197 US TNCs to analyse the degree of denationalisation in 1972. They find that of the 100 largest firms, 61 were foreign (of which 39 were US); of the 300 largest, 150 were foreign (97 US). Foreign subsidiaries were on average much larger than local private firms, but smaller than public-sector enterprises. US firms accounted for 36 per cent, and other foreign firms for 16 per cent, of the assets of the top 300 firms; of total GDP,

TNCs accounted for 18 per cent in 1962 and 23 per cent in 1970 (US firms for 15 per cent and 18 per cent respectively). Thus, TNCs represented a large and growing force in Mexican manufacturing. As for structure, Newfarmer and Mueller found that Mexican industries were highly concentrated relative to the US, with over three-fourths of production coming from industries where one or more leading producers was a TNC. They also found 'a high correlation between the presence of MNCs in various markets and their overall concentration' (p. 62).[42]

b. Brazil

Newfarmer and Mueller also provide similar data on Brazil, where the US accounts for 36 per cent of foreign capital stock, and where of the 500 largest non-financial corporations in 1972 TNCs number 158 (US firms 59). TNCs are again much larger than domestic private firms, but smaller than state enterprises. They increased their share of assets in five out of seven advanced industrial sectors, the main countervailing force in the other two coming from the government rather than private enterprises. As in Mexico, industry is highly concentrated, with four plants accounting for 50 per cent of output in 176 out of 302 manufacturing industries. TNC presence is associated with concentration:[43] This association would be stronger if data were available by firm rather than by plant, since TNCs are very likely to operate several plants.

c. Argentina

Some data on Argentina are given by Sourrouille (1976), who finds that foreign firms contributed some 30 per cent of total manufacturing output in 1970, far more than twenty years previously. Moreover, 'in 1970/73 two-thirds of the foreign industrial produce stemmed from subgroups where they dominated over 75 per cent of the market . . . and 75 per cent came from sub-groups where they dominated over 50 per cent of the market' (p. 27).[44] The growth of TNCs was 60 per cent higher than average industrial growth.

d. Central America

Willmore (1976) calculates the degree of foreign dominance for Guatemala, where he finds that in 22 industries in which at least one leading firm is foreign, 'the degree of concentration rises as foreign control of leading firm rises' (p. 506). He concludes that foreign entry raises the level of concentration.

Scattered data of this sort are available for other countries—Chile,[45] Colombia,[46] India,[47] South Korea,[48] Malaysia,[49] and Singapore[49]— but they do not contribute greatly to our understanding of the problem at hand. The general upshot of the work done seems to confirm *a priori* expectations, that TNCs are a significant and growing force in the manufacturing sectors of most LDCs, that they are present in industries with high degrees of concentration, and that they are generally larger than domestic private firms.[50] We are, however, unable to say confidently from the evidence whether or not TNCs *cause* higher levels of concentration. TNCs certainly flourish in sectors that are marked by high levels of oligopoly, but the causes of oligopolisation may well lie elsewhere, in scale economies of production, R and D, marketing, finance, or some such factor: to the extent that several modern industries are inherently oligopolistic, the presence of TNCs may not as such cause higher concentration. However, it is quite plausible that in LDCs their entry does *speed up* the natural process of concentration, and that the weakness of local competitors (with the exception of enterprises fostered by the state) enables them to achieve a much *higher degree of market dominance*, in sectors in which they are active, than would be the case in developed economies.[51] Much more detailed empirical work, with more sophisticated tests than have been used till now, will be needed before these matters are clarified.

CONDUCT

In this section we shall consider only two aspects of TNC conduct – takeover as a means of entry, and financing behaviour.

While there is a vast literature on the theory and experience of firms' conduct in expanding or entering new markets, especially on *takeover and merger behaviour*,[52] relatively little work in this area has been done on LDCs. Several host governments in LDCs have, however, expressed concern about takeovers of local firms by TNCs; it has been generally felt that TNCs have, in their immense financial and other resources, an 'unfair advantage' over local competitors, and can, therefore, buy them out at a price which understates their true value. Furthermore, TNCs may, by predatory market conduct, stifle local competition, or so emasculate it that local firms are forced to sell out to them, thus speeding up the process of 'denationalization' and increasing 'dependence' on foreigners.[53] Such fears are not confined to LDCs; they have been voiced in European countries in the 1960s, and the control of

Transnationals, Domestic Enterprises: A Survey

acquisitions by large firms (mostly transnational) remains the major concern of anti-monopoly policy.

The US Tariff Commission's (1973) study of US TNCs noted their preference for entering new markets by mergers or takeovers, and gave various reasons for this preference: immediate access to markets and brand names; control over proprietary technology; access to operating plant and personnel; and valuation at less than true worth. In LDCs the second and third reasons may not be important, but the others may be significant enough to explain Vernon's (1974) finding that by the end of the 1960s almost 65 per cent of 2904 subsidiaries of 396 US and other TNCs in LDCs had been set up by acquisitions rather than by new investments.

The Newfarmer and Mueller (1975) study produces data on Brazil and Mexico which show a lower overall figure for takeover activity in TNCs than those given by Vernon, but which suggest that such activity has risen sharply in recent years, and that TNCs strongly prefer entry by takeover in low-technology sectors (like food processing, textiles, paper, and others) where established local firms offer clear advantages to new entrants. Thus, in Mexico, less than 10 per cent of affiliates were established via acquisitions before 1950, but by 1971-2 this had risen to 75 per cent; for the period 1960-72, 20 per cent of the growth of US TNCs' assets was accounted for by takeovers.[54] Similarly, in Brazil, less than 10 per cent of new entries before 1950 took the form of acquisitions; by the early 1970s takeovers accounted for well over half of new affiliates. Almost 25 per cent of the growth of US assets in Brazil was accounted for by acquisitions during 1960-72.

Similar data are not, as far as I can tell, available for others LDCs, but it seems likely that where takeovers by TNCs are permitted, they have been actively used as a method of entry into sectors where successful local firms offered distinct benefits to new entrants, like established market networks, efficient plant, or a skilled labour force. These factors apply with much less force to high-technology industries, where TNCs would gain little from acquiring local enterprises. If this is indeed true, it would appear that TNC takeovers, generally adding little by way of technology, may not have been very beneficial to host LDCs: they may have yielded high profits to TNCs by the injection of famous brand names supported by sophisticated marketing, but their social gains may have been quite small. Only detailed work on the economic effects of particular takeovers can show how true this is; and such work has not yet been undertaken.

Let us now consider *financing*. A great deal of the literature on TNCs suggests that they use their strong financial position to gear themselves exceptionally highly in LDCs, thus raising the profitability of their equity investment (and depriving local enterprises of domestic savings) and reducing their exposure to exchange risk.[55] While general presumptions of this sort are too numerous to list here, empirical support for them has usually been provided by showing figures on the sources of financing (parent firm, retained profits, local equity, and local/foreign debt) of TNC subsidiaries: in the absence of comparisons with patterns of financing of the TNCs in their home countries, and of local firms in the host country, however, such figures may be quite misleading. A counter to the usual argument is provided by Lall (1976) in his examination of the comparative financing patterns of a sample of firms (divided into TNC and others, as well as into locally and foreign controlled) in India and Colombia. Lall finds that financing patters differ markedly between the countries, testifying to the importance of the different institutional and economic environments, but that 'there is little evidence to support statements that MNCs have significantly different borrowing requirements from other firms'. Even if TNCs have privileged access to local finance, the evidence for the two countries suggests that they 'conform to local financing practices rather than using their borrowing power to an abnormal extent'. Lall's argument is supported by Gershenberg's (1976) findings for a sample of TNCs and local firms in Uganda.[56]

An aspect of TNC behaviour which has received a great deal of attention recently is *transfer-pricing*; as this does not directly involve domestic firms, however, readers are referred to the existing literature.[57] Other aspects of conduct – such as the pricing of final products, advertising, innovation, dividend remittance[58] – have not been studied in detail with a view to assessing the impact of TNCs on local industry, or to comparing their respective practices. Some impressionistic evidence exists, but not of sufficient coverage or weight to merit separate discussion.

PERFORMANCE

There are several issues which may be considered under 'performance', but we shall concentrate on three which have attracted attention in the context of TNCs, and which fall within the general scope of industrial economics: profitability, productivity, and the choice of technology. Other issues such as employment creation[59] (part of this comes under the choice of technology), exports[60] or management efficiency[61] are deliberately excluded from this survey. We have already remarked on evidence from Brazil and Mexico that, in terms of *size*, TNC subsidiaries seem to be much larger than domestic firms. This difference is found to be confirmed and statistically significant for India but not for Colombia; a general inference is drawn that the larger and more industrially advanced a host economy, the more will TNC affiliates tend to exceed their local competitors in size.[62] This is an interesting observation, but needs greater empirical examination.

It was noted above, and may bear repeating, that practically all the work on profitability, productivity, and technological choice relating to TNCs and local firms has contented itself with comparing these aspects of their performance rather than trying to evaluate the impact of one on the other. Clearly, the latter question is the more important one, but in view of the grave difficulties in empirically investigating it, the present survey can only discuss the former.

i. Profitability

While some scattered data are available on the profitability of TNCs in LDCs,[63] there are relatively few studies which try to statistically analyse and explain the relative profitability of TNCs and other firms. The aggregate data indicate that TNCs are fairly profitable in LDCs, and on average perform better than local firms. While this accords with the general theoretical consideration that TNCs possess certain oligopolistic advantages that give them an element of market power (and thus superior profitability) not possessed by other firms,[64] it may be misleading if the average profitability of TNCs reflects, not their superior performance, but the fact that they happen to be concentrated in industries with higher profits (due, say, to higher risk, greater barriers to entry, better capacity-utilisation or higher rates of growth), or that they are larger (if size is associated with profitability). If the explanation lies in industrial composition or size, local firms of comparable size and specialisation may show equally high profitability—'transnationality' as such may not add to earning capacity.[65]

The main problem in studying the profitability of TNCs is the potential for undeclared profits remitted abroad by transfer pricing, which by its nature is practically impossible to detect and allow for. All studies for LDCs mention this, and we may bear it in mind in interpreting their results.

Willmore (1976) is unable, for a sample of 33 foreign and 33 matched local firms in Costa Rica, to reject the null hypothesis that the former are no more profitable than the latter. He reports a similar finding by Rosenthal (1973) for Guatemala that 'if anything, average rates of return on domestic industrial plants were higher than those for foreign plants'. Lall (1976) has compared the profitability of TNCs and other firms, and foreign- and locally-controlled firms, for a sample of 109 firms in India and Colombia; he comes to the conclusion, after using analysis of variance, that the declared profits of TNCs and others do not differ significantly from each other. Gerschenberg (1976) arrives at the same result for his sample in Uganda.

All these studies are at variance with *a priori* expectation about TNC performance and with many of the findings for developed countries. Part of the explanation may lie with transfer pricing problems (but this would not be very significant for countries like India where the extent of import-dependence in manufacturing is very small and where a large part of imports is channelled through the State Trading Corporation); part may lie with the relative smallness of the samples, or with accounting and measurement problems; part may lie with host government policies that may have affected the profitability of foreign firms; and part may lie with market structure and entry-barrier variables that affect foreign and local firms equally.[66] If market structure and policies are stronger influences on profitability than origin of ownership or the fact of transnationality, as seems likely from the evidence, some widely held beliefs about the nature of TNCs in LDCs may need to be revised.[67]

ii. Productivity

The measurement and comparison of inter-firm productivity is fraught with difficulties. It is not clear how inputs (especially different kinds of labour and capital) and outputs should be measured nor how their relationships should be interpreted. Productivity varies widely with the nature of the industry, the technique of production used, scale economies, managerial efficiency, capacity utilisation, labour-force skills, market power, and so on.[68] Since the purpose of such productivity comparisons (in this case of TNCs with local firms) is presumably to gain an insight into how 'efficiently' firms use 'labour' and 'capital',[69] ideally one should separate out extraneous factors not related to individual firms' efficiency. However, depending on how 'efficiency' is defined (e.g. the ability to maximise value added for a given size of firm, in a given industry, from a given bundle of inputs with a given technology, or to bring new technologies into use, or to improve technology over time, or to realise economies of scale, or simply to 'learn'), different influences may be regarded as relevant or not. There are problems of methodology which need careful handling: to simply compare local and foreign firms, of different sizes, in different industries, facing different market conditions, or using vastly different technologies in the same industry, may be misleading if these factors are not explicitly accounted for. These points should be borne in mind in reviewing existing studies.

Vaitsos (1976) has collected estimates for labour and capital productivity for a large sample (about 3,200) of firms in Peru. He has allowed for different sizes of firms, but his measures of productivity (total output over balance-sheet figures for fixed assets and total employment) leave much to be desired. Since he does not distinguish between different industries, his general findings[70] that foreign firms seem to be more efficient than local ones, particularly in their use of labour, need to be carefully interpreted. Average productivity differences may be caused mainly by the industrial composition of the two groups of firms, a presumption which is supported by figures given in the appendix tables to Vaitsos' report. The absence of statistical tests makes it difficult to say how significant industrial differences are, but it appears from the figures given that in low-technology sectors[71] foreign firms have similar capital productivity but much higher labour productivity, perhaps indicating a more efficient use of similar technology; in high technology sectors[72] foreign firms have much higher capital as well as labour productivity (sometimes with less capital/worker), indicating the use of more advanced technology, scale economies, or better management.

Fajnzylber's (1975) study of Mexico groups firms into light consumer goods, consumer durables, intermediates, and capital goods. Measuring productivity by value-added over employment and capital, he finds that foreign firms have higher labour productivity overall than local firms (2.0 times), with the difference being greatest in light consumer goods (2.5) and least in consumer durables (1.4). Somewhat surprisingly, he finds that the capital productivity of foreign firms is uniformly lower, being 0.8 of that of local firms on average, highest in light consumer goods (0.9), and least in intermediate goods (0.6). Whether this is due to the nature of the technology, the distribution of firms within these broad groups, their size, the existence of excess capacity, or poor management is impossible to say.

On Argentina, Sourrouille (1976) provides information on labour productivity of foreign and local enterprises (measured by output per employee) by industry groups.[73] For 1967, foreign firms' productivity was 2.1 times that of local firms on average, with the difference being highest in transport equipment (5.1), electrical appliances (5.0), machinery (2.6), and petroleum products (2.6), and lowest in chemicals (1.4), textiles and rubber (1.3), and food (0.9). Again, the figures do not enable us to trace the sources of these differences, since data on size, technology, capacity utilisation, and so on are not given.

Jo (1976) compares the capital intensity and labour productivity of foreign and local firms in different industries in South Korea. He finds that on average foreign firms have labour productivity 1.8 times that of local firms, lower than local firms in sectors like clay, metal products, food, wood, and electrical machinery, and higher in textiles, chemicals, machinery, and transport equipment. As this pattern is closely related to differences in capital intensity between the two groups (more capital intensity being associated with higher productivity), we may infer that differences in productivity are explained more by the sort of technology used (and perhaps size) than by efficiency in the running of operations.

None of these studies allows us to say whether TNCs *as such* are more efficient in their use of capital and labour than domestic firms. Differences between them certainly seem to exist, but whether this is due to industrial distribution, size, technology, market conditions, x-efficiency, or other factors cannot be determined from the evidence presented.[74] Lall and Streeten (1977) examine labour and capital productivity of different groups of firms in their Colombian and Indian samples, but fail to find satistically significant differences between TNCs and other firms. Industry groupings turn out highly significant, as may be expected, but the sample is too small to test for differences within industry groups.

Balasubramanyam (1973) compares productivities and capital-intensities *within* industries for a sample of 85 Indian firms of which 28 are local without foreign licensing, 42 local with foreign licensing, and 15 foreign. He finds such a diversity of experience across different industries for different measures of productivity that foreign licensing or ownership as such does not seem to exercise an independent influence; in any case, the smallness of the sample of foreign firms does not permit any general inference about their performance.[75]

In his study of Central America, Willmore (1976) finds that capital output ratios of foreign firms is significantly lower than that of local firms, but is unable to explain whether this is because of differences in labour-output or capital-labour ratios.

We are, therefore, led to adopt an agnostic position about the relative productivities of TNCs and local firms, at least as far as 'efficiency' is concerned. It is likely that TNCs achieve greater output or value-added

Transnationals, Domestic Enterprises: A Survey   47

per worker because they are concentrated in industries which are capital-intensive, they use more modern technology or are able to reap economies of scale.[76] Depending on the nature of the technology, they may or may not achieve higher capital productivity. Not much more can be said about their performance with the evidence that we possess. There is certainly no firm basis for saying that TNCs are more efficient or more productive than local enterprises of similar size, in similar activities and using similar technology: on the other hand, they do seem to be larger, specialised in oligopolistic sectors, and use more advanced technology than firms in LDCs.

iii. Choice of Technology

One of the areas of great interest and controversy in the study of TNCs in developing countries has been that of the 'appropriateness' of technology. There are several recent works reviewing the general literature on the choice of technology and employment creation in LDCs.[77] so we shall confine ourselves to the narrower issue of the role of TNCs. There are three separate questions involved:

1. whether the technologies used by TNCs are *adaptable* to low-wage, labour-abundant conditions in LDCs;
2. whether TNCs *do in fact adapt* the technologies they transfer; and
3. whether TNCs adapt *better or worse* than local firms.

As far as the *adaptability* of TNC technologies is concerned, the position is far from clear. Much of the general literature on capital-labour substitutability in developing countries has argued that technologies are fairly flexible, using anecdotal evidence from particular industries or production functions derived from aggregated data.[78] However, doubts have been expressed about whether the technology is really flexible once the products (and so income distribution and tastes) are specified,[79] about the production function methodology used to produce high elasticity estimates,[80] and about the economic and commercial viability of labour-intensive technologies, even for simple products where alternatives actually do exist.[81] This is not the venue for a discussion of general factor-substitution problems, but it does appear that efficient technologies may be fairly 'rigid' in a plausible range of economic conditions in LDCs. This 'rigidity' applies especially to TNC technologies (since they tend to predominate in complex, continuous-process, capital-intensive, and modern industries), with the qualifications that 'peripheral' processes like handling, transport, storage,

48 *The Multinational Corporation*

administration, etc., may be amenable to substitution, and also that the 'core' process itself may, by adaptation of machinery, greater machine speeds and more shifts, subcontracting, use of lower quality inputs, and less rapid changes of technique and models, also be made to use more labour.[82] The total resultant adaptability may not be very great as far as TNCs are concerned, but some flexibility does exist.

The evidence on the *actual* adaptation by TNCs is in line with this reasoning. One of the main sources of the TNCs' special 'advantage' which enables them to grow is precisely the possession of advanced technology, combined in a profitable package with marketing, administrative and financial factors, which can be applied with little adaptation to different areas. It is not to be expected, therefore, that they will undertake *major, expensive alterations* to suit the relatively small markets of LDCs, or to take advantage of differences in labour costs which form a small proportion to total cost. Minor on-the-spot adaptations may be made to suit local conditions, to meet official requirements, or to save foreign exchange, but by their very nature TNCs do not specialise in the simple, labour-intensive products which can be adapted to LDC factor endowments. The following paragraphs recount the evidence on this.

Reuber (1973) finds for his sample that about 70 per cent reported no adaptations. The changes in technique that were made were mainly to scale down plant and equipment to lower production volumes; 'there were relatively few instances of adaptation to take advantage of low labour costs or to make up for the absence of skilled labour in the host 'country' (p. 126). Government regulation, raw material quality, and demand characteristics also induced some changes.

Stewart (1974) collects evidence from different sources that very little adaptation was made to basic production technologies in several cases; she also notes, however, that Philips, Ford, General Motors, and some other TNCs were trying to develop appropriate *products* for LDCs. (There is little evidence in more recent years that such attempts have been very successful. All these firms are still operating their modern, capital-intensive plants, producing the latest array of products, in LDCs.)

Baranson (1967) lists several minor technological adaptations in the Cummins diesel plant in India, mainly to suit the smaller scale of production. While these tended to use old techniques that were more labour intensive, they were not made explicitly in order to exploit low-wage costs in the host country.

Courtney and Leipziger (1975) study nearly 1,500 US affiliates in

LDCs, using Cobb-Douglas production functions to estimate two sorts of adaptation: to the technique transferred by the parent (ex ante substitution) and to the running of a given plant (ex post substitution). While the production function approach, especially at the two and three digit industrial classification level used by the authors, is open to serious criticism,[83] and the findings are crucially dependent on these estimates, they argue that ex ante technology exported by TNCs differs between developed and less-developed areas but not systematically in a capital or labour-intensive direction. In nine out of eleven cases, however, the given process is run more labour-intensively in LDCs to take advantage of lower wage-rates.

Morley and Smith (1974) in their plant-level investigation of TNCs in Brazil, find little scope for adaptation of technology to low-wage conditions. The main adaptations come, as noted by Reuber and Baranson, from the need to scale down plants.

Allen (1973a,b), in his study of US and Japanese firms in South East Asia, fails to find any significant technological adaptation by TNCs to local conditions.

A study of can-making in Kenya, Tanzania, and Thailand by Cooper *et al.* (1975) finds that there does exist some scope for efficient factor substitution, and that different TNCs behave differently in response to conditions in LDCs. Some TNCs (vertically integrated and innovative can-makers as well as food packagers for whom can-making is a peripheral activity) prefer to use 'standardised' plant in different areas; however, one TNC shows greater flexibility in searching out and adapting technology. The precise reasons for this difference are not clear from the available evidence.

Several studies have noted the adaptability of peripheral activities[84] and remarked on the willingness of TNCs to use more labour in LDCs.[85]

As for the question of whether TNCs adapt *better or worse* than local firms, the findings are extremely mixed and based on rather shaky data and methodology. The ideal procedure would be to compare matched sets of foreign and local firms, making similar products, with equal access to the relevant technology and facing identical market conditions. While existing studies cannot, for obvious reasons, live up to this ideal, most of them have contented themselves with comparing large and diverse groups of local and foreign firms. Only two studies have, in my knowledge, tried to compare matched pairs; Cohen (1975) and Mason (1973) both fail to find consistent patterns of factory intensity in their samples of local and foreign firms once industry differences are accounted for, and are, therefore, unable to conclude whether or not TNCs are better or worse at adapting technologies.[86]

There are several more general comparisons of the factor intensity of foreign and local firms, some using data aggregated over different sectors, others differentiating between industries. For all of these, we may bear in mind the conceptual and practical problems mentioned previously:

Balasubramanyam (1973) compares factor intensities of Indian firms without foreign technology or capital with those of Indian firms with foreign licensing and those with foreign capital. He finds, within given industries, that the first and third groups are less capital-intensive than the second, but does not provide any clear evidence on the performance of foreign investors as such.

Reidel (1975) finds for Taiwanese export-based industries that there is no consistent pattern of difference between the factor-intensities of foreign and local firms within specific sectors, especially when multivariate analysis is used.

Lall and Streeten (1977) do not find that transnationality makes a statistically significant difference to capital-intensity for their aggregated sample of 109 Indian and Colombian firms, but that the industry grouping does.

Vaitsos (1976) finds that foreign firms are more capital-intensive in Peru for all sizes except the largest ones, where local firms are more capital-intensive. The value of this finding is much reduced by its aggregation over industries.

Fajnzylber (1975) finds in Mexico that foreign firms use 2.5 times more capital per employee on average than local firms. He differentiates between light consumer, durable, intermediate, and capital goods, but the degree of aggregation is still high.

Jo (1976) reports for South Korea that relative capital-intensities vary markedly over industries with no consistent pattern emerging for TNCs, though on average foreign firms are more capital-intensive. Import-substituting firms are far more capital-intensive than export-based ones.

Agarwal (1976) finds for thirty-four Indian industries (at the three digit level) that TNCs are more capital-intensive than local firms. This is contradicted by Leipziger's (1976) comparison of US and local Indian firms. Using Cobb-Douglas production functions, which has drawbacks noted above, Leipziger finds that US firms import less capital-intensive technology ex ante, but use more fixed capital per man ex post because they have to pay higher wages.

Solomon and Forsyth (1977) find for Ghana that foreign firms are more capital-intensive than local firms within given sectors, but that they are markedly less skill-intensive. The usefulness of this finding is limited by the fact that they cover industries (furniture, bread, footwear, shirts, etc.) where large TNCs hardly exist.

Wells (1973) notes that TNCs may be better at adaptation than local firms in Indonesia, especially when put under competitive pressure.[87]

Pack (1976) finds that in Kenya engineering-trained managers (of whom more are possessed by TNCs) are better at adapting technology than commercially trained ones. Pack's study, unfortunately, focuses on 'traditional' sectors not much frequented by TNCs; in any case, his findings are challenged by Solomon and Forsyth above and by Gershenberg (1976) for Uganda. Gershenberg argues that TNCs use more capital-intensive techniques than local firms.

A number of studies under way are investigating this problem,[88] and may cast more light on a confused situation. The mass of conflicting evidence, the occasional use of imprecise methodology, the inherent problems of definition and measurement, all do not support any strong statement about the relative performance of TNCs and local firms as far as adaptation is concerned.

IV CONCLUDING REMARKS

The issues covered in this survey have been important ones for theory and policy, but the results of the search through the literature have been disappointing. Far more empirical work is needed on both direct linkages and industrial structure and performance before we have a clear picture of what TNCs do and how best to use their presence to promote development. There are many unwarranted generalisations which are accepted unquestioningly by writers on TNCs and by concerned policy-makers, about their good effects, or bad ones, on domestic enterprises and industrial structure and performance. The evidence does not bear out any strong statement on either side; all it provides is a need for caution and further research.

NOTES

1. This paper is substantially adapted from a larger survey prepared for the UN Centre on Transnational Corporations on 'Transnationals and

52   *The Multinational Corporation*

   Linkages with Domestic Enterprises in LDCs'. The Centre's sponsorship of
   the original paper is gratefully acknowledged.
2. For a summary see Lall and Streeten (1977).
3. See Scitovsky (1954) and Hirschman (1958).
4. Hirschman (1958) pp. 205–6.
5. For a summary see Lall and Streeten (1977). This study found that over half
   the sample firms imported goods worth over 30 per cent of their total value
   of sales – over 65 per cent if India is excluded – but that this high degree of
   import dependence did not differ significantly between TNCs and other
   firms.
6. See Mason (1967), who attempts to quantify the local linkages of US foreign
   investments using aggregate industry data, measuring backward linkages
   simply by the 'ratio of local expenditure to total sales' and forward linkages
   by the 'ratio of local sales to total sales'. See Hufbauer and Adler (1968) for
   estimates of local and foreign buying propensities of US TNCs.
7. Vaitsos (1976) gives comparative data on the import propensities of local
   and foreign firms in Peru for 1973, which show that foreign firms had higher
   imports in eleven out of twelve broad industry groups. He notes, however,
   that this does not necessarily imply that local firms created more linkages
   (p. 40); such aggregate data do not permit a detailed examination of the
   technologies and products involved.
8. Daftary and Borghey (1976) provide rather sketchy data on local purchases
   by thirteen TNCs, and conclude that few of these have set up significant
   local linkages, except with the domestic packaging industry (pp. 75–6).
9. See Jo (1976), who reports that foreign firms have higher import-
   propensities than local firms, and that supply, cost, and quality problems
   limit the growth of local purchasing.
10. Thoburn (1973), in the course of his study of the tin and rubber sectors,
    touches upon the role of foreign engineering firms in Malaysia. He finds that
    they helped in the development of local suppliers in processes of low capital
    intensity and few scale economies; 'but in all cases the firms concerned were
    already in existence when the link with foreign firms was formed' (p. 113).
11. See Chapters 5 and 14 of the annotated bibliography on TNCs by Lall
    (1975) for other references on LDCs.
12. We shall consider subcontracting for export below.
13. Watanabe (1972a), p. 425.
14. Baranson (1967) and (1969).
15. Lall (1977) notes that foreign automobile assembly plants in Malaysia have
    not created significant domestic linkages; despite the government's ex-
    pressed desire to increase local content, the absence of statutory controls on
    imports has led the TNCs to continue to depend heavily on imports.
16. I am informed that ECLA (Santiago, Chile), in collaboration with the UN
    Centre on TNCs, is launching studies of linkages of TNCs in Brazil with
    particular reference to public sector enterprises.
17. This is, of course, a reflection of the general problems of import-substituting
    industrialisation discussed by Little, Scitovsky, and Scott (1970).
18. 'Subcontracting' is defined differently by different authors (see Michalet
    (1977)): some mean all production which is contracted for export, whether
    it is by local subsidiaries of TNCs or by domestic firms; others use the term

more narrowly to refer only to production – for export or domestic sale – by domestic enterprises. I prefer the narrow definition, since production by TNC subsidiaries as part of a worldwide strategy is hardly 'subcontracting' in the normal sense. On subcontracting see Helleiner (various), Watanabe (various), Sharpston (1975), and Adam (various).
19. See de la Torre (1974) and Helleiner (1976). In very small and backward LDCs, however, even simple and undifferentiated products may be made by vertically integrated TNCs. The lack of any relevant industrial experience may greatly curtail linkages with local enterprises, though it may have other favourable effects on development. See Morrison (1976).
20. For a detailed analysis of these factors see Sharpston (1975).
21. UNCTAD (1975) notes that this is happening in South Korea, Taiwan, Hong Kong, and Singapore. However, König (1975) finds that Mexico, despite its industrial development, is unable to provide 'border industries' with even 1 per cent of their inputs; he places the full blame for this on inefficiencies caused by protection.
22. See UNCTAD (1975), Chang (1971), Finger (1975), Finan (1975), US Tariff Commission (1970), and Lim and Pang (1976). Some products of the electronics industry, mainly in consumer electronics, *are* amenable to local manufacture in their entirety, and so fall into the third group.
23. For general discussions of the determinants of export-orientated foreign investments and their costs and benefits see Helleiner (1973) (1976), Adam (1972) (1975), Michalet (1977), de la Torre (1974); for an analysis of the significance of labour skills in trade see Hirsch (1975) and for a recent theoretical analysis of TNCs and trade see Hirsch (1976); for a description of the role of multinational buying groups see Hone (1974); and for an examination of the tariff provisions in developed countries which lead to 'offshore assembly' see Finger (1975).
24. Rising wage costs in Singapore have led TNCs to upgrade the skill content of their activities rather than leave the country. See Lim and Pang (1976) and Lall (1977).
25. East European countries are also entering the field, and their use of 'Industrial Co-operation Agreements', under which Western firms provide technology, and usually also equipment and intermediate inputs, in return for processed goods, seems to have provided major benefits to their smaller establishments without incurring the problem of direct TNC investment. This arrangement, discussed by Hewett (1975), may serve as a model to the more advanced LDCs.
26. See König (1975), Baerresen (1971), Walker (1969), Fernandez (1973), Sahagun (1976), and Watanabe (1974a).
27. Reidel (1974) and Evers *et al.* (1977), the latter concentrating on textiles.
28. Lim and Pang (1976) on the electronic industry.
29. Van Houten (1973).
30. Reidel (1975).
31. Especially in Helleiner (1976), Watanabe (1972a), and Sharpston (1975).
32. As noted above, however, this has not occurred for 'border industries' in the advanced but highly protected economy of Mexico, even in textiles, despite the efforts of some TNCs to increase local content in order to qualify for GSP privileges. See König (1975) pp. 92–4.

33. For general international comparisons of industrial structures of developed countries see Bain (1966), Pryor (1972), Horowitz (1971), Dyas and Thanheiser (1976), and Panič (1976).
34. Meller (forthcoming), mentioned in the *Annual Report* of the National Bureau of Economic Research (Washington, DC: 1976).
35. White (1974) and Sharwani (1976). White finds that overall concentration in Pakistan is higher than in the US, UK, or Germany, and about the same as Japan and Chile.
36. Petras (1969) and Zeitlin (1974).
37. Hazari (1966), Ghosh (1974), (1975), Gupta (1968), Sawhney and Sawhney (1973). Most Indian studies show a marked decrease in overall concentration with the process of industrial growth.
38. House (1973) and (1976).
39. Industrial organisation literature is replete with controversies on these problems of theory and methodology; for some recent studies see Needham (1976), Schmalensee (1976), and Phillips (1976).
40. See Caves (various), de Jong (1973), Horst (various), Rowthorn (1971), and Hymer (1976).
41. With the exception of my study of Malaysia (see Chapter 3), which was prepared after this survey was completed.
42. The growing proportion of foreign ownership and the relationship between TNC presence and concentration in Mexico are also noted by Fajnzylber and Tarragó (1976) and Sahagún (1976).
43. Also see Evans (1971, 1974) on Brazil. M. C. Tavares of FINEP, Rio de Janeiro, is presently conducting a study of 800 firms (foreign and local) in Brazil, covering their effects on industrial structure and comparing their performance.
44. Also see Chudnovsky (1976) and Katz (1974) for data on Argentina.
45. Zeitlin (1974), and a CORFO study mentioned by Vaitsos (1976) in a footnote on p. 24.
46. Chudnovsky (1973).
47. The Reserve Bank of India *Bulletins* publish periodic data on sales of foreign companies, but these have not been utilised to calculate the evolution of foreign ownership in the country. Kidron (1965) gives some early figures.
48. Jo (1976) distinguishes export-orientated from other foreign firms, and finds that foreign dominance is much stronger in import-substituting than exporting industries. Surprisingly, the bulk of foreign firms in South Korea are quite small, presumably because of their concentration in textiles, apparel, and electric and electronic components.
49. Lall (1977) finds that 48 per cent of manufacturing output and 51 per cent of fixed assets in West Malaysia were foreign controlled in 1972; and that up to 77 per cent of manufacturing output and 88 per cent of manufactured exports were contributed by foreign controlled firms in 1975 in Singapore.
50. This will be touched upon again in the section on performance.
51. This may not, of course, be true of LDCs where government policies strictly regulate TNC entry and expansion (like India); the bulk of the evidence on 'denationalisation' comes from countries which have traditionally followed liberal policies on foreign investment.

52. For general reviews see Singh (1971, 1975) and de Jong (1976); for the relevance of merger theory to TNCs see Baumann (1975).
53. For a colourful expression of such beliefs see Barnett and Müller (1974).
54. These findings cast doubt on the generality of Reuber's (1973) finding for his sample that 'in the large majority of cases foreign investors launch their projects in LDCs by establishing new facilities rather than through takeovers. This evidence coincides with that collected in another study for Mexico' (p. 212). Unfortunately this study, by S. Rothenberg, is not available here, but its out-of-date data (it was published in 1957) may account for its findings.
55. See, for instance, Reuber (1973), pp. 88–91. Data on financing patterns of US TNCs are given by Leftwich (1974), while financial strategies open to TNCs are analysed in general terms by Robbins and Stobaugh (1974).
56. In their study of the Singapore electronics industry, Lim and Pang (1976) found that small local firms complained of having much more difficulty than large TNCs in obtaining bank finance. Their data did not, however, permit a testing of whether this was due to difference in size or to the 'foreignness' of TNC subsidiaries.
57. See Kopits (1976a,b), Vaitsos (1974a) and Chapters 5 and 6 below.
58. See Kopits (1976a) for a survey of attempts to explain TNC remittance behaviour in response to different tax rates. Few of these deal with LDCs, and those that do use over-simplified models of TNC behaviour (which ignore the existence of oligopolistic rents and interdependence as well as risk and uncertainty) that greatly reduce their practical interest. No systematic comparisons of the reinvestment behaviour of TNCs and local firms are available, but see Lall and Streeten (1977) for some evidence.
59. For recent surveys see Sabolo and Trajtenberg (1976) and Vaitsos (1974b, 1976).
60. See Helleiner (1976) and Lall and Streeten (1977), ch. 7.
61. See Negandhi and Prasad (1975) for a comparison of the management performance of US TNCs and local firms in selected LDCs.
62. Lall and Streeten (1977), ch. 6.
63. See the references on Mexico, Brazil, Argentina, India, and Korea above.
64. See Caves (1971), Dunning (1973), Horst (1975, 1976), Hymer (1976), and Vernon (1971).
65. Empirical work on US TNCs in developed countries (Horst (1975), Wolf (1975)) does seem to confirm the superior profitability of TNCs over other firms; it also suggests that TNC earnings are less volatile during business cycles than those of firms confined to particular national markets.
66. On the importance of market structure and policy in affecting corporate profitability in different developed countries, see Adams (1976).
67. It may be the case, however, that TNC entry itself changes market structure and so the profitability of different industries.
68. See Bhalla (1975), Lim (1976b), Merrett (1971), and OECD (1966).
69. The problem of technological choice is closely related, but is considered separately below. On the measurement of technical efficiency in LDCs and an interesting analysis of firms in Chile see Meller (1976); unfortunately, this study does not distinguish between foreign and local firms.
70. Vaitsos finds that foreign controlled firms (20 per cent or more foreign

equity) have higher labour productivity for all sizes of firms than locally controlled ones, the differential being highest for intermediate-sized firms and fairly low for the smallest and largest ones. Foreign firms have lower capital productivity for small sizes, slightly higher for the intermediate, and much higher for the largest firms.
71. Food and beverages, textiles, wood and furniture, pulp and paper, leather, construction, and glass.
72. Chemicals, rubber, petroleum, metal products, and automobiles. Rather oddly, tobacco falls into this group in terms of its productivity.
73. See Sourrouille (1976), appendix tables on pp. 84–5.
74. Meller (1976), in his study of over eleven thousand firms in twenty-one Chilean industries, is unable to distinguish between efficient and inefficient establishments on the basis of size, capital-labour ratios, or administration-worker ratios within particular industries. Clearly, the role of managerial efficiency, technology (not measured by simple capital-labour ratios), or other factors is extremely important.
75. An RBI (1974) study of six industry groups in India, tracing productivity changes over 1964–70 for four groups of firms finds a similar diversity, which renders any generalisation impossible.
76. Lim (1976a) finds that in Malaysia foreign firms operate their plant longer and more intensively than local counterparts. This is due, according to him, not to their greater x-efficiency or managerial superiority, but to larger size and greater capital intensity.
77. See Bhalla (1975), Gaude (1975), Morawetz (1974), Stewart (1974), and White (1976b).
78. See references in previous footnote, as well as Pack (1974, 1976), Cooper et. al. (1975), and Pickett, Forsyth, and McBain (1974).
79. Stewart (1974).
80. O'Herlihy (1972), Morawetz (1976), Gaude (1975), and Pickett and Robson (1977), p. 211.
81. On sugar manufacturing see Forsyth (1977), and on textiles see Pickett and Robson (1977). It is interesting to note that Pickett and Forsyth seem to have considerably modified their views since their 1974 paper, where they showed a much greater belief in the feasibility of extensive factor substitution.
82. See Helleiner (1975) for a good survey of the issues relating technology transfer to LDCs by transnationals. Also see Hellinger and Hellinger (1976) on Latin America and Pack (1976) on Kenya. On a visit to a foreign car-assembly plant in Singapore, I was informed that considerably more labour was employed than in advanced countries by using old equipment, though it was also necessitated by the large number of models that were assembled on one line.
83. The parents and affiliates may be using technologies of different ages, producing different products, having different degrees of capacity utilisation, and so on, all of which would affect the calculation. The Courtney and Leipziger finding that constant returns to scale apply to seventeen out of twenty-two cases is also highly suspect. On methodical issues see O'Herlihy (1972) and Gaude (1975).
84. See references in Helleiner (1975), Pack (1976) and Vaitsos (1974b).

85. This willingess may not be due solely to economic consideration. Social and political factors may, as Pickett and Robson (1977) note for textiles, cause all types of firms in LDCs to indulge in a certain 'prodigality' in their use of capital and labour.
86. Cohen's sample covers Singapore, Taiwan and S. Korea; Mason's covers Mexico and Singapore.
87. The role of competition in stimulating appropriate adaptation is supported for Pakistan by White (1976), though he does not study TNCs separately.
88. Helleiner (1975) reports a study by Helen Hughes of 1400 firms in Israel, Colombia, Malaysia, and the Philippines, which finds that TNCs had higher capital-in-place to labour ratios, but used their capital more intensively than local firms. Anne Krueger of the NBER is investigating 1000 US TNCs' factor substitution in LDCs, as reported in the 1976 *Annual Report* of the NBER.

REFERENCES

Adam, G. (1972), 'Some implications and concomitants of worldwide sourcing', *Acta Oeconomica*, pp. 309–23.
—— (1975), 'Multinational corporations and worldwide sourcing' in H. Radice (ed.), *International Firms and Modern Imperialism* (Harmondsworth: Penguin).
Adams, W. J. (1976), 'International differences in corporate profitability', *Economica*, pp. 367–79.
Agarwal, J. P. (1976), 'Factor proportions in foreign and domestic firms in Indian manufacturing', *Economic Journal*, pp. 589–94.
Allen, T. W. (1973a), *Direct Investment of United States Enterprises in South East Asia* (Bangkok: ECOCEN).
—— (1973b), *Direct Investment of Japanese Enterprises in South East Asia* (Bankok: ECOCEN).
Baerresen, D. W. (1971), *The Border Industrialisation Program of Mexico* (Lexington: D. C. Heath).
Bain, J. S. (1966), *International Differences in Industrial Structure* (New Haven: Yale University Press).
Balasubramanyam, U. N. (1973), *International Transfer of Technology to India* (New York: Praeger).
Baranson, J. (1967), *Manufacturing Problems in India: the Cummins Diesel Experience* (Syracuse: Syracuse University Press).
—— (1969), *Automotive Industries in Developing Countries* (Washington, DC: IBRD).
Barnet, R. J., and Müller, R. (1974), *Global Reach: the Power of the Multinational Corporations* (New York: Simon and Schuster).
Baumann, H. G. (1975), 'Merger theory, property rights, and the pattern of US investment in Canada', *Weltwirtschaftliches Archiv*, pp. 676–98.
Bhalla, A. S. (1975) (ed.), *Technology and Employment in Industry* (Geneva: ILO).
Brown, M., and Perrin, J. (1977), 'Engineering and industrial projects' (Paris: OECD Development Centre) CD/R/(77)2, mimeo.

Caves, R. E. (1971), 'International corporations: the industrial economics of foreign investment', *Economica*, pp. 1-27.

—— (1974a), 'Causes of direct investment: foreign firms' shares in Canadian and United Kingdom manufacturing industries', *Review of Economics and Statistics*, pp. 279-93.

—— (1974b), 'International trade, international investment and imperfect markets' (USA: Princeton University) Special Papers in International Economics, no. 10.

Chang, Y. S. (1971), *The Transfer of Technology: Economics of Offshore Assembly, the Case of Semiconductor Industry* (New York: UNITAR) Report no. 11.

Chudnovsky, D. (1973), 'Foreign manufacturing firms' behaviour in Colombia', D.Phil. thesis, St. Antony's College, Oxford. Published in Spanish as *Empresas Multinacionales y Ganancias Monopolicas* (Buenos Aires: Siglo xxi, 1974).

—— (1976), *Dependencia Technologica y Estructura Industrial: El Caso Argentino* (Buenos Aires: FLASCO (mimeo)).

Cohen, B. (1975), *Multinational Firms and Asian Exports* (New Haven: Yale University Press).

Cooper, C., Kaplinsky, R., Bell, R., and Satyarakwit, W. (1975), 'Choice of techniques for can-making in Kenya, Tanzania and Thailand', in A. S. Bhalla (1975) above.

Courtney, W. H., and Leipziger, D. M. (1975), 'Multinational corporations in less-developed countries: the choice of technology', *Oxford Bulletin of Economics and Statistics*, pp. 297-304.

Daftary, F., and Borghey, M. (1976), 'Multinational enterprises and employment in Iran', World Employment Programme, Working Paper no. 14, mimeo (Geneva: ILO).

De Jong, F. J. (1973), 'Multinational enterprises and the market form' in G. Bertin (ed.), *The Growth of the Large Multinational Corporation* (Paris: Centre National de la Recherche Scientifique).

De Jong, H. W. (1976), 'Theory and evidence concerning mergers: an international comparison' in A. P. Jaquemin and H. W. De Jong (eds), *Markets, Corporate Behaviour and the State* (The Hague: Nijhoff).

De La Torre, J. (1974), 'Foreign investment and export dependency', *Economic Development and Cultural Change*, pp. 135-50.

Dunning, J. H. (1973), 'The determinants of international production', *Oxford Economic Papers*, pp. 289-336.

Dyas, G. P., and Thanheiser, H. T. (1976), *The Emerging European Enterprise: Strategy and Structure in French and German Manufacturing Industry* (London: Macmillan).

Evans, P. B. 1971), 'Denationalisation and development: a study of industrialisation in Brazil', Ph.D. thesis (Harvard University).

—— (1974), 'Direct investment and industrial concentration', unpublished manuscript.

Evers, B., de Groot, G., and Wagenmans, W. (1977), 'Hong Kong: development and perspective of a clothing colony', (Tilburg (Netherlands): Development Research Institute) translated summary of Progress Report no. 6 (mimeo).

Fajnzylber, F. (1975), 'Las Empresas Transnacionales y el Sistema Industrial de Mexico', *El Trimestre Economico* (Oct.-Nov.).
—— and Tarragó, T. M. (1976), *Las Empresas Multinacionales: Expansion a Nivel Mundial y Proyyeccion en la Industria Mexicana* (Mexico: Fondo de Cultura Economica).
Fernandez, R. A. (1973), 'The border industrialisation program on the US-Mexico border', *Review of Radical Political Economics*, Spring, pp. 37-52.
Finan, N. (1975), 'The international transfer of semiconductor technology through US based firms' (New York: National Bureau of Economic Research, Working Paper no. 118).
Finger, J. M. (1975), 'Tariff provisions for offshore assembly and the exports of developing countries', *Economic Journal*, pp. 365-71.
Forsyth, D. J. C. (1977), 'Appropriate technology in sugar manufacturing', *World Development*, pp. 189-202.
Gaude, J. (1975), 'Capital-labour substitution possibilities: a reviewer of empirical evidence', in A. S. Bhalla (1975) above.
Gershenberg, I. (1976), 'The performance of multinational and other firms in economically less-developed countries: a comparative analysis of Ugandan data' (Nairobi: Institute of Development Studies, Discussion Paper 234 (mimeo)).
Ghosh, A. (1974), 'The role of large industrial houses in Indian industries, 1948-68', *Indian Economic Journal* (Apr.-June).
—— (1975), 'Concentration and growth of Indian industries, 1948-68', *Journal of Industrial Economics*, pp. 203-22.
Gupta, V. E. (1968), 'Cost functions, concentration and barriers to entry in twenty-nine manufacturing industries of India', *Journal of Industrial Economics*, pp. 57-72.
Hazari, R. K. (1966), *The Structure of the Corporate Private Sector: a Study of Concentration, Ownership and Control* (London: Asia Publishing House).
Helleiner, G. K. (1973), 'Manufactured exports from less-developed countries and multinational firms', *Economic Journal*, pp. 21-47.
—— (1975), 'The role of multinational corporations in the less developed countries' trade in technology', *World Development*, pp. 161-89.
—— (1976), 'Transnational enterprises, manufactured exports and employment in the less developed countries', *Economic and Political Weekly* (Annual number, February), pp. 247-62.
Hellinger, D., and Hellinger, S. (1976), *Unemployment and the Multinationals: A Strategy for Technological Change in Latin America* (Port Washington (N.Y.): Kennikat Press).
Hewett, E. A. (1975), 'The economics of East European technology imports from the West', *American Economic Review* (May), pp. 377-82.
Hirsch, S. (1975), 'The product cycle model of international trade', *Oxford Bulletin of Economics and Statistics*, pp. 305-17.
—— (1976), 'An international trade and investment theory of the firm', *Oxford Economic Papers*, pp. 258-70.
Hirschman, A. O. (1958), *The Strategy of Economic Development* (New Haven: Yale University Press).
Hone, A. (1974), 'Multinational corporations and multinational buying groups', *World Development* (Feb.) pp. 145-50.

Horowitz, I. (1971), 'An international comparison of the international effects of concentration on industry wages, investment and sales', *Journal of Industrial Economics* (Apr.) pp. 166–78.

Horst, T. (1972), 'Firm and industry determinants of the decision to invest abroad: an empirical study', *Review of Economics and Statistics*, pp. 258–66.

—— (1974), 'Theory of the firm' in J. H. Dunning (ed.), *Economic Analysis and the Multinational Enterprise* (London: Allen & Unwin).

—— (1975), 'American investment abroad and domestic market power' (Washington, DC: Brookings Institution) mimeo.

—— (1976), 'American multinationals and the US economy', *American Economic Review Papers and Proceedings*, pp. 149–54.

House, W. J. (1973), 'Market structure and industry performance: the case of Kenya', *Oxford Economic Papers* (Nov.).

—— (1976), 'Market structure and industry performance: the case of Kenya revisited', *Journal of Economic Studies*, pp. 117–32.

Hufbauer, G. C., and Adler, F. M. (1968), *US Manufacturing Investment and the Balance of Payments* (Washington, DC: US Treasury Department).

Hymer, S. (1976), *The International Operations of National Firms: A Study of Direct Foreign Investment* (Cambridge, Mass.: The MIT Press).

Jo, Sung-Hwen (1976), 'The impact of multinational firms on employment and incomes: the case study of South Korea' (Geneva, ILO, World Employment Programme) Working Paper no. 12, mimeo.

Katz, J. (1974), *Oligopolio, Empresarios Nacionales y Corporaciones Multinacionales* (Buenos Aires: Siglo) p. xxi.

Kidron, M. (1965), *Foreign Investments in India* (London: Oxford University Press).

König, W. (1975), 'Towards an evaluation of international subcontracting activities in developing countries' (Washington, DC: UN ECLA) (mimeo).

Kopits, G. F. (1976a), 'Taxation and multinational firm behaviour: a critical survey', *IMF Staff Papers*, pp. 624–73.

—— (1976b), 'Intra-firm royalties crossing frontiers and transfer-pricing behaviour', *Economic Journal*, pp. 791–805.

Lake, A. (1976), 'Transnational activity and market entry in the semiconductor industry' (New York: National Bureau of Economic Research) Working Paper no. 126.

Lall, S. (1975), *Private Foreign Manufacturing Investment and Multinational Corporations: An Annotated Bibliography* (New York: Praeger).

—— (1976), 'Financial and profit performance of MNCs in developing countries: some evidence from an Indian and Colombian sample', *World Development*, pp. 713–24.

—— (1977), 'Transfer pricing in assembly industries: a preliminary analysis of the issues in Malaysia and Singapore' (London: Commonwealth Secretariat) (mimeo).

—— and Streeten, P. P. (1977), *Foreign Investment, Transnationals and Developing Countries* (London: Macmillan).

Leftwich, R. B. (1974), 'US multinational companies: profitability, financial leverage and effective income tax rates', *Survey of Current Business* (May) pp. 27–36.

Leipziger, D. M. (1976), 'Production characteristics in foreign enclave and

domestic manufacturing: the case of India', *World Development*, pp. 321-5.
Lim, D. (1976a), 'Capital utilisation of local and foreign establishments in Malaysian manufacturing', *Review of Economics and Statistics*, pp. 209-17.
—— (1976b), 'On the measurement of capital utilisation in less developed countries', *Oxford Economic Papers*, pp. 149-59.
Lim, L., and Pang, Eng-Fong (1976), 'The electronics industry in Singapore: structure, employment, technology and linkages' (University of Singapore: Economic Research Centre) mimeo.
Little, I. M. D., Scitovsky, T., and Scott, M. F. (1970), *Industry and Trade in Some Developing Countries: A Comparative Study* (London: Oxford University Press).
McLinden, J. E. (1972), 'World outlook for electronics', *Columbia Journal of World Business*, May-June, pp. 65-71.
Mason, R. H. (1967), 'An analysis of benefits from US direct foreign investments in less-developed areas', Ph.D. thesis (Stanford University).
—— (1973), 'Some observations on the choice of technology by multinational firms in developing countries', *Review of Economics and Statistics*, pp. 349-55.
Meller, P. (1976), 'Efficiency frontiers for industrial establishments of different sizes', *Explorations in Economic Research*, pp. 379-407.
—— (forthcoming), 'International comparisons of industrial concentration in Latin America' (New York: National Bureau of Economic Research, 1976 (submitted for publication)).
Merrett, S. (1971), 'Snares in the labour productivity measure of efficiency: some examples from Indian nitrogen fertiliser manufacture', *Journal of Industrial Economics* (Nov.) pp. 71-84.
Michalet, C.-A. (1977), 'International subcontracting' in OECD Development Centre's 'Experts' Meeting on International Subcontracting and Reinforcing LDCs' Technological Absorption Capacity', (Paris: OECD) mimeo.
Morawetz, D. (1974), 'Employment implications of industrialisation in developing countries: a survey', *Economic Journal*, pp. 491-542.
—— (1976), 'Elasticities of substitution in industry: what do we learn from econometric estimates?', *World Development*, pp. 1-15.
Morley, S. A., and Smith, G. W. (1974), 'The choice of technology: multinational firms in Brazil', Rice University Program in Development Studies, no. 58, mimeo; Later published in *Economic Development and Cultural Change* (1977).
Morrison, T. K. (1976), 'International Subcontracting: improved prospects in manufactured exports for small and very poor LDCs', *World Development*, pp. 327-32.
Moxon, R. W. (1974), 'Offshore production in the less-developed countries: a case study of multinationality in the electronics industry', *The Bulletin* (New York: New York University Graduate School of Business Administration, July).
Müller, R., and Morgenstern, R. D. (1974), 'Multinational corporations and balance of payments impact in LDCs: an econometric analysis of export pricing behaviour', *Kyklos*, pp. 304-21.
Needham, D. (1976), 'Entry barriers and non-price aspects of firms' behaviour', *Journal of Industrial Economics*, pp. 29-43.

Negandhi, A., and Prasad, B. (1975), *The Frightening Angels* (Kent, Ohio: Kent State University Press).
Newfarmer, R. S., and Mueller, W. F. (1975), *Multinational Corporations in Brazil and Mexico: Structural Sources of Economic and Non-Economic Power* (Washington, DC: US Senate Subcommittee on Multinational Corporations).
OECD (1966), *Productivity Measurement* vol. iii (Paris).
O'Herlihy, C. St. J. (1972), 'Capital/labour substitution and developing countries: a problem of measurement', *Bulletin of the Oxford University Institute of Economics and Statistics*, pp. 269-80.
Pack, H. (1974), 'Capital-labour substitution—a microeconomic approach', *Oxford Economic Papers*, pp. 388-404.
—— (1976), 'The substitution of labour for capital in Kenyan manufacturing', *Economic Journal*, pp. 45-58.
Panic, M. (1976), *The UK and West German Manufacturing Industry 1954-72: A Comparison of Structure and Performance* (London: National Economic Development Office).
Petras, J. (1969), *Politics and Social Forces in Chilean Development* (Berkeley: University of California Press).
Phillips, A. (1976), 'A critique of empirical studies of relations between market structure and profitability', *Journal of Industrial Economics*, pp. 241-9.
Pickett, J., Forsyth, D. J. C., and McBain, N. S. (1974), 'The choice of technology, economic efficiency and employment in developing countries' in E. O. Edwards (ed.), *Employment in Developing Countries* (New York: Columbia University Press).
—— and Robson, R. (1977), 'Technology and employment in the production of cotton cloth', *World Development*, pp. 203-16.
Pryor, F. (1972), 'An international comparison of concentration ratios', *Review of Economics and Statistics*, pp. 130-40.
RBI (1974), 'Survey of foreign financial and technical collaboration in Indian industry—1964-70', *Reserve Bank of India Bulletin* (June) pp. 1040-83.
Reidel, J. (1974), *The Industrialisation of Hong Kong* (Kiel: Institut für Weltwirtschaft).
—— (1975), 'The nature and determinants of export-oriented direct foreign investment in a developing country: a case study of Taiwan', *Weltwirtschaftliches Archiv*, pp. 505-28.
Reuber, G. L. *et al.* (1973), *Private Foreign Investment in Development* (Oxford: Clarendon Press).
Robbins, S. M., and Stobaugh, R. B. (1974), *Money in the Multinational Enterprise* (New York: Basic Books).
Rosenthal, G. (1973), 'The role of private foreign investment in the development of the Central American Common Market', Guatemala (manuscript).
Rowthorn, R., in collaboration with Hymer, S. (1971), *International Big Business, 1959-1967* (London: Cambridge University Press).
Sabolo, Y., and Trajtenberg, R. (1976), 'The impact of transnational enterprises on employment in developing countries: preliminary results' (Geneva; ILC, WEP) Working Paper no. 6, mimeo.
Sahagùn, V. M. B. *et al.* (1976), 'The impact of multinational corporations on employment and incomes: the case of Mexico' (Geneva: ILO) World

Employment Programme Working Paper no. 13, mimeo.
Sawhney, P. K., and Sawhney, B. L. (1973), 'Capacity-utilisation, concentration and price-cost margins: results on Indian industries', *Journal of Industrial Economics*, pp. 145–53.
Schmalensee, R. (1976), 'Advertising and profitability: further implications of the null hypothesis', *Journal of Industrial Economics*, pp. 45–54.
Scitovsky, T. (1954), 'Two concepts of external economies', *Journal of Political Economy*, pp. 143–52.
Sharpston, M. (1975), 'International subcontracting', *Oxford Economic Papers*, pp. 94–135.
Sharwani, K. (1976), 'Some new evidence on concentration and profitability in Pakistan's large-scale manufacturing industries', *Pakistan Development Review*, pp. 272–89.
Singh, A. (1971), *Takeovers* (London: Cambridge University Press).
—— (1975), 'Takeovers, economic natural selection and the theory of the firm: evidence from the postwar UK experience', *Economic Journal*, pp. 497–515.
Solomon, R. F., and Forsyth, D. J. C. (1977), 'Substitution of labour for capital in the foreign sector: some further evidence', *Economic Journal*, pp. 283–9.
Sourrouille, J. V. (1976), 'The impact of transnational enterprises on employment and income: the case of Argentina' (Geneva: ILO), World Employment Programme Working Paper no. 7, mimeo.
Stewart, F. (1974), 'Technology and employment in LDCs', *World Development*, (Mar.) pp. 17–46.
Thoburn, J. T. (1973), 'Exports and the Malaysian engineering industry: a case study of backward linkage', *Oxford Bulletin of Economics and Statistics*, pp. 91–117.
UNCTAD (1975), *International Subcontracting Arrangements in Electronics between Developed Market-Economy Countries and Developing Countries* (New York: United Nations).
United Nations (1973), *Multinational Corporations in World Development* (New York: United Nations).
US Tariff Commission (1970), *Economic Factors Affecting the Use of Item 807.00 and 806.30 of the Tariff Schedules of the United States* (Washington, DC: Government Printing Office).
—— (1973), *Implications of Multinational Firms for World Trade and Investment and for US Trade and Labour* (Washington, DC: GPO).
Vaitsos, C. V. (1974a), *Intercountry Income Distribution and Transnational Enterprises* (Oxford: Clarendon Press).
—— (1974b), 'Employment effects of foreign direct investments in developing countries' in E. O. Edwards (ed.), *Employment in Developing Nations* (New York: Columbia University Press).
—— (1976), 'Employment problems and transnational enterprises in developing countries: distortions and inequality' (Geneva: ILO) World Employment Programme Working Paper no. 11, mimeo.
Van Houten, J. F. (1973), 'Assembly industries in the Caribbean', *Finance and Development* (June).
Vernon, R. (1971), *Sovereignty at Bay* (New York: Basic Books).
—— (1974), 'Multinational enterprises in developing countries: an analysis of national goals and national policies' (Vienna: UNIDO (mimeo)).

Walker, H. O. (1969), 'Border industries with a Mexican accent', *Columbia Journal of World Business* (Jan.–Feb.) pp. 25–32.

Watanabe, S. (1971), 'Subcontracting, industrialisation and employment creation', *International Labour Review*, pp. 51–76.

—— (1972a), 'International subcontracting, employment and skill promotion', *International Labour Review*, pp. 425–49.

Watanabe, S. (1972b), 'Exports and employment: the case of the Republic of Korea', *International Labour Review*, pp. 495–526.

—— (1974a), 'Constraints on labour-intensive export industries in Mexico', *International Labour Review*, pp. 23–45.

—— (1974b), 'Reflections on current policies for promoting small enterprises and subcontracting', *International Labour Review*, pp. 405–22.

Wells, L. T. (1973), 'Economic man and engineering man; choice of technology in a low wage country', *Public Policy*, pp. 39–42.

White, L. J. (1974), *Industrial Concentration and Economic Power in Pakistan* (Princeton: Princeton University Press).

—— (1976a), 'Appropriate technology, x-inefficiency and the competitive environment: some evidence from Pakistan', *Quarterly Journal of Economics*, pp. 575–89.

—— (1976b), 'Appropriate factor proportions for manufacturing in less developed countries: a survey of the evidence' (Princeton: Woodrow Wilson School, Research Program in Development Studies) no. 64, mimeo.

Willmore, L. (1976), 'Direct foreign investment in Central American manufacturing', *World Development*, pp. 499–518.

Wolf, B. N. (1975), 'Size and profitability among US manufacturing firms: multinational versus primarily domestic firms', *Journal of Economics and Business*, Fall, pp. 15–22.

Zeitlin, M. (1974), 'Economic concentration, industrial structure, national and foreign capital in Chile, 1966', *International Industrial Organisation Review*, pp. 195–205.

3 Multinationals and Market Structure in an Open Developing Economy: The Case of Malaysia[1]

I INTRODUCTION

The relationship between industrial market structure and foreign investment has been extensively studied in recent years, but almost exclusively to analyse the sorts of structures that give rise to multinational companies (MNCs), and then mainly in the context of advanced economies.[2] The opposite chain of causation, from MNC entry to market structures in host countries, has been relatively neglected. Only occasional note has been taken of this issue in theoretical literature,[3] and only a few empirical studies in developed countries[4] and less developed ones[5] have made rather desultory attempts to analyse it statistically.

In every case, however, the empirical procedure has relied simply upon relating some measure of market concentration to some index of MNC presence in different industries. No attempt has yet been published, for developed or less developed countries, assessing how MNC entry affects market concentration within a comprehensive model of the determinants of industrial structure. Without such a model, however, it is impossible to assess whether foreign entry has an influence on market structure *independently* of the industrial variables which are commonly thought to determine it, whether it is merely *associated with* structural characteristics that are inherent in different industries, or whether it *speeds up* the process of structural change which may occur even in its absence.

There are several conceptual and practical difficulties in the conduct of an exercise intended to clarify these issues: these will be noted below. One of these is a virtual absence of empirical studies of the determinants of market structure in LDCs, even without having foreign investment as an explanatory factor.[6] This paper starts by attempting a comprehensive explanation of market structure in a developing country – Peninsular Malaysia – to see whether the conventional theories of industrial economics have any validity in economies just starting to industrialise. It then introduces foreign investment as a separate explanatory factor, to clarify its relationship with inter-industry differences in concentration levels in the manufacturing sector for 1972, and with the other determinants of market structure.

Section II discusses general considerations related to the role of foreign investment and industrial market structure in a developing host country. Section III gives some background information on foreign investment in Malaysia and the variables used. Sections IV and V present the results for 46 industries for which data are available, and for consumer and non-consumer goods industries separately. Section VI draws the main conclusions.

II MARKET STRUCTURE AND FOREIGN ENTRY IN A DEVELOPING ECONOMY

The literature on industrial structure in developed countries has identified several influences on the level of market (seller) concentration (the precise nature of the relationships between some of these and concentration levels is controversial, but we cannot enter into the broader debate here): economies of scale; capital intensity; minimum capital requirements; market size; market growth; and advertising intensity.[7] The first three have generally been found to be positively, and the fourth negatively, correlated with concentration levels, while the final two have had ambiguous relationships.

While on *a priori* grounds we would expect these variables to bear more or less the same relationship to concentration levels in LDCs as in industrialised countries, there may be some special factors about the former that may affect the outcome. For instance, most LDCs have dualistic production structures in manufacturing, with a modern sector, serving mainly urban markets, coexisting with a traditional one which uses completely different techniques, produces different products and serves different groups of consumers. As the available (census) data for LDCs include the traditional sector, it is possible that the relationships observed in industrial economies may be different (weaker or stronger) in LDCs. Or, to take another example, the influence of advertising may

An Open Developing Economy: The Case of Malaysia   67

be different in a market with less exposure to mass media, with mass illiteracy or with primitive retailing systems. Only empirical analysis can indicate how well the structural relationships discovered in the advanced travel to the third world.

What impact might a substantial entry of foreign investment have on industrial structure in a less-developed country? One of the most significant differences between developed and less-developed countries that play host to foreign manufacturing investment lies precisely in the sorts of industrial structures that confront the foreign entrant. In developed countries, market structures may be assumed to be fairly similar to those of the capital exporting country, and the impact of foreign entry may not in general greatly alter the forces that determine concentration (technology, product differentiation, and the like), unless particular circumstances like a major technical breakthrough or a weak currency lead to a wave of mergers and takeovers spearheaded by MNCs.[8] In most less-developed countries, however, where local enterprise, if it is present at all, is relatively small, weak and technologically backward, and industrial structures reflect this state of underdevelopment, the entry of MNCs may act as a powerful agent for the transmission of change and modernisation.

It is by now a commonplace in the literature that industries that give rise to MNCs are concentrated, and that MNCs are possessed of large size and various monopolistic advantages over potential competition abroad, such as easy access to capital, specialization in capital and skill intensive activities, advanced technology and heavy product differentiation.[9] The transfer of such attributes to an LDC, with low or nonexistent barriers to entry offered by local firms and with relatively small industrial markets, may be expected to have the following sequence of effects.

In the short run, it may reduce concentration, directly by adding to the numbers of local suppliers (if the mode of entry is not by takeover) and indirectly by inducing competing MNCs to follow suit.[10] This may occur regardless of the economic viability of serving a small market by a larger number of plants, especially if the host government offers tariff or non-tariff protection to new investors.

In the longer run, assuming that the government lets market forces run their course, the entry of MNCs may be expected to increase concentration, for two reasons. First, regardless of the MNCs' market conduct, the *attributes* of these enterprises can raise barriers to entry for local firms: MNCs often introduce advanced, usually larger-scale and more capital-intensive technology; they generally produce a wider, more differentiated and better marketed range of products; they utilise newer managerial and organisational skills; they have better access to financial, technical and marketing resources abroad; and they may be more prepared to challenge 'live-and-let-live' rules of the game observed by local oligopolists than local entrants.

Second, their *conduct* may speed up the process of concentration. MNCs are generally the leading forces in the developed countries in diversifying across industries, in affecting takeovers and in lobbying policy makers, and they may be expected to transfer these highly developed strategies to all the host countries in which they operate. Thus, in LDCs MNCs may purchase local firms on especially favourable terms because of their strong hold over technology or input markets (as Newfarmer (1978) notes for the Brazilian electrical sector); they may be able to outlast local competitors in price-cutting wars because of financial staying power; or they may be able to win more favourable concessions from host governments. The market power and tactics of MNCs may also cause higher concentration by inducing defensive mergers among local firms.

In the long run, therefore, it is plausible that substantial MNC presence will raise concentration levels, partly perhaps by their conduct and partly by their role as the agent of transferring highly developed modes of operation to small and backward economies. It may be noted that the effect on concentration levels does not as such tell us anything about the *desirability* of MNC entry: a rise in concentration levels by itself has no normative implications in the context of dynamic industrialisation. In so far as the efficiency of industrial operations is raised, new technology utilised, better products offered and competitive pressures generated, the increase of concentration may well be a necessary accompaniment to beneficial change. However, in so far as MNCs reach dominating positions by predatory anti-competitive conduct or by extracting special official favours, it may be regarded as undesirable. The most interesting question in this context is precisely this: does MNC entry raise concentration only by changing industrial parameters, such as capital-intensity or advertising intensity, or does it exercise an independent influence after all the other factors have been taken into account?

An important analytical problem here is to distinguish the effect of MNC entry from what may have happened in the 'alternative situation'. Clearly, some new technology, skills and products would have been developed by local firms, or imported by them from abroad, and some anticompetitive strategies would have been employed by local market

An Open Developing Economy: The Case of Malaysia 69

leaders. The change in industrial structure may have been similar to that occasioned by MNC entry. It is, however, very likely that the pace of change would have been much slower: the presence of large, advanced and aggressive MNCs is likely to provide a far more powerful stimulus to change than the autonomous growth of national enterprises. The *net* effect of MNC entry – the difference between the actual and alternative situations – is impossible to measure with the data at hand. Our procedure, of analysing only interindustry differences in the actual situation, thus imparts an upward bias to our estimates of the effects of TNC entry. But it is believed that it still provides a correct assessment of the general nature and direction of the impact.

III DATA AND VARIABLES

Malaysia provides an excellent case study for the task in hand, both because it has traditionally followed very liberal policies towards foreign investment and so has a large, well-established and diversified foreign presence in manufacturing industry, and because it is one of the few developing countries that publishes sufficient census data to enable such an investigation to be conducted. The recently published volume 2 of the Malaysian Government Department of Statistics' *Survey of Manufacturing Industries, Peninsular Malaysia, 1972*[11] gives separate data on foreign and local 'establishments' (firm-level figures are not given) for sales, employment, value added and wages in 46 industries at the 4-digit level. It also provides, in volume 1, figures on fixed assets, size distribution, advertising, employment by function and so on for each industry, but these are not separated between local and foreign firms. The Appendix of this chapter shows the extent of foreign participation in employment (our measure of foreign presence) and concentration levels (4-plant concentration ratios) for the 46 industries.

Some background information on the foreign sector in Malaysia will be relevant to this study. In 1972, foreign establishments (549 in number) accounted for 56 per cent of total value added, 52 per cent of sales and 33 per cent of employment in the manufacturing sector (3685 establishments in total, including foreign ones) in the country. The UK was the largest foreign investor, with 32 per cent of foreign value added, followed by Singapore (26 per cent) and the US (9 per cent). The rest was divided between various developed and a few other less-developed (mainly Hong Kong and India) countries, though the latter accounted only for about 2 per cent of foreign value added.

Malaysian firms (henceforth 'firm' is used interchangeably with 'establishment') were, as may be expected, much smaller on average than foreign ones: average value added in the former came to some 14 per cent of value added in the latter. They were also far less capital-intensive: fixed assets per employee (in thousands of Malaysian dollars) came to 6.2 in local firms, as compared to 17.3 for UK, 16.9 for US, 14.0 for Japanese and 16.9 for 'other' (presumably mainly European) firms. Malaysian firms also paid lower average wages, 1.8 per annum, as compared to British (4.1), American (2.8) or 'other' (3.0) firms, and achieved lower value added per employee.[12] These aggregate figures strongly support the presumption advanced above about foreign investment introducing 'modern' techniques, scales and skills into industry.

There are, however, marked differences *within* the foreign sector. Firms from the developed countries, most of them the 'real' multinationals (i.e. very large, diversified and technologically advanced firms), seem to be a different species from firms from other LDCs, mostly Singaporean ones. The latter (260 in number) seem to be in an intermediate stage between the large MNCs and local firms, in terms of size (they are four times larger than local firms as compared to twelve times for UK firms), capital intensity (fixed assets per employee 6.6) or wages (2.6).[13] The phenomonenon of LDC multinationals has aroused some academic interest recently, and some of these 'intermediate' characteristics have been remarked upon.[14] The point of interest in the present context is whether the 'real' MNCs exercise a greater effect on market concentration than the 'intermediate' ones. We do not have the data to test for this properly, since the Survey does not give national origins for every industry. It does, however, provide sufficient indications for us to get a fair idea of the sectors in which the foreign firms are predominantly Singaporean[15] (we shall return to this below), and so to attempt a tentative distinction between the two sorts of foreign investors. The variables employed in statistical analysis are as follows.

The *dependent* variable, C_4, is the 4-plant minimum concentration ratio in Malaysian manufacturing industry at the 4-digit level. There are several well-aired problems with this measure of concentration, but it does remain the easiest to compute and to compare across countries and there is some evidence that it captures the essential elements of concentration as well as alternative (Herfindahl and entropy) measures.[16] The Appendix, which gives our data, also presents comparable ratios for a number of UK industries. The 28 industries for which UKC_4 is shown are also (with one or two exceptions, like paper and electrical machinery, where comparable UK ratios could not be calculated without great aggregation problems) those in which the 'real' MNCs are predominant; the others are largely the domain of investors from LDCs. Since UKC_4 is also used below as an independent variable, its inclusion serves to narrow the sample to 'real' MNC dominated sectors and so to distinguish their effect more distinctly.

The *independent* variables are:

SCALE ECONOMIES

The measurement of scale economies has always been a difficult exercise for economists in the absence of specific engineering data. A number of indirect measures have been constructed, each of which suffers from certain disabilities.[17] We have selected the following:

MEPS
Minimum efficient plant scale of production in relation to market size, defined as the average size of plant of the largest plants accounting for 50 per cent of industry sales expressed as a percentage of total industry sales. This measure assumes that these largest plants exhaust available technical economies of scale, and it has the great advantage that it incorporates the size of the market into the measurement of efficient scale. However, it has been noted that this measure is usually highly collinear with concentration (simple correlation coefficient between C_4 and MEPS for Malaysia is round 0.90) and that, where cost curves are flat after certain level, it captures, not just scale economies in production, but also elements of market power, different specialisation in products, different sorts of technology and so on, between large and small firms.[18] Thus this variable may be (and is, in our case) highly collinear with other independent variables and may, because of its strong relationship to the dependent, totally swamp their effects. This is not to say that it is a completely misleading indicator of scale economies, but that its use should be tempered with caution.

CAR
The cost advantage ratio, defined as value-added per employee in large plants (supplying the top 50 per cent of the market) divided by value-added per employee in small plants.[19] This measure also faces problems raised by the value-added data catching the influence of market power, different product mix, and so on, but the problems here seem less severe than those identified for MEPS.

MEPCA

A combination of MEPS and CAR, obtained by multiplying the two. This increases the effect of entry barriers when the minimum efficient size of plant is higher *and* the relative value added of large plants is greater.[20] This measure slightly diminishes some of the statistical difficulties raised by MEPS, but not to a great extent: however, it is useful to report some results using the variable.

CAPITAL VARIABLES

The capital intensity of production may make entry difficult for firms which cannot raise the minimum amount of capital necessary for efficient production. We have tried two measures, which are highly collinear with each other (simple correlation coefficient 0.73) but are shown separately.

K/L
Fixed assets per employee.[21]

MKR
Minimum capital requirements, measured by MEPS multiplied by the fixed assets-to-sales ratio for each industry.

MARKET SIZE (MSZ)

Measured by value added in each industry. Since market size is already included in MEPS and MEPCA it is not used in conjunction with these in the regressions.

MARKET GROWTH (MGR)

Measured by the percentage growth of output of each industry in the period 1968–72.

ADVERTISING INTENSITY (AD)

The advertising-to-sales ratio for each industry, as a measure of product-differentiation entry barriers.

An Open Developing Economy: The Case of Malaysia 73

UK CONCENTRATION LEVELS (UKC$_4$)

A control variable to incorporate those technological factors leading to concentration that are not captured by the above variables.[22] This variable was only obtainable for 28 observations, mainly comprising TNC-dominated industries.

FOREIGN PRESENCE (FP)

Measured by the foreign share of employment in each industry. A measure based on foreign share of sales was also tried, but was so highly correlated with the employment measure (correlation coefficient 0.95), and its results were so similar to those reported here, that it was dropped.

These are the variables used for empirical analysis. They incorporate practically all the determinants of structure which have been tried for the developed countries, and enable us to test, for the first time, how they work for a small LDC.

IV FINDINGS FOR THE ENTIRE SAMPLE

This section presents the results for all the industries together. Section V presents results for the consumer and non-consumer industries separately.

The statistical tool employed was ordinary least-squares regression analysis. The dependent variable and UKC$_4$ were not transformed: all other variables were expressed in natural logarithms. Linear formulations gave very similar results, but the semi-leg formulation proved more significant (*a priori* expectations also favour a non-linear formulation).

A simple regression of C_4 on log gave:

$C_4 = 17.28$ FP $- 15.78 \qquad R^2 = 0.32 \qquad F = 21.12$
  (4.60)   (t − value in parentheses)

The effect of foreign presence is positive and significant at 99 per cent; the simple correlation coefficient between them is 0.65. However, this correlation between concentration and foreign presence is expected, and does not show *how* the influence of foreign entry upon structure works, or whether FP has an independent influence once other industrial variables are taken into account. Only multiple regression can help resolve these issues.

Concentration was also highly correlated with MEPS (0.90) and MEPCA (0.82), and fairly highly with K/L (0.50), MKR (0.49) and CAR (0.47). Since a high incidence of collinearity is expected among the independent variables, and since the relationship of FP to the others is of analytical significance, let us look at the simple correlation coefficients for the variables (Table 3.1). We have not shown UKC_4 here because it greatly reduces the number of industries; we shall return to it later.

The first column of the table shows the correlations between foreign presence and the other independent variables. The extremely high correlation between FP and MEPS indicates that foreign investment is very prominent in industries where large firms account for significant proportions of output. This may be because of their tendency to build efficient-sized plants; it may also be due to other factors which cause *both* large size of plant as well as high foreign participation. The correlations of FP and MEPS with K/L and MKR suggest that capital intensity may be related to MNCs by the latter's introduction of large scale, modern technology (in so far as new technology is embodied in the value of net fixed assets). The relatively low correlation of AD with FP and MEPS is somewhat surprising, but this may be because local advertising does not fully capture the effect of product differentiation or

TABLE 3.1 Simple correlation coefficients for (logs of) independent variables

	FP	MEPS	CAR	MEPCA	AD	MSZ	MGR	K/L	MKR
FP	1.00								
MEPS	0.633	1.00							
CAR	0.179	0.420	1.00						
MEPCA	0.457	0.819	0.841	1.00					
AD	0.337	0.294	0.425	0.428	1.00				
MSZ	0.200	−0.128	0.115	−0.010	0.175	1.00			
MGR	0.048	0.119	−0.005	0.065	−0.294	0.162	1.00		
K/L	0.549	0.514	0.141	0.393	0.004	0.064	0.222	1.00	
MKR	0.496	0.502	0.216	0.449	0.058	0.679	0.417	0.728	1.00

An Open Developing Economy: The Case of Malaysia   75

the 'spill-over' effects of MNCs' international promotion in raising firm size or attracting MNCs.

CAR is not highly correlated with FP. Somewhat surprisingly, its correlation with MEPS is also not as high as may be expected. The fact that its coefficient with AD is about the same as with MEPS, and that it has low correlation with the capital variables, lead us to suspect that it is factors like product-mix and advertising which affect CAR (by raising marker power) more than technological ones, but it is difficult to say anything more with confidence.

The two capital variables are highly correlated. However, their relationship to MSZ is puzzling. The fact that K/L is insignificantly, and MKR strongly, related to market size may be spurious; certainly an examination of the variables above does not provide a ready explanation.

With these relationships in mind, let us examine the results of the regression analysis for the sample, still excluding the variable UKC_4. Table 3.2 sets out some of the results obtained. Results for independent variables with very high collinearity are not shown (in particular MEPS with FP and the capital variables: when tried together FP retained its sign but lost significance, the others changed sign and also lost significance).

If we ignore FP for a minute, we find that the results serve to confirm most of the relationships discovered in advanced countries. MEPS (and its close construct MEPCA) have powerful effects on C_4. So strong are these effects, however, that they raise doubts about the exact meaning and explanatory power of this variable.[23] Nevertheless, the fact that CAR has significant and positive effects, as do both capital variables, suggests that scale economies and capital intensity do influence concentration. AD has a positive and generally significant effect (except in equation 2 where MEPCA seems to overwhelm it); it becomes most significant when combined with either of the capital variables, suggesting an interaction between the two barriers to entry. Market size is always significant and negative (even when tried with MEPCA), while market growth is negative but insignificant when tried without market size, but positive and significant when tried with it. This is in line with Kamerschen's finding for the US that market growth has ambiguous effects on concentration,[24] and suggests that growth increases concentration once the negative effect of industry size has been accounted for.

Foreign presence has a positive and significant effect on concentration whether tried without the capital variables or (as in equations 7 and 12) with them. It functions best when combined with CAR, MSZ

TABLE 3.2 Regression results for determinants of concentration: 46 industries

Equation	FP	MEPS	CAR	MEPCA	AD	MSZ	MGR	K/L	MKR	Const.	R^2
(1)		26.82[a] (12.06)			1.34 (1.12)		−1.68 (−1.13)			−65.08	0.83
(2)	8.40[a] (2.92)			12.28[a] (6.63)	−0.965 (−0.59)					−85.99	0.72
(3)	17.30[a] (5.78)				4.37[b] (2.11)	−6.95[b] (−2.42)		14.83[a] (4.13)		−75.04	0.49
(4)			13.79[a] (4.35)			−8.18[a] (−3.69)				−46.05	0.59
(5)					8.02[a] (4.76)	−16.48[a] (−5.05)			14.79[a] (6.51)	12.77	0.60
(6)	17.44[a] (5.79)		13.09[a] (4.14)			−8.77[a] (−3.85)	3.86[b] (2.02)			−65.67	0.62
(7)	12.33[a] (2.58)				3.57[c] (1.65)			5.57 (1.24)		−36.92	0.42
(8)			8.90[b] (2.01)		4.22[b] (1.84)				5.85[a] (2.73)	−57.89	0.37
(9)			9.85[a] (2.36)		3.76[b] (1.71)			11.85[a] (3.29)		−86.14	0.42
(10)				14.26[a] (11.10)		−2.82[b] (−1.70)				−77.63	0.74
(11)	19.21[a] (5.35)					−8.09[a] (−2.97)	4.02[b] (1.75)			−8.20	0.35
(12)	13.29[a] (2.72)				3.21[c] (1.36)		−0.78 (−0.25)		2.40 (0.80)	−15.03	0.35
(13)			15.08[a] (3.89)			−6.81[a] (−2.52)	3.92[c] (1.66)	11.40[a] (2.93)		−99.43	0.41
(14)		21.91[a] (12.75)								−51.56	0.78

NOTE

R^2 corrected for degrees of freedom; t statistic in parentheses; one-tail tests used.
[a] indicates significant at 99%.
[b] indicates significant at 95%.
[c] indicates significant at 90%.

An Open Developing Economy: The Case of Malaysia

and MGR (equation 6). When combined with AD, K/L or MKR, it retains significance, but reduces the others' significance, and the equations as such (7 and 12) deteriorate in their explanatory power. In general, the findings suggest that *foreign investment serves to raise concentration over and above the level accounted for by other industrial variables as tested above*. However, *it also serves raise concentration via the industrial variables*, by raising capital-intensity and minimum capital requirements, and, rather less so, through local advertising. It is also possible that foreign firms are, through the various advantages they possess (not captured in the above variables), able to raise the minimum efficient scale of production as measured here, but the exact direction of cause and effect is open to debate. The evidence at hand does not enable us to say precisely how the independent effect of FP on C_4 manifests itself: it may be through predatory conduct, through technological and marketing factors (which lead to the disappearance of small or traditional producers), or through gaining special concessions, not captured by our industrial variables, or a combination of these.

It is possible that the results obtained are due, not to MNCs causing higher concentration, but to higher concentration attracting MNCs. While this cannot be directly tested by means of cross-section analysis, certain *a priori* considerations lead us to support the former rather than the latter hypothesis. First, MNCs contemplating entry into an underdeveloped, small country are unlikely to pay much attention to the existence of local oligopolies (as an indicator of high potential profits). They possess highly developed sources of market power in their own industries, which they undoubtedly have the confidence to apply, when market size and costs are appropriate, without having to note the structure of local industry. Second, the technological, marketing and organisational differences between MNCs and local enterprises in a country like Malaysia are so large that it seems eminently plausible that MNC entry greatly alters the barriers to entry. Third, the evidence shows enormous size differences between foreign and local firms, again lending more weight to our hypothesised causation than the reverse. And, finally, the fact that FP has an independent effect on C_4 suggests that causation runs from MNC entry to concentration, rather than from the industrial variables associated with concentration to foreign entry.

The inclusion of UKC_4 as an explanatory variable enables us to introduce further industrial determinants of structure and to concentrate on 28 sectors where large, modern TNCs are most active. The relationship between concentration levels in the UK and Malaysia is given by the following simple linear regression:

$$C_4 = 0.604 UKC_4 + 36.59 \qquad R^2 = 0.27 \qquad F = 11.07$$
$$(3.33) \qquad\qquad\qquad (t \text{ value in parentheses})$$

The coefficient and the equation are both significant at 99 per cent, indicating a similarity in the factors at work in determining structures in the UK and Malaysia. However, the relatively low R^2 suggests that a number of important determinants are quite different, attributable to the very different levels of industrial development.[25]

The simple correlation coefficients for this sample (not reported here) are very similar to these shown in Table 3.1, except that coefficient for FP and MEPS rises even higher (to 0.712), as does the one for FP and K/L (to 0.626), suggesting a stronger relationship between MNC presence, large plant-size dominance and capital-intensity. The AD coefficient with FP remains the same, strengthening the suspicion the local advertising is not greatly affected by foreign presence. As for UKC_4, it shows a positive and fairly strong correlation with FP (0.412) and with MEPS (0.486) but with none of other independent variables. The former supports the finding of other studies that MNCs hail from relatively concentrated industries at home;[26] the latter implies that plant-level concentration in the UK probably has a similar relationship to efficient plant scale as found in Malaysia – whether for technological or for other reasons is difficult to say.

Table 3.3 sets out some of the main results of the regressions for the 28 industries using UKC_4. Not surprisingly, when combined with other variables, UKC_4 becomes statistically less significant. More unexpectedly, there is very little perceptible effect on the performance of the other variables. The strength of FP, K/L and MKR does not increase. The presence of multinationals continues to exercise a positive independent influence on concentration, but the coefficients are not noticeably higher than for foreign investment as a whole. AD seems to become weaker for the smaller sample, though it still seems to act as a significant barrier to entry when combined with MKR. Capital barriers are significant and positive, but not more as than for the full sample. On the basis of this limited evidence, then, it cannot be said that, given the industrial determinants of concentration, the 'real' MNCs have a stronger effect on structure than small foreign investors.

TABLE 3.3 Regression results for determinants of concentration: 28 industries

	UKC_4	FP	$MEPS$	CAR	$MEPCA$	AD	MSZ	MGR	K/L	MKR	$Const.$	R^2
(1)	0.17 (1.68)		24.25^a (9.44)								−65.20	0.83
(2)	0.19 (1.31)	17.06^a (4.78)		9.90^a (3.04)			−6.04^b (−0.200)				−37.03	0.67
(3)	0.20 (1.18)			6.46^c (1.60)		5.45^b (2.24)	−13.08^a (−2.93)			12.81^a (3.65)	−24.05	0.59
(4)	0.25^b (1.87)				12.49^a (6.33)						65.43	0.71
(5)	0.32^b (1.82)			12.42^a (3.07)			−6.13^c (−1.57)		12.66^c (2.71)		74.52	0.50
(6)	0.31^b (2.06)	14.67^a (4.13)		8.06^b (2.15)		0.20 (0.09)					−52.55	0.61
(7)	0.22^b (1.82)	8.85^a (2.67)			9.87^a (4.68)	−0.65 (−0.36)					−82.86	0.76
(8)	0.31^b (1.83)	17.50^a (4.17)					−3.27 (−0.95)	1.84 (0.58)			−16.10	0.54
(9)	0.53^a (3.08)									6.41^b (2.19)	−75.41	0.36

NOTE
See Table 3.2, p. 76.

TABLE 3.4 Selected simple correlation coefficients for consumer and non-consumer industries

Non-consumer goods

FP	1.00	0.702	−0.072	0.113	0.585	0.596	FP
MEPS	0.601	1.00	0.222	0.007	0.368	0.340	MEPS
CAR	0.434	0.549	1.00	0.265	−0.309	−0.137	CAR
AD	0.528	0.591	0.506	1.00	−0.306	−0.192	AD
K/L	0.630	0.573	0.541	0.541	1.00	0.814	K/L
MKR	0.560	0.517	0.205	0.410	0.632	1.00	MKR
	FP	MEPS	CAR	AD	K/L	MKR	

Consumer goods

V FINDINGS FOR CONSUMER AND NON-CONSUMER GOODS INDUSTRIES

The division of the sample into sub-groups of consumer and non-consumer goods industries was undertaken to check certain *a priori* expectations about the different impact of the product differentiation and capital variables on these groups. Consumer goods industries were expected to show a higher correlation between foreign presence and product differentiation barriers, and a greater influence of these barriers on concentration, than non-consumer goods industries. They were also expected to show a lower influence of the capital variables, since it may be argued that in a developing country the impact of foreign technology on capital-intensity would be sharper on non-consumer goods industries (where there is less scope for substituting traditional for modern products and techniques) than in consumer industries.

An examination of the simple correlation coefficients for the two groups bears out these expectations to some extent. Table 3.4 shows a selection of coefficients, combining both groups for ease of comparison. Each group has (fortuitously) equal numbers of observations, 23 each; when UKC_4 is included, we get 15 observations for consumer goods and 13 for non-consumer goods industries.

For consumer goods industries foreign presence is highly correlated with practically every other independent variable. While its correlations with MEPS and the two capital variables are similar to those observed for non-consumer industries, suggesting that foreign entry introduced large size of plant and capital-intensive techniques in both sectors, its correlation with AD indicates that product differentiation is strongly associated with foreign investment in consumer goods and not in other industries. AD is also highly correlated with the capital-intensity and scale-economy variables for consumer goods industries, while for non-consumer goods it is negatively related to the capital variables and insignificantly to the others. The higher incidence of collinearity for consumer goods industries reduces the scope for meaningful regressions, but it does illustrate the marked differences in the behaviour of the variables in comparison to other industries.

Table 3.5 sets out some regression results for the two groups of industries. The effects of FP on C_4 in simple regressions are as follows:

Consumer Goods: $C_4 = 16.74$ FP $- 12.42$ $R^2 = 0.29$ $F = 8.73$
$\qquad\qquad\qquad\quad$ (2.95) $\qquad\qquad\qquad$ (t value in parentheses)

Non-Consumer Goods: $C_4 = 17.90$ FP $- 19.25$ $R^2 = 0.33$
$\qquad\qquad\qquad\qquad\quad$ (3.42)
$\qquad\qquad\qquad\quad$ F $= 11.71$

Foreign presence has a positive and significant (at 99 per cent) effect on concentration in both samples, but it is slightly stronger for non-consumer goods industries. It is interesting that the simple regression of Malaysian on UK concentration ratios shows a much closer similarity between the consumer goods sectors ($R^2 = 0.74$) than for the non-consumer sectors ($R^2 = 0.24$), indicating that technological differences between them are much more prominent in the latter.

The regression equations in Table 3.5, a dozen for each sector (with last four in each being for reduced samples including UKC_4), show some notable differences. FP continues to be a stronger and more significant influence on concentration in non-consumer than consumer goods. Furthermore, the inclusion of the UKC_4 variable (i.e. concentrating on MNC-dominated industries) seems to show – and we must be cautious because of the smallness of the samples – that the effect of FP is greatly increased for non-consumer goods while it is dominished for consumer goods. This may suggest that, for consumer goods, industrial and technological factors making for concentration are being communicated by 'intermediate' foreign investors more strongly than by the 'real' MNCs, but that, in non-consumer goods industries, the large MNCs are the most powerful channel for introducing concentrating forces from the advanced countries.

AD has a positive effect on concentration for both groups, with slightly, but very slightly, higher significance in consumer goods industries. This is an unexpected but not an unprecedented finding;[27] in view of the lack of correlation between FP and AD in the non-

TABLE 3.5 Regression results for determinants of concentration: consumer and non-consumer goods industries

	UKC_4	FP	MEPS	CAR	MEPCA	AD	MSZ	MGR	K/L	MKR	Const.	R^2
Consumer goods												
(1)		15.94a (2.33)		12.17b (2.45)			−5.99c (−1.59)				−44.38	0.46
(2)		14.76b (2.42)				5.08c (1.73)	−6.17c (−1.65)				15.36	0.44
(3)				7.16 (1.20)		4.34c (1.36)	−4.94 (−1.32)		14.34c (1.67)		−65.01	0.42
(4)			26.77a (7.08)			0.28c (1.50)		−1.60 (−0.74)			−62.04	0.81
(5)						8.05a (3.95)	−14.54a (3.74)			14.34a (4.53)	5.45	0.66
(6)					13.11a (6.70)		−1.95 (−0.76)				−70.84	0.67
(7)		14.72b (1.87)				5.24c (1.69)	−6.30c (−1.62)	0.98 (0.25)			9.33	0.40
(8)		10.82c (1.87)		8.75c (1.63)		2.71 (0.84)					−41.92	0.43
(9)	0.46b (2.01)			4.18 (0.81)			−2.40 (−0.53)		22.18b (2.11)		−113.0	0.67
(10)	0.58b (2.71)	9.78c (1.81)									−1.36	0.58
(11)	0.65a (4.96)			0.06 (0.01)		6.18b (2.82)				5.77c (1.96)	24.24	0.79
(12)	0.51c (1.84)	8.32 (1.22)		7.83c (1.42)		−1.36 (−0.25)					29.69	0.59

An Open Developing Economy: The Case of Malaysia   83

	UKC_4	FP	MEPS	CAR	MEPCA	AD	MSZ	MGR	K/L	MKR	Const.	R^2
Non-consumer goods												
(13)		17.87[a] (4.94)					−10.47[a] (−3.47)				−49.51	0.68
(14)		15.98[a] (3.63)					−13.15[a] (3.41)	5.68[c] (1.53)			16.93	0.60
(15)		20.39[a] (4.24)				4.69 (0.98)	−11.43[b] (−2.12)				29.29	0.54
(16)				16.57[a] (3.29)		9.59[b] (1.94)	−23.12[a] (−3.35)			14.86[a] (3.80)	44.97	0.48
(17)				15.45[b] (2.54)		8.20[c] (1.68)	−13.24[b] (−2.36)		18.33[a] (4.02)		−96.49	0.56
(18)			30.96[a] (10.56)			4.19[c] (1.75)		−0.28 (−1.16)			−99.56	0.88
(19)					15.95[a] (7.88)		−0.26 (−0.98)				−94.69	0.80
(20)				13.22[b] (2.41)			−16.97[a] (−4.80)			11.55[a] (4.17)	−20.08	0.62
(21)	−0.04 (−0.28)	26.02[a] (8.33)		14.18[a] (5.24)			−9.15 (−0.04)				−115.5	0.90
(22)	0.03 (0.13)	26.77[a] (5.09)				11.67[c] (2.10)	−0.68 (0−.11)	9.62 (1.96)			−127.6	0.76
(23)	0.05 (−0.33)	24.46[a] (8.65)		12.98[a] (4.20)		2.88 (0.81)					−114.5	0.90
(24)	0.01 (0.02)			17.01[c] (2.16)			−14.12[c] (−1.52)		14.68 (1.66)		−65.56	0.26

NOTE
See Table 3.2, p. 76.

consumer goods industries, it supports our earlier reading that foreign investment and product differentiation can act independently to raise concentration. However, the generally low significance of AD in consumer goods industries is probably due to collinearity with FP; when tried without the latter (equation 5) it becomes highly significant. There is, therefore, some ground to suppose that FP and AD act together to raise concentration in consumer goods.

The scale variable CAR performs better for non-consumer than for consumer goods industries, as does market size. Both support the presumption that technological variables making for larger minimum size of plant are more powerful for the non-consumer industries. Market growth has similar, rather ambiguous, effects. The capital variables seem to perform equally well for both groups, belying the expectation they would tend to cause greater concentration for non-consumer goods industries. This does not imply, of course, that the two groups have similar capital intensities, simply that, given their respective technologies, capital intensity as such (this also applies to advertising) does not lead to greater concentration in one or the other groups.

In general, the independent influence of foreign investment in increasing concentration persists through both groups of industries, but *is stronger in non-consumer goods industries, these also being the industries where the industrial structures between home and host countries are more disparate.* Thus, it seems to act as an active agent for propagating structural change. As before, however, our data do not enable us to say whether the effect manifests itself through predatory conduct, product differentation 'spill overs', or technology; i.e. they do not permit us to say whether the effect is beneficial or not. Such an evaluation can only be made by further empirical investigation.

VI CONCLUSIONS

The main findings of the investigation of the determinants of industrial concentration in Malaysia may be summarised as follows.

1. The factors which have been found to influence concentration in advanced industrial countries also determine it in a small, relatively unindustrialised country. Barriers to entry exercised by scale economies, capital requirements and product differentiation are all found to be significant in promoting concentration. Market size is negatively correlated with concentration, and market growth has minor, and rather ambiguous, effects.

An Open Developing Economy: The Case of Malaysia 85

2. The structure of industry in Malaysia is, insofar as a limited comparison shows, similar to the structure in the UK, but the similarity is far greater for consumer goods industries than for non-consumer goods industries. While concentration in both groups of industries is determined by the same sets of factors, technological variables seem to play a stronger role in non-consumer goods industries.

3. The introduction of foreign investment as an explanatory variable shows that higher foreign presence in an industry is associated with higher levels of concentration. The effect of foreign presence is exercised partly through other independent variables and partly quite independently of them, i.e. foreign investment increases concentration by introducing new processes and products and raising the capital intensity of production, and also by influences (such as predatory conduct, spillover effects of international promotion or gaining concessions from the government) not captured by the other variables. It should be noted that no policy conclusion may be drawn on the basis of our finding. We cannot say, with the evidence at hand, whether the increase in concentration associated with foreign investment is desirable for industrial efficiency and technical change or not: a mixture of 'good' and 'bad' influences seems to be involved, but further research is needed to disentangle them.

4. Foreign investment has a greater impact on concentration in non-consumer goods industries (probably because the industrial structure in Malaysia is distinctly more different from that in advanced countries from which MNCs come) than in consumer goods industries. In the latter, foreign presence is closely correlated with high levels of advertising; in the former, foreign entry is more related to capital intensity, but its independent influence (presumably by the introduction of new processes) is very strong.

5. Concentration is positively influenced by foreign investment both by small firms from neighbouring LDCs and by large multinationals from advanced countries. Some limited evidence suggests that the only difference between them, at least as far as concentration is concerned, is that MNCs are a more powerful factor for non-consumer goods industries than LDC foreign investors. For the sample as a whole, given their relative spheres of influence, both seem to be equally effective in transmitting the impulses that shape industrial structure. This inference is, however, very tentative, since the sample evidence does not permit a very clear distinction between the two sorts of investors.

6. Finally, a word of caution about the methodology of the study as a whole. Cross-section analysis of industrial structure at a given point of

time may not be the ideal way of analysing the impact of the entry of foreign firms. A 'before and after' analysis, using time-series data for particular industries and making specific international comparisons, may be more appropriate. Furthermore, a more detailed consideration of how government policies may have affected market structure in particular industries would have added more flesh to the statistical skeleton. However, a more exhaustive and detailed study was not, given the resources and data available, possible for the present author. It is hoped that the results obtained, which seem plausible and interesting, will provide an incentive to further work in this area.

APPENDIX

TABLE A.3.1 Malaysia concentration level (4-plant), comparative UK concentration,[1] and foreign participation in employment, 1972

Consumer goods				Non-consumer goods			
Industry	Malaysia 4-plant concent.	UK[2] 4-plant concent.	Foreign Participation (in Malaysia)	Industry	Malaysian 4-plant concent.	UK[2] 4-plant concent.	Foreign Participation (in Malaysia)
1. Ice crea	87	73	63	25. Rubber smokehouses	50	n.a.	50
2. Pickles & sauces	30	n.a.	20	26. Palm oil factories	21	n.a.	50
3. Sago & tapioca	33	n.a	0	27. Saw mills	7	n.a.	8
4. Rice mills	16	n.a.	0	28. Planning windows, etc.	39	n.a.	14
5. Biscuits	46	65	57	29. Paper, products	51	n.c.	43
6. Bakeries	23	1	7	30. Animal feeds	48	16	43
7. Cocoa & chocolate	56	40	24	31. Industrial chemicals	52	4.2[6]	61
8. Noodles	49	n.a.	16	32. Chemical fertilizers	63	38	93
9. Coffee	18	n.a.	0	33. Misc. chemicals	72	18	43
10. Ice	15	n.a.	31	34. Clay, china, earthware	20	22[7]	10
11. Rubber	57	27	44	35. Cement, concrete	69	48	49
12. Soft drinks	41	24	66	36. Iron & Steel milling	60	15	71
13. Tobacco	76	23	43	37. Fabricated structurals	68	n.c.	23
14. Textiles	25	n.c.	33	38. Architectural metals	32	n.c.	16
15. Footwear	92	21	7	39. Wire products	39	12	31
16. Clothing	36	n.c.	96	40. Metal boxes	58	15	57
17. Furniture	18	10	10	41. Brass, copper aluminium	48	15[8]	36
18. Printing	19	4[3]	23	42. Boilers, tanks	55	10[9]	60
19. Paint	57	32	86	43. General engineering, repair	15	n.c.	10
20. Soaps	94	52	79	44. Refrigeration, etc. machinery	90	10[10]	72
21. Cosmetics	41	16[4]	84	45. Electrical machinery	28	n.c.	68
22. Pharmaceuticals	49	12	54	46. Plastic	18	3	13
23. Bicyles	72	61[5]	46				
24. Rubber remilling	11	n.a.	58				

NOTE 1. 4-plant minimum concentration, calculated on comparable basis as share of largest 4 plants (by employment size) in total industry sales.
2. n.a. means not available because industry does not exist (or is not separately mentioned) in UK; n.c. means not available on comparable basis to Malaysian classification.
3. General printing and publishing, excluding newspapers and periodicals.
4. Toilet preparations.
5. Including motor-cycles.
6. Average of organic and inorganic chemicals.
7. Pottery only.
8. Average of brass and copper, and aluminium.
9. Iron castings.
10. Refrigeration machinery, space-heating, ventilating and air-conditioning equipment.

SOURCES
Department of Statistics, *Survey of Manufacturing Industries, Peninsular Malaysia, 1972*, vol. 2 (Kaula Lumpur: 1977); Department of Industry, *Census of Production 1972* (London: HMSO).

An Open Developing Economy: The Case of Malaysia 87

NOTES

1. I am very grateful to Ajit Singh and Dermot McAleese for comments on an earlier draft of this paper.
2. Recent surveys are provided by Caves (1974), Dunning (1977) and Horst (1975).
3. See, for instance, Caves (1974) and Dunning (1974).
4. Mainly Steuer (1973), Dunning (1973) and Rosenbluth (1970).
5. Newfarmer and Mueller (1975), Newfarmer (1978), Connor and Mueller (1977) and Evans (1977). The first three of these studies find a relationship between foreign presence and high levels of industrial concentration in various sectors of Brazil and Mexico – a result which conflicts with the more agnostic findings in developed countries – but they do not attempt to explicitly analyse the effects of MNC entry on concentration. Evans discusses the pharmaceutical industry in Brazil, where he finds that MNCs tended to reduce concentration. Newfarmer (1978) finds, on the other hand, that the takeover behaviour of TNCs in the electrical equipment industry in Brazil led to a sharp increase in concentration levels. For a survey of the literature of MNCs and industrial structure in developing countries see Chapter 2 above.
6. Ghosh (1975) discusses some influences on changes in concentration levels in India: Meller (forthcoming) compares concentration in 10 Latin American Countries, apparently using market size as the main explanatory variable; Nam (1975) uses more variables but the specification of his scale-economy and capital-requirements variables is unsatisfactory and leaves several difficulties, noted below, out of account.
7. See, among others, Ornstein et al. (1973), Ornstein (1976), Henning and Mann (1976), George and Ward (1975), Caves and Uekusa (1976) and papers by Guth, Kamerschen and Weiss in the readings edited by Yamey (1973).
8. Rosenbluth (1970) considers these factors for Canada in the 1960s and concludes that there is no discernible relationship between concentration and foreign control. Similar findings are reported for the UK by Dunning (1973) and Steuer (1973).
9. See Caves (1974), Dunning (1977), Horst (1975) and Wolf (1977).
10. On the use of takeovers by MNCs as a method of entry see Newfarmer (1978). On oligopolistic interaction in MNC entry, see Knickerbocker (1973), and, for the case of pharmaceuticals in Brazil, Evans (1977).
11. Volume 1 provides aggregate figures for all industries. Volume 2 was published in 1977, and provides detailed figures on 4-digit industries; a copy of this volume was kindly supplied to me before publication by the Chief Statistician. A firm is classified as 'foreign' if over 50 per cent equity is held abroad.
12. Survey of Manufacturing Industries, vol. 1, op. cit., table 5.
13. Hong Kong and Indian firms are even closer to local firms in terms of size, capital intensity and wages, but due to their tiny share of Malaysian manufacturing we ignore them here.
14. See the papers by L. T. Wells and C. F. Diaz-Alejandero in Agmon and Kindleberger (1977) and Lecraw (1977).

15. I would also like to acknowledge the help of Zainal Yusof, currently writing a doctoral dissertation at Oxford on foreign investment and employment structure in Malaysia, for his help in explaining the Malaysian situation.
16. See Vanlommel, Brabender and Liebaers (1977) for a comparison of different measures based on Belgian data.
17. See Caves et al. (1975) and Ornstein et al. (1973).
18. See Caves et al. (1975). These problems are worse when MEPS is used to explain firm-level concentration. Since we are trying to explain plant-level concentration, however, some of the problems raised by MEPS are reduced.
19. This is the reciprocal of the 'cost disadvantage ratio' of Caves et al. (1975).
20. This is a variant of a construct employed by Caves et al. (1975).
21. Because capital-intensity is generally associated with the 'lumpiness' that gives rise to economies of scale, Ornstein et al. (1973) in fact use K/L as a proxy for scale economies rather than utilise MEPS.
22. Caves and Uekusa (1976) use this variable (with US data) to explain market structure in Japan. The two main factors which may lead to concentration and are not captured by Malaysian data are R and D intensity and the 'spillover' effects of advertising done by the parent MNC. The use of a control variable should capture these influences.
23. See Caves et al. (1975) and Ornstein et al. (1973).
24. In Yamey (1973). Ghosh (1975) finds for India, however, that over a longer period, 1948–68, growth did significantly diminish concentration. Ghosh's study is not comparable to ours since he studies *changes* in concentration levels.
25. George and Ward (1975) show, in a similar exercise for 20-plant concentration ratios in the UK and Continental countries, that the similarity between advanced economies is much greater. For the UK and Germany, the correlation coefficient is 0.63, the UK and France 0.72, and the UK and Italy 0.59; for Germany and France, 0.75, Germany and Italy 0.80; and France and Italy 0.77 (p. 32, Table 4.4). Connor and Mueller (1976) compare concentration levels in the US with Brazil and Mexico. The two LDCs have very similar structures but US levels are much lower, and its pattern is quite different from the other two. This supports our inference about differences in levels of development causing differences in structure between the UK and Malaysia.
26. See Horst (1975).
27. See Ornstein (1976) for a similar finding for the US. His explanation is that advertising and concentration are both caused by the 'large firm' effect.

REFERENCES

Agmon, T. and Kindleberger, C. P. (ed.) (1977), *Multinationals from Small Countries* (Cambridge, Mass.: MIT Press).
Caves, R. E. (1974), 'Industrial Organisation', in: J. H. Dunning (ed.) *Economic Analysis and the Multinational Enterprise* (London: Allen & Unwin) pp. 115–46.

Caves, R. E., Khalilzadeh-Shirazi, J. and Porter, M. E. (1975), 'Scale Economies in the Statistical Analyses of Market Power', *Review of Economics and Statistics*, pp. 133-40.
Caves, R. E. and Uekusa, M. (1976), *Industrial Organisation in Japan* (Washington DC: Brookings Institution).
Connor, J. M. and Mueller, W. F. (1977), *Market Power and Profitability of Multinational Corporations in Brazil and Mexico*, Report to the subcommittee on Foreign Economic Policy, US Senate (Washington DC: GPO).
Dept. of Statistics (vol. 1, 1975; vol. 2, 1977), *Survey of Manufacturing Industries, Peninsular Malaysia, 1972* (Kuala Lumpur: Govt. of Malaysia).
Dunning, J. H. (1973), *United States Industry in Britain* (London: Financial Times).
—— (1974), 'Multinational Enterprises, Market Structure, Economic Power and Industrial Policy', *Journal of World Trade Law*, pp. 575-613.
—— (1977), 'Trade, Location of Economic Activity and the MNE: A search for the Eclectic Approach', in: B. Ohlin et al. (ed.), *The International Allocation of Economic Activity* (London: Macmillan) pp. 395-418.
Evans, P. B. (1977), 'Direct Investment and Industrial Concentration', *Journal of Development Studies*, pp. 373-86.
George, K. D. and Ward, T. S. (1975), *The Structure of Industry in the EEC: An International Comparison*, University of Cambridge, Department of Applied Economics, Occasional Paper, 43 (London: Cambridge University Press).
Ghosh, A. (1975), 'Concentration and Growth of Indian Industries, 1948-68', *Journal of Industrial Economics*, pp. 203-22.
Henning, J. A. and Mann, H. M. (1976), 'Advertising and Concentration: A Tentative Determination of Cause and Effect', in: R. T. Masson and P. D. Qualls (eds.), *Essays on Industrial Organisation in Honour of Joe S. Bain* (Cambridge Mass.: Ballinger) pp. 143-54.
Horst, T. (1972), 'Firm and Industry Determinants of the Decision to Invest Abroad: An Empirical Study', *Review of Economics and Statistics*, pp. 358-66.
—— (1975), 'American Investments Abroad and Domestic Market Power' (Washington DC: Brookings Institution). mimeo. Subsequently published in F. Bergsten, T. Horst and T. Moran, *American Multinationals and American Interests* (Washington DC: Brookings, 1978).
Knickerbocker, F. T. (1973), *Oligopolistic Reaction and Multinational Enterprise* (Boston: Harvard University, Graduate School of Business Administration).
Lecraw, D. (1977), 'Direct Investment by Firms from Less Developed Countries', *Oxford Economic Papers*, pp. 442-57.
Meller P. (forthcoming), 'International Comparisons of Industrial Concentration in Latin America' (New York National Bureau of Economic Research), Draft.
Nam, W. H. (1975), 'The Determinants of Industrial Concentration: The Case of Korea', *Malayan Economic Review*, pp. 37-48.
Newfarmer, R. S. (1978), 'TNC Takeovers in Brazil: The Uneven Distribution of Benefits in the Market for Firms', University of Notre Dame, Indiana, Working Paper. Forthcoming in *Multinational Conglomerates and the Economics of Dependent Development* (JAI Press).

Newfarmer, R. S. and Mueller, W. F. (1975), *Multinational Corporations in Brazil and Mexico: Structural Sources of Economic and Noneconomic Power*, Report to the Subcommittee on Multinational Corporations, US Senate (Washington DC: GPO).

Ornstein, S. I., Weston, J. F., Intriligator, M. D. and Shrieves, R. E. (1972), 'Determinants of Market Structure', *Southern Economic Journal*, pp. 612–25.

Ornstein, S. I. (1976), 'The Advertising-Concentration Controversy', *Southern Economic Journal*, pp. 892–902.

Rosenbluth, G. (1970), 'The Relation between Foreign Control and Concentration in Canadian Industry', *Canadian Journal of Economics*, pp. 14–38.

Steuer, M. et al. (1973), *The Impact of Foreign Direct Investment on The United Kingdom* (London: HMSO).

Vanlommel, E., Brabander, B. de, and Liebaers, D. (1977), 'Industrial Concentration Measures', *Journal of Industrial Economics*, pp. 1–20.

Wolf, B. M. (1977), 'Industrial Diversification and Internationalisation: Some Empirical Evidence', *Journal of Industrial Economics*, pp. 177–91.

Yamey, B. S. (ed.) (1973), *Economics of Industrial Structure* (Harmondsworth: Penguin).

Part Two

Intra-Firm Trade and Transfer Prices

4 The Pattern of Intra-Firm Exports by US Multinationals[1]

I INTRODUCTION

This paper reports on an attempt to explain inter-industry differences in the pattern of intra-firm exports (exports from parent MNCs to affiliates abroad) by US manufacturing firms in 1970. The growth of intra-firm exports of manufactures in the past two decades has been noted with interest in the literature, though much of this interest has centred on the possibilities of transfer price manipulation by MNCs.[2] No serious effort has, to my knowledge, yet been made to examine the economic factors which account for the wide inter-industry differences observed in the propensity to use intra-firm rather than unrelated-party (or 'open market') trade, despite the significance of these differences for understanding MNC strategy and for formulating policies to deal with the potential dangers of transfer price manipulation.[3]

Two factors place handicaps in the way of such an examination. First, there is little theory which deals specifically with this problem; conventional trade theory, which does not distinguish between inter- and intra-firm trade, certainly offers little guidance. The study of vertical integration in industrial economics comes closest to analysing the factors that account for the pattern of intra-firm trade, but we need to supplement it with considerations specific to the operations of MNCs, where 'vertical integration' in the form of common ownership already exists and where the international nature of the phenomenon adds a new set of influences. Second, and more significantly, data on intra-firm trade are scarce, and those that are published are highly aggregated.[4] Thus a detailed investigation which deals with specific products, arguably the ideal level of analysis, cannot be undertaken.

The present study suffers from both handicaps, and its limitations must be acknowledged at the start. It is, however, hoped that what does emerge is of interest, and that this preliminary attempt will lead to further investigation. We proceed as follows: section II describes some relevant characteristics of intra-firm exports for the US; section III discusses factors that may be expected to account for inter-industry differences in intra-firm trade; section IV describes the variables; and section V gives the results of the empirical tests.

II INTRA-FIRM EXPORTS BY US MNCs

In another paper (see chapter 5) I traced the growth of intra-firm trade by US firms from 1962 to 1970, and noted difficulties in comparing figures for different years created by changes in sample coverage (of the parent MNCs as well as of the definition of affiliates). The massive study conducted by the US Tariff Commission (1973), which contains by far the most comprehensive data on intra-firm trade by industry, and is the source of data used in this paper, also faced similar problems. It had to rely on data from a sample of 298 MNCs, extrapolated, on the basis of a 1966 survey of all MNCs, to provide estimates for the whole universe of MNCs for 1970. It also had to interpolate items of information suppressed by source agencies for reasons of confidentiality.[5] Furthermore, it confined its estimates of intra-firm trade to MOFAs (majority-owned foreign affiliates) of US firms, leaving out minority-owned affiliates which may account for substantial trade with parent companies. It did not provide a breakdown of the destination of intra-firm exports, of their composition, of the nature of the firms indulging in such exports, all of which are relevant to explaining their industrial distribution.[6] Nevertheless, these are the best data available, and we have to make do with them.

Of total US manufactured exports of $31.7 billion in 1970, MNCs accounted for $21.7 billion or 68 per cent. Of this latter sum $8.8 billion (41 per cent of MNC exports and 28 per cent of total US exports) was exported to MOFAs and 'charged on the books of parent MNCs'.[7] However, some of the exports were undertaken on behalf of other US firms. By themselves, MNC exports to MOFAs totalled $7.7 billion (35 per cent of MNC and 24 per cent of US exports) in 1970:[8] in the rest of this paper we shall concentrate on these intra-firm exports.

Appendix 1 sets out the detailed figures on 1970 intra-firm exports of US MNCs by industry. Such exports are expressed as two percentages, both of which form the dependent variables in regressions described below: IFX, or intra-firm exports as a percentage of total exports by

MNCs, and IFP, intra-firm exports as a percentage of production by MOFAs receiving those exports. There is a substantial variation in propensities to use intra-firm channels to export from the US, both between two-digit industries and, within the two-digit level, between three-digit industries. For industries like soaps, plastics, chemical combinations, instruments and office and calculating equipment, intra-firm trade accounts for well over half of total exports by MNCs; for others, like beverages, industrial chemicals, primary metals, electrical equipment or timber and wood products it accounts for under 20 per cent. Given the quantitative significance of US intra-firm trade and its inter-industry variations, it is surprising that no attempt has been made to analyse its economic determinants.

There are several interesting facts which are relevant to a study of this phenomenon that are not shown by the Tariff Commission figures nor discussed in its study.

First, the destination of intra-firm exports. A study for 1965 shows that of total intra-firm exports of $4.6 billion, 35 per cent went to Canada alone and another 36 per cent to Europe.[9] If we make an allowance for Australasia and South Africa, the share of developed countries may reach 80 per cent; less-developed countries accounted for less than a quarter of the total.

Second, the same study shows that, in 1965, 49 per cent of total intra-firm exports were goods 'for resale without further manufacture' and another 7 per cent were 'exports sold for parents' account on a commission basis',[10] making the total share of finished goods for resale 56 per cent. Goods 'for further processing and assembly' comprised another 36 per cent, capital equipment 5 per cent and unallocated 3 per cent. A very large part of intra-firm exports was, therefore, simply finished products being channelled through affiliates in order to serve third parties; intermediate goods, which were used in affiliates' manufacturing, comprised only slightly over a third of the total.

Third, of the total intra-firm exports of goods by manufacturing MNCs for resale and on commission basis, some 53 per cent was channelled through manufacturing affiliates and the remainder through other (mainly distribution) affiliates.[11] Thus, manufacturing affiliates served significantly as sales and service outlets for their parent companies, quite apart from engaging in their main industrial activity. These affiliates also absorbed a large share of intra-firm exports of intermediate goods for their own use (49 per cent of the total).

Fourth, a major reason for the growth of intra-firm exports (and reimports) by certain US firms in recent years has been the granting of special duty drawbacks on items which were sent abroad for processing and then finished and marketed in the US.[12] This provision (items 807.00 and 806.30 of the US Tariff Schedules) allows import duty to be paid only on the value-added component of foreign manufacture rather than on the full value of the imported goods, giving a great incentive to the industries concerned to set up facilities abroad to use cheap semi-skilled labour and so extend intra-firm trade. Thus, such industries as metal fabrication, electronic equipment, automobile parts, textiles and apparel and instruments have benefited significantly from these schedules, and the growth of their intra-firm trade may to some extent be traced to them.

The Tariff Commission's study does not differentiate between different kinds of intra-firm exports or between sales and manufacturing affiliates. Nor does it try to assess the impact of tariff provisions in stimulating particular industries' growth of intra-firm trade. The figures it provides thus amalgamate a variety of different factors. They contain exports of finished goods which are marketed by manufacturing and distribution affiliates. They contain intermediate products which are used in production by manufacturing and other affiliates, and the resulting output is sold in host countries, other foreign countries, or exported back to the US. To explain the propensity to use intra-firm exports, therefore, we must look for determinants which encompass all these factors.

III DETERMINANTS OF INTRA-FIRM EXPORT BEHAVIOUR

The reasons for undertaking intra-firm exports are rather similar to the conventional economic reasons for undertaking vertical integration, and we may fruitfully start our search for explanations by looking at this literature.[13]

Vertical integration refers to the tendency of a firm or an industry to internalise, by bringing under common ownership, production or marketing functions directly connected to its own activity. The choice of a parent MNC to sell, and so of the affiliate to buy, a product internally rather than to trade with third parties, represents a similar decision to internalise a transaction – with one major difference. Vertical integration in general describes the act of merging of ownership (or the taking over of one firm by another), while the internalisation of trade by MNCs refers to the choice between external and internal markets of firms which are already under common ownership and control.

The fact of foreign investment as such may also be viewed as the 'internalisation' of the markets for certain intangible advantages. The literature on MNCs postulates that the expansion of firms abroad occurs in response to, and in an attempt to internalise the benefits arising from, the possession of certain 'monopolistic advantages' such as advanced technology, product differentiation, skills of various sorts, access to capital and so on.[14] The fact that internalisation is preferred to open market sales of these advantages is taken to reflect imperfections in what may broadly be labelled 'information' markets. These imperfections raise the cost of transacting open market sales, because of the difficulties inherent in fully appropriating the gains from the possession of superior 'information' in open markets, and result in 'market failure'.[15]

The choice of MNCs to resort to intra-firm trade may also be viewed as a response to market failure in commodity markets, which renders recourse to external transactions either impossible or relatively costly. However, the imperfections which cause failure in information markets, and so lead firms to resort to direct investment rather than to the sale of their intangible advantages, are not the same as, though they may sometimes be related to, imperfections causing failure in commodity markets. Failure in information markets may be closely related to failure in commodity markets when the commodities involved embody new information (i.e. when they are produced with new technology). In such cases, the reasons for investing abroad (technological superiority) will be close to the reason for internalising trade (highly 'specific' products not available on open markets). In other conditions, however, the reasons for the two will be quite different. Several of the following set of reasons for resorting to intra-firm trade are not strong reasons for undertaking foreign investment (we shall remark on the similarities between the two later). To start with, therefore, it seems justified to keep the two phenomena separate.

The conventional theory of vertical integration[16] provides a number of plausible reasons for the internalisation of commodity trade. We have selected those which seem relevant to intra-firm trade, and added some by drawing on the specific experience of MNCs. The first factor discussed below applies to intra-firm exports of finished products, and is analogous to explanations of forward integration. The others apply mainly to export of intermediate products, and are analogous to explanations of backward integration.

MARKETING REQUIREMENTS

An MNC may prefer to rely on affiliates for the sale of finished products abroad for various reasons: first, the desire to control distribution facilities, where these are exceptionally profitable; second, the existence of a need for a great deal of specialised after-sales service, maintenance and updating (because of the possibilities of pooling technical resources with manufacturing affiliates this may lead MNCs to use such affiliates to act also as pure sales outlets); third, the need for assimilating and communicating information to and from consumers on their requirements, designs, plans, and so on; and, fourth, the need where relevant for keeping direct representation in order to maintain government contacts, monitor or influence policy, or win large orders.

SPECIFICITY OF PRODUCT

The more specific is an intermediate input to the firm concerned, the more will it tend to rely on internal rather than external supplies. 'Specificity' refers to such characteristics as uniqueness (high-technology products made by the MNC, not available on open markets), high quality (precision, performance or high tolerance, available externally only at high cost or after considerable search) and suitability to demanding or variable requirements (available externally only after close relationships with suppliers are established).

RISK AND UNCERTAINTY

Even for non-specific intermediate commodities the risks of disruption, delay, price changes, quality variation and the like can clearly lead firms to rely on internal sources of supply. For MNCs, the strength of this inducement will depend on the political and economic state of international markets as well as on conditions in particular host countries in which they happen to be located.

UNEXPLOITED CAPACITY AND SCALE ECONOMIES

A parent MNC which has spare capacity or unexhausted plant economies of scale would prefer to use its own facilities to supply affiliates rather than let them go to open markets. A firm may do this even when the cost of internal trading to the enterprise as a whole is higher than that of buying externally, if it feels obliged (owing to political, strategic or trade union pressures) to use its existing facilities in its home country.

'DIVISIBILITY' OF PRODUCTION PROCESSES

Certain industries use processes which can economically be divided, and parts of them relocated in cheap-labour areas abroad.[17] Where these cheap-labour areas do not possess their own firms capable of undertaking the task, or where the MNCs concerned prefer to set up their own affiliates to capitalise on technological advantages (the best example being the semi-conductor industry), the internalisation of the cost advantage will lead to the growth of direct investment together with that of intra-firm trade. In cases where local firms in cheap-labour areas *can* undertake the job efficiently, of course, the MNC may realise the cost advantage by subcontracting (and so increase inter- rather than intra-firm trade).[18] For US firms, slightly less than half of such activity has taken place through direct investment and intra-firm trade.[19]

HOME GOVERNMENT POLICY

The policies of the home (i.e. US) government may influence the extent of intra-firm trade, reducing it, on the one hand, by requiring parent companies to use domestic installed capacity to supply affiliates, or increasing it, on the other, by permitting or even encouraging the transfer abroad of 'divisible' processes (as defined above). There is little evidence that the first has been practised; the second, however, is, as we saw in section II, an important element of US policy. The provisions of Tariff Schedules 807.00 and 806.30 have promoted the growth of intra-firm exports by industries whose processes are 'divisible', though there is good reason to believe that these exports would have grown even in the absence of such provisions.[20]

HOST GOVERNMENT POLICY

The policies of host governments with respect to foreign investment, imports and domestic purchasing can influence the extent of intra-firm exports. This is particularly true of less-developed countries which, on the one hand, create a high initial dependence on imported (often intra-firm) inputs by attracting foreign investments into highly protected activities, and, on the other, seek to reduce the import content of production over the longer run by forcing foreign firms to use local

100   *The Multinational Corporation*

inputs. Thus, the distribution of MNC affiliates over countries at different levels of industrial development and with different policies will affect their propensities (and abilities) to indulge in intra-firm trade.

TRANSFER-PRICING

MNCs may wish to increase the extent of intra-firm trade simply in order to enlarge the scope for using transfer-prices to remit profits or evade taxes.[21] This inducement is likely to be stronger for operations in LDCs than in developed countries, but it may also operate for the latter.

These are the factors which we expect to influence the pattern of intra-firm exports by different US industries. It is apparent that some of them (like specificity of product) are closely related to factors (technological superiority) which also account for foreign investment, while others are not so closely related. As with most such investigations, the empirical testing falls far short of theoretical requirements, but the next section shows what we have been able to accomplish with the material at hand.

IV THE VARIABLES

The variables used for empirical testing are given below; the sources of data are described in Appendix 2. The *dependent* variable is intra-firm exports at the industry level, deflated by two sets of figures:

IFX
Intra-firm exports for each industry expressed as a percentage of total MNC exports for that industry. This variable shows the propensities of parent firms in each industry to use internal rather than external outlets for their exports.

IFP
Intra-firm exports for each industry expressed as a percentage of sales of affiliates receiving these exports. This variable shows the propensity of subsidiaries to purchase from internal rather than external sources. The two formulations of the dependent variable are designed to capture propensities from both sides of the intra-firm transaction.

The *independent* variables are:

RD
Research and development expenditures as a percentage of industry sales in the US. This variable, measuring the technological intensity of each industry, is intended to capture the innovational cause of 'specificity' of products. The higher is RD and the more specific a product, the greater is the expected incidence of intra-firm exports.

VAL
Value-added per employee, the 'Lary measure' of the flow of physical capital and skill services, for each industry in the US. This variable partly captures the skill element in each industry that may contribute to product 'specificity', and partly it captures an element of capital intensity, which in turn may contribute to scale economies in each sector. This measure suffers from the handicap that it catches a number of influences, such as market power, not related to skill or capital-intensity, but it does have the advantage that it is easy to calculate.

SALES
A dummy variable to denote the marketing requirements of each industry, taking the value of 1 when after-sales service requirements were high and 0 when they were low. The need for after-sales service was worked out from figures provided by Bailey (1975) who gives 'marketing-support' (mainly advertising and market research) costs separately from 'selling-related' (field service, technical support and other kinds of after-sales activities) for a number of US industries. Where selling-related costs were more than double the marketing support costs, and when the industry spent a relatively high amount on sales and technical services, the industry was deemed to have high after-sales service requirements.

AD
Advertising as a percentage of sales, a further indicator, but a negative one, of the need for specialised after-sales service. It is postulated that highly advertised goods (in the US) are mass-produced commodities sold directly to consumers, and so require little specialised follow-up by skilled personnel who need to be controlled by the producer. Products where a great deal of design and information exchange goes on between producer and buyer, and where the need for marketing *via* affiliates is higher, naturally need lower levels of advertising. Thus, *AD* is expected to be negatively related to the dependent variables.

TAR

A dummy variable taking the value 1 when the industry used Tariff Schedules 807.00 and 806.30, and 0 when it did not. This variable captures the influences of both the 'divisibility' of production processes and of home government policy: since the two go so closely together, we cannot separate them here.

FA

Foreign assets as a percentage of domestic assets of each US industry, a measure of the foreign spread of each sector. We argued above that the reasons which make for greater foreign investment (the 'internalisation' of intangible monopolistic advantages) were not the same as, though they may sometimes be similar to, those that make for the internalisation of commodity trade. The extent of foreign investment may, however, be used as a proxy variable to catch four different types of influences on intra-firm exports. First, it can reflect the existence of intangible advantages (like efficient and immediate communication between parent and affiliate) that lead to greater intra-firm trade by increasing the relative cost of collecting information on external markets. Thus, the more international an industry, the more 'specific' its trade may become for those products where intra-firm information becomes relatively cheap to gather. Second, a greater international spread may expose an industry to greater social, political and economic risk, and so may lead it to rely more on internal sources of supply. Third, some industries may invest abroad to keep a direct presence in countries where such representation is necessary to win contracts, adapt designs, and exert political influence. Thus, greater foreign spread may reflect greater marketing requirements, which in turn may reflect the existence of highly 'specific' products. Fourth, it may act as a proxy for inducements to indulge in transfer-price manipulations. The more widespread an industry's operations, the more the opportunities to benefit from tax, tariff and other differences between countries, and the greater the incentives to use intra-firm trade (to allow tax minimisation on global profits by changing the prices assigned to such trade).

Despite all our efforts, a number of potential influences on intra-firm exports could not be captured at all, or were only unsatisfactorily captured by the proxy variables. Thus, such factors as risk and uncertainty, excess capacity, scale economies or the geographical distribution of MNC trade,[22] are inadequately represented in our empirical tests. The inability to take these factors into account is a serious gap in this study, but with the data available it is practically impossible to test a more comprehensive model. Furthermore, the high level of aggregation of the data must certainly conceal large variations within industry groups, but there is no way of correcting for this.

The data provided by the Tariff Commission (1973) are collated in such a way as to give 32 observations for IFX and 30 for IFP. Two- and three-digit industries are combined in the sample; however, where a three-digit industry (e.g. drugs) is used, the relevant two-digit category (chemicals) is dropped. This procedure is unexceptionable as long as the extent of aggregation for the industries in the final sample is not dissimilar or misleading. The table in Appendix 1, which shows the sample industries (all the two-digit ones without three-digit breakdown, e.g. paper, rubber etc., were used), indicates that our procedure is likely to be correct.

V THE RESULTS

The statistical procedure used was ordinary least squares linear regression. A set of logarithmic formulations was also tried, but did not give noticeably better results. We do not report their results. Table 4.1 sets out the main results, showing three equations for the dependent IFX and four for IFP.

TABLE 4.1 Determinants of inter-industry differences in US intra-firm exports, 1970

Dependent	RD	$(RD)^2$	AD	FA	VAL	TAR	SALES	Const.	R^2
1. IFX	0.361[a]				0.08[c]			14.07	0.20
	(2.47)				(1.53)				
2. IFX				0.119[a]	0.301	16.25[b]		7.18	0.30
				(3.34)	(0.77)	(1.93)			
3. IFX				0.110[a]				20.77	0.28
				(3.61)					
4. IFP				0.102[c]		22.53[b]	43.17[a]	40.34	0.49
				(1.70)		(1.74)	(2.87)		
5. IFP			−0.53[b]			18.17[c]	57.90[a]	65.06	0.49
			(−1.98)			(1.38)	(4.55)		
6. IFP	2.22[a]	−0.02[b]	−0.615[c]			28.20[b]		49.50	0.42
	(2.65)	(−1.73)	(−1.53)			(2.01)			
7. IFP	2.30[a]	−0.02[b]				36.52[a]		30.17	0.40
	(2.77)	(−1.95)				(2.72)			

NOTES
R^2 corrected for degrees of freedom; t-values in brackets. One-tail tests used.
[a] Denotes significant at 99 per cent.
[b] 95 per cent.
[c] 90 per cent.

Multicollinearity problems existed among some of the independent variables, and should be noted at the outset. RD was highly correlated with the dummy SALES (simple correlation coefficient of 0.77) suggesting that high-technology industries also have to provide heavy after-sales service and maintain large sales-related staff. Both SALES and RD were also significantly correlated with FA (0.51 and 0.63 respectively) indicating that technological advantage, and the need to follow up the sales of high-technology products with affiliate servicing, constitute important factors in promoting foreign investment.[23] VAL was correlated with AD (0.65), indicating a relationship between value-added and advertising-based market power. The other variables had relatively low correlation coefficients. The results shown exclude cases with severe collinearity problems.

The results are, in general, interesting and, given the nature of the data, not as poor as may have been feared. The model works better for IFP than for IFX: the determinants identified here are more significant when intra-firm exports are calculated as an input into affiliate sales rather than as proportions of total MNC exports. The independent variables are able to explain nearly half of the variation in IFP and somewhat less than a third for IFX. This is a moderately successful preliminary attempt, but factors which we could not account for clearly are of significance in determining intra-firm exports.

The explanatory variables which perform best are RD, FA, TAR and SALES. Of these, RD is uniformly positive and always highly significant.[24] However, it is possible that at very high levels of technology the relationship may be reversed, for two reasons. First, the industry may, according to product cycle theory,[25] export innovative products at the beginning of the cycle to unrelated buyers because it has not yet started foreign production; or, second, because economies of scale in R & D are so large that it is uneconomical to invest abroad. To test for this possibility, a quadratic formulation was tried (equations 6 and 7); it gave significant results, supporting the hypothesis than an inverse U-shaped relationship exists between IFP and RD.

The extent of foreign investment, as measured by FA, is positively and significantly related to both dependent variables. It has a much stronger effect on IFX than on IFP: this may be because IFP already contains a measure of the international spread of the industry (foreign sales) in the denominator. The results indicate that the more internationally diversified industries have a higher propensity to use intra-firm exports, but because FA captures the effect of several possible influences we cannot establish the exact causation more clearly.

TAR has a strong, positive and significant effect on both dependent variables, confirming the influence of economic pressures forcing industries with 'divisible' processes to expand intra-firm trade, and of US tariff policy in encouraging such expansion. Curiously enough, TAR has a very low correlation coefficient with FA (0.09), probably because the volume of capital investment involved in offshore processing is relatively low in relation to total foreign investment.

The after-sales service dummy SALES has the most powerful positive effect on IFP. It is also positive for IFX but usually fails to reach significance (not shown in Table 4.1). As noted above, SALES is collinear with RD and FA, but its coefficient in relation to IFP is higher and more significant than either of these variables. As far as intermediate goods exports are concerned, SALES may be picking up the influence of technology on product specificity. However, as far as finished goods exports go, the indications are that the need to control the after-sales function provides a strong incentive to channel exports, particularly of high-technology products, through affiliates.

AD has the predicted sign and reaches significance for the dependent IFP; providing some grounds for arguing that heavily promoted goods may be efficiently marketed through unrelated dealers. VAL barely reaches significance for IFX and behaves erratically for IFP (not shown): whether this is due to its misspecification as a proxy for skill and scale factors, or to the unimportance of these factors themselves in affecting intra-firm trade, is difficult to say.

Despite the extent of unexplained variation and despite the level of aggregation of the data, it appears that the pattern of intra-firm trade is amenable to rational economic explanation. The forces which make for vertical integration within countries also seem to make for the internalisation of commodity trade between countries. The use of better measures of risk and uncertainty in internal markets, of host government policy, excess capacity and scale economies, and the use of more disaggregated data for the dependent variables, should greatly improve the performance of our model.

VI CONCLUDING REMARKS

Our attempt to explain the pattern of US intra-firm exports has met with some success. The usefulness of the tools of industrial economics in clarifying the phenomenon bears out the validity of this approach (now increasingly popular[26]) in analysing problems in international trade and capital movements more generally. The factors which, in our model, affect the pattern of intra-firm exports are: technological intensity, the extent of foreign investment, the 'divisibility' of production processes and the need for after-sales service.

There remain clear gaps in the present empirical investigation. We need to focus on specific products rather than on industries. We need to add variables to account for risk, scale economies, capacity utilisation and host government policy. And we need longer coverage over which to study the problem. All these, however, require much more detailed data than are presently published by the US; other capital exporting countries provide far less than the US government does.

APPENDIX 1

TABLE A.4.1 Intra-firm exports of US MNCs by industry, 1970 ($ million)

Industry	Total exports	Intra-firm exports	IFX (%)	IFP (%)	Industry	Total exports	Intra-firm exports	IFX (%)	IFP (%)
Food products	1062	362	34	5	*Non-electrical machinery*	3795	1674	44	15
Grain Mills	227	106	47	8	Farm machinery	192	192	49	20
Beverages	58	11	19	1	Industrial[a]	1694	457	27	12
Combination	40	9	23	n.a.	Office[b]	576	431	75	17
Other	737	236	32	5	Computing	399	298	75	17
Paper	609	150	25	7	Other	734	296	40	20
Chemicals	2342	845	36	7	*Electrical machinery*	2060	575	28	8
Drugs	361	138	38	5	Household[c]	157	39	25	5
Soaps and cosmetics	130	70	54	3	Equipment	978	151	15	7
Industrial	1198	181	15	9	Electronic	734	210	29	8
Plastics	318	279	88	12	Other	191	175	92	12
Combinations	114	114	100	n.a.	*Transport equipment*	6750	2748	41	17
Other	221	63	29	8	*Textiles, Apparel*	244	97	40	6
Rubber	383	148	39	6	*Lumber, wood furnishing*	352	40	11	10
Primary and fabricated metals	2237	278	12	4	*Printing publishing*	144	36	25	6
Primary	976	51	5	6	*Stone, clay, glass*	267	86	32	6
Fabricated (excluding aluminium, brass and copper)	554	131	24	4	*Instruments*	848	522	62	18
Aluminium	627	56	9	2					
Other	80	40	50	6	*Other manufacturing*	625	146	23	3
					ALL MANUFACTURING	21,718	7707		

NOTES
IFX: Intra-firm exports as percentage of total exports by MNCs.
IFP: Intra-firm exports as percentage of total MOFA sales (i.e. local sales plus exports, including exports to U.S.).
n.a.: data not available.

Two-digit industries are in italics.
[a] Data for MOFA production of industrial and 'other' were shown jointly by the Tariff Commission; it was assumed that the IFP for latter was higher because of IFX figures.
[b] Data for MOFA production of office and computing equipment were shown jointly; it was assumed that same IFP applies to both.
[c] Data for MOFA production of household and other electrical machinery were shown jointly; latter was assumed to have much higher IFP than former because of IFX figures.

SOURCE
U.S. Tariff Commission (1973) pp. 367, 374.

APPENDIX 2

Data Sources
All the data on intra-firm exports, foreign production and assets are taken from the US Tariff Commission (1973). Advertising data are gathered from the *Statistical Abstract of the United States 1972*, Comanor and Wilson (1974), and (after adjustment) from Bailey (1975). Value added figures were taken from the *Statistical Abstract*. Information on use of Tariff Schedules 807.00 and 806.30 was taken from the US Tariff Commission (1970). The after-sales service dummy was constructed on the basis of data given in Bailey (1975); some interpolations had to be made for missing industries. R & D figures were taken, with a few interpolations, from the National Science Foundation, *Research and Development in Industry 1973* (Washington, DC, 1975).

NOTES

1. I am very grateful to Gerry Helleiner and John Knight for helpful comments on an earlier draft.
2. See, for instance, chapter 5 below.
3. The relevance of these considerations for policy-makers in less-developed countries is discussed at greater length in chapter 6.
4. See US Tariff Commission (1973).
5. See US Tariff Commission (1973) pp. 267–70.
6. Some indications of these are provided by Bradshaw (1969) for an earlier period, and are mentioned below.
7. US Tariff Commission, p. 361. This figure is mentioned here because earlier studies used this definition of intra-firm exports.
8. Ibid., p. 367. If we combine intra-firm exports from MOFAs, the total comes to $18.5 billion, 49 per cent of the total exports of MNCs plus MOFAs.
9. Bradshaw (1969), table 14.
10. Ibid., table 1.
11. Ibid., table 6.
12. US Tariff Commission (1970).
13. See Stigler (1951), Adelman (1955), Oi and Hunter (1965), Blair (1972) and Porter and Spence (1977).
14. See Kindleberger (1969), Caves (1971), Dunning (1973, 1977), Hirsch (1976), Buckley and Casson (1976) and Magee (1977).
15. For an elegant theoretical analysis of transaction costs and market failure see Arrow (1971).
16. Two recent textbooks, Jacquemin and de Jong (1977) and Howe (1978) provide simple and concise treatments; for a more theoretical analysis see Porter and Spence (1977).

17. The viability of such relocation depends on several factors, such as the nature of the process (continuous-process chemical manufacture would be difficult to divide), the weight-to-value ratio of the goods involved, transport costs to the cheap labour areas, the nature of production skills required, the importance of labour in total costs, and scale economies.
18. See Helleiner (1973).
19. US Tariff Commission (1970), pp. 6–7.
20. Ibid., pp. 230–31. It is in fact likely that the profitability of moving divisible processes abroad led powerful MNCs to influence US government policy, rather than the other way round; see Helleiner (1977).
21. This factor applies to trade in finished as well as intermediate products. It is, however, probably a more powerful inducement to intra-firm exports of intermediate products, because the risk of getting 'caught out' is less here than for finished products.
22. It may be argued that policies of LDC governments cannot affect intra-firm exports significantly, since only about 20 per cent of total US intra-firm exports go to LDCs. However, they may well be important for particular industries – we cannot tell.
23. A similar point is made in a theoretical analysis of the determinants of foreign investment by Hirsch (1976).
24. Buckley and Pearce (1977) find, in a study of 156 MNCs from several countries, that nationality and industry groups make significant differences to the propensity to use intra-firm exports (neither of these is relevant to our study), and that high-technology firms have higher intra-firm exports than low-technology ones (which confirms our findings).
25. Vernon (1966). Vernon's theory is posed in terms of products, but Magee (1977) argues that it may also apply to whole industries.
26. See Caves (1971) and Dunning (1973).

REFERENCES

Adelman, M. A. (1955), 'Vertical Integration and Market Growth', reprinted in Yamey (1973).
Arrow, K. J. (1971), 'Political and Economic Evaluation of Social Effects and Externalities', in M. D. Intriligator (ed.), *Frontier of Quantitative Economics* (Amsterdam: North-Holland).
Bailey, E. L. (1975), *Marketing-Cost Ratios of US Manufacturers* (New York: Conference Board).
Blair, J. M. (1972), *Economic Concentration* (New York: Harcourt, Brace, Jovanovich).
Bradshaw, M. T. (1969), 'US Exports to Foreign Affiliates of US Firms', *Survey of Current Business* (May) pp. 34–51.
Buckley, P. J. and Casson, M. (1976), *The Future of the Multinational Enterprise* (London: Macmillan).
Buckley, P. J. and Pearce, R. D. (1977), 'Overseas Production and Exporting by the World's Largest Enterprises – a Study in Sourcing Policy' (University of Reading, Discussion Papers in International Investment and Business Studies, no. 37).

Caves, R. E. (1971), 'International Corporations: the Industrial Economies of Foreign Investment', *Economica*, pp. 1–27.
Comanor, W. S. and Wilson, T. A. (1974), *Advertising and Market Power* (Cambridge, Mass.: Harvard University Press).
Dunning, J. H. (1973), 'The Determinants of International Production', *Oxford Economic Papers*, pp. 289–336.
—— (1977), 'Trade, Location of Economic Activity and the MNE: a Search for an Eclectic Approach', in B. Ohlin *et al.* (ed.), *The International Allocation of Economic Activity* (London: Macmillan).
Helleiner, G. K. (1973), 'Manufactured Exports from Less-Developed Countries and Multinational Firms', *Economic Journal*, pp. 21–47.
—— (1977), 'Transnational Enterprises and the New Political Economy of US Trade Policy', *Oxford Economic Papers*, pp. 102–16.
Hirsch, S. (1976), 'An International Trade and Investment Theory of the Firm', *Oxford Economic Papers*, pp. 258–70.
Howe, W. S. (1978), *Industrial Economics: an Applied Approach* (London: Macmillan).
Jacquemin, A. P. and de Jong, H. W. (1977), *European Industrial Organisation* (London: Macmillan).
Kindleberger, C. P. (1969), *American Business Abroad* (New Haven: Yale University Press).
Magee, S. P. (1977), 'Information and the Multinational Corporation: an Appropriability Theory of Direct Foreign Investment', in J. N. Bhagwati (ed.), *The New International Economic Order* (Cambridge, Mass.: MIT Press).
Oi, W. Y. and Hunter, A. P. (1965), 'A Theory of Vertical Integration in Road Transport Services', reprinted in Yamey (1973).
Porter, M. E. and Spence, A. M. (1977), 'Vertical Integration and Different Inputs' (University of Warwick, Research Paper 120).
Stigler, G. J. (1951), 'The Division of Labour is limited by the Extent of the Market', *Journal of Political Economy*, pp. 185–93.
US Tariff Commission (1970), *Economic Factors Affecting the Use of Items 807.00 and 806.30 of the Tariff Schedules of the United States* (Washington, DC: GPO).
US Tariff Commission (1973), *Implications of Multinational Firms for World Trade and Investment and for US Trade and Labor* (Washington, DC: GPO).
Vernon, R. (1966), 'International Investment and International Trade in the Product Cycle', *Quarterly Journal of Economics*, pp. 190–207.
Yamey, B. S. (1973), (ed.), *Economics of Industrial Structure* (Harmondsworth: Penguin).

5 Transfer-Pricing by Multinational Manufacturing Firms[1]

I INTRODUCTION

This paper deals with the determinants and implications of the pricing of intra-firm trade by manufacturing firms operating in different countries. Intra-firm trade is defined here as transactions involving international shipments of commodities (including capital, intermediate and finished goods, but excluding technology or services) between branches or affiliates under the control of one firm. Only firms in the manufacturing sector (called multinational enterprises, MNEs, for short) are considered: while similar issues of transfer-pricing have arisen in primary sectors, they seem to have been understood more clearly and dealt with in an explicitly bargaining framework.

In the manufacturing sector the problem of transfer-pricing has remained a curious blind spot in the rapidly growing academic literature on the MNE and its effects on trade and development. The two major studies on the balance-of-payments effects of overseas investment on the capital-exporting countries, Hufbauer and Adler (1968) on the US, and Reddaway (1967) on the UK, have not even recognised the problem, while a great deal of the theoretical discussion of MNEs, for example, in Kindleberger (1969) and (1970), or Johnson (1969), has barely noted the existence of intra-firm trade[2] – the implication being either that such trade is very similar in its economic effects to inter-firm trade (between unrelated parties), or that it is quantitatively insignificant. Even some of the economists who have recognised that intra-firm trade creates problems (Dunning, (1972); Vernon, (1971); Brooke and Remmers, (1970), seem to have underestimated its full extent.

The argument of this paper is that the determination of prices in intra-firm trade takes place according to considerations rather different from those in inter-firm trade (section II), that intra-firm trade is not an insignificant proportion of trade by MNEs or world manufactured trade (section III), and that it raises serious issues about the effects of MNEs on trade, welfare and national control (section IV). The discussion is conducted with special reference to the less-developed countries which play host to MNEs, and some data from Colombia is adduced to illustrate the potential impact of transfer-pricing.

II DETERMINANTS OF TRANSFER-PRICING

The fact that a transaction involving a transfer or sale of goods takes place *within* a firm, regardless of whether or not the firm spans different countries, and the firm is free within broad limits[3] to assign whatever price it likes to those goods, means that the traditional theory of pricing in competitive, oligopolistic or monopolistic markets ceases to apply to the process of transfer-pricing. The essential difference is simply that in transactions on the open market or between unrelated firms, the buyers and sellers are trying to maximise their profits at *each other's expense*, while in an intra-firm transaction the price is merely an accounting device and the two parties are trying to maximise *joint profits*. It is possible that the accounting price may approximate the arm's length price of the goods (the price which would obtain in an open market, or in a transaction between unrelated parties), but certainly there is no presumption that this should be so: any other price is equally plausible, and the conditions mentioned below will determine whether the actual transfer-price will deviate from the arm's length price.

Any discussion of the transfer-pricing problem has to assume that there exists a yardstick by which the effect of the price can be measured; there must, in other words, be an arm's length price, and the goods may be 'overpriced' if transfer prices are higher, and 'underpriced' if they are lower, than this price.[4] It is not necessary for there to be an open market price; from the firm's point of view all that is required is that it should know at what price (or within what range) it would be prepared to sell to unrelated concerns. When a good is over-priced, therefore, the firm transfers funds *via* the pricing channel from the buying to the selling units; declared profits are thus understated and overstated respectively in comparison with the situation where no intra-firm transactions take place. The converse happens with underpricing.

Let us start with the case where a parent MNE in country A has a wholly owned subsidiary in country B, the goods transferred have an open market price, there is no official check on the transfer-prices set

112   The Multinational Corporation

(though such prices may be assumed to be always positive), the same transfer-price is declared in both A and B, and there is no internal constraint on declaring profits or losses in either place. Let us say that transfer-prices are being 'used' (to transmit profits) when they do not correspond to open market or arm's length prices, and consider in turn the inducements to and constraints on the 'use' of transfer-pricing in this way.[5] The simplifying assumptions are relaxed in the following sections.

A preliminary point to note is that the profits actually made in each country of the MNE's operation, given by the market conditions and costs of production (including the cost to the firm of intra-firm transfers), are not in any way directly affected by the level of transfer-prices set.[6] We shall proceed on assumption that each unit maximises its real profits in its centre of operations, just as if it were an independent firm, and that the determination of transfer-prices rests only on the question of where and how the profits are to be declared.

INDUCEMENTS TO THE USE OF TRANSFER-PRICES

If the parent firm in A and the subsidiary in B both made profits, effective tax rates on remissible profits (taking into account withholding taxes) were equal, there were no restrictions on remissions and no price controls on the output in either country, import duties did not exceed the effective tax rates, the exchange rate of the two currencies was stable, and there were no political or other pressures on the level of declared, present or future, profits, then there would be no inducement to use transfer-prices deliberately to move profits from one country to another. If transfer-prices did diverge from their open market level, it would be the result of chance or lack of contact with the market rather than a conscious policy on the part of the MNE, since the conditions have been so defined that it makes no difference over the short or long term where profits are declared.[7]

Clearly these conditions are extremely restrictive, and many of them do not apply to less-developed host economies in particular, inducing MNEs to use intra-firm transactions to move profits to centres which are better for profit declaration. The inducements to such transfer-pricing may be grouped under two broad headings: those which maximise the present value of the MNE's overall profits, and those which minimise present and future risk or uncertainty about the value of profits.

Maximise Present Profits
Bearing in mind that the MNE is concerned to maximise the value of

Transfer-Pricing 113

profits of *all its operations taken together*, and abstracting for the moment from the problems of risk minimisation, we can postulate a number of conditions in which transfer-pricing will be used.

i. Loss in one centre of operations. It may be argued that when the MNE makes losses in one of the countries it operates in, it would be induced to remit profits to that country so as to minimise its overall tax burden. Vaitsos (1974) has tried to construct a theory of transfer-pricing on the grounds that MNEs make losses in their home countries (in our example, country A) because of heavy overhead and research expenditures there. The firm in A will therefore overprice its exports to B or underprice imports from it. The argument is, however, of limited applicability. Besides the question of whether MNEs in fact make losses on their domestic operations, the inducement will operate only if A's government does not allow losses to be carried forward into the future for tax purposes or if the firm expects the losses to continue beyond the period of tax offsets.[8] Similarly, if the firm in B is making a loss, the MNE may move funds there if losses cannot be carried forward *and* if they cannot be offset against the tax burden in A. As most countries allow losses to be carried forward (but not indefinitely) and some capital exporting countries (notably the US) do allow tax offsets against losses made by subsidiaries, the incidence of this sort of inducement is probably rather small.

ii. Taxes, tariffs and subsidies. The best known inducement to the use of transfer-pricing is international differences in tax and tariff rates, see Horst (1971); Copithorne (1971); Tugendhat (1971); Brooke and Remmers (1970); export subsidies may also be introduced as a factor affecting the calculation. If tax rates are higher in B than in A, and the parent MNE supplies imports to the subsidiary, it would pay the firm to overprice these transactions and move profits to A as long as the difference in effective tax rates exceeds the tariff in B on those imports. If tariffs are higher, it would pay to underprice the imports.[9] Similarly, if the subsidiary is exporting to the parent it would pay to underprice the transactions as long as the tax rate differential plus the saving in import duty in A exceeded the export subsidy in B. If trade is taking place in both directions, the MNE many underprice imports into B to avoid duties and underprice its exports to A to take advantage of exports subsidies in B and lower taxes in A.[10] The extent to which profits can be moved around freely depends, of course, on the volume of intra-firm trade, the structure of the firm and the vigilance of the relevant authorities, discussed later.

iii. Multiple exchange rates. In some countries which have multiple exchange rates (for instance, Colombia before 1966), the rate applicable to profit remittances tends to be unfavourable relative to the one applicable to capital or intermediate goods imports, effectively imposing an additional tax on declared profit remittances.

iv. Quantitative restrictions. Limits imposed on the remittance of profits create a very strong inducement to use the transfer-pricing mechanism, especially when other channels, such as royalties and management and technical fees to the parent firm, are also controlled. If the subsidiary is exceptionally profitable, and the MNE does not wish to re-invest the profits in B, it may remit them by over-pricing imports into B *regardless of the extra tariff cost*, since any gain in profits abroad would be a net benefit. Furthermore, if the amount of permissble dividends were calculated as a percentage of the MNE's net worth (equity plus re-investments),[11] the firm would be induced to overprice its initial equity contribution which took the form of capital equipment to inflate the capital base.

v. Existence of local shareholders. The existence of local shareholders in the subsidiary in B may induce the MNE to overprice its imports into B for three reasons: first, to increase its own share of the total profits at the cost of the local shareholders; second, to inflate the initial value of capital equipment contributed by way of equity participation; and, third, to act in collusion with the local partners in order to provide funds for accumulation abroad or for resale in the black market.[12]

vi. Exchange rate speculation. If the exchange rate of either A or B is expected to change and the MNE cannot or will not speculate openly, it may use transfer prices to reinforce the normal leads and lags which minimise its obligations in the devaluing currency. The profitability of such speculation would depend on the amount of devaluation expected and the cost of using transfer prices in terms of additional taxes and tariffs. There is a distinction to be drawn between active speculation for gain (as postulated here), which is basically short-term and liable to be reversed after the rates have been readjusted (or the crisis averted), and long-term hedging against a basically weak currency (mentioned below). The former is likely to be used by MNEs in developed countries (Brooke and Remmers, 1970 and 1972) in periods of exchange crises, while the latter is likely to occur in developing countries, particularly those with inflation.

Minimise Risk and Uncertainty

The long-term profitability of an MNE is subject to various pressures in the different areas it operates in, and the judicious use of transfer-pricing to show low levels of profits may well contribute to insuring its future earning, or even its existence, against all sorts of threats.

i. Balance-of-payments and exchange rate pressures. Some countries may be deemed bad risks because of the threat of impending restrictions on remittances, periodic devaluations, and the like, and the MNE may adopt a long-term strategy of moving profits out *via* transfer-pricing.

ii. Political and social pressures. These may range from trade union pressures for a larger share of declared profits to government threats to nationalisation because of 'exploitation'. In fact, any host country which tries to control or limit the activities of MNEs may be considered a more or less undesirable area to declare high profits in, and for long-term safety, regardless of tax-tariff or other short-term factors, the transfer-pricing mechanism may be used to send profits abroad. Expectation of individual firms are likely to differ considerably as far as this is concerned, however, and the built-in deterrent that the discovery of such a policy would itself exacerbate the situation may induce firms not to over-indulge. Nevertheless, the environment of a particular host country in the eyes of the MNE may well be one of the most important factors influencing the long-term use of the transfer-pricing channel; the inbuilt secrecy is ideal in situations where there are long-term threats to its operations arising from its profitability.

iii. Direct threats to profits. The declaration of high profits may cause a number of reactions which directly reduce the MNE's profitability. First, the government may, where appropriate, lower the level of *protection* on the firm's final output. If the level of protection is determined by the government on the basis of the firm's cost of production plus some reasonable allowance for profit, the MNE can easily raise the protection, and its profits, by inflating its costs by overpricing intra-firm imports. The existence of such an instrument in the hands of the MNE gives it a strong weapon when bargaining for concessions with host governments, one which they may not even be aware of.

Second, a similar case arises when governments impose *price controls* on products manufactured by MNEs (pharmaceuticals is the most common example) the level at which prices are fixed being determined again by the costs of production. This happens most often when protection is granted by the banning of imports rather than by tariffs, and domestic prices are sought to be kept in check by direct means. There is evidence that overpricing of imports has been caused by this factor in India (Bhagwati, 1967) and Colombia (see below).

Third, the danger of increased *competition* from other MNEs or local manufacturers, attracted by high declared profits, may also cause transfer-pricing to be used in exceptionally profitable countries (Vaitsos, 1974). A similar danger is that the host government may insist on profitable foreign enterprises *selling shares* to local investors, reducing both the rewards earned by the MNE as well as its control over the operation. If the process of gradual nationalisation has already started, high profits may speed it up. The government may also decide to take a larger share of the profits for itself by raising the level of *taxation* or imposing *special levies* on the firm.

These are the various inducements to the use of transfer-pricing by MNEs to transmit profits clandestinely from one country to another. Although there is no necessary presumption that the mechanism would be operated to the detriment of countries other than the home-country of the MNE, or of less-developed host countries generally – given exchange-rate instability, tax differentials, trade union pressures, and so on, it may well be worked against the home country[13] – the cards are in fact stacked heavily against the less-developed economies. Not only do their tax rates tend to be higher, their import duties on intermediate inputs relatively low, their balances-of-payments often in crisis, and quantitative restrictions often in force, but their political, social and economic environment also tends to be inimical to the free operation and expansion of MNEs. With a few exceptions, their governments try to limit and control MNE activities, to enlarge local shareholding in them, to lower their profits and ultimately even to get rid of them. It is difficult to imagine circumstances in which an MNE would want to ship profits *to* such countries (barring the few countries which are tax havens). In order to ensure that transfer-pricing was not used against it, a host economy would therefore have to conform politically and economically to many of the norms of the developed world – not an aim which most poor countries subscribe to, and certainly not one which should be demanded as a condition for increasing the activities of MNEs.

While many of the inducements to transfer-pricing have been noticed, most writers have assumed that the mechanism is not very much 'misused'. They have perhaps been impressed by limitations on its unrestricted use, mostly on the basis of evidence given by the firms themselves; some restrictions undoubtedly do exist, and we now examine what they are and how strictly they operate.

Transfer-Pricing 117

LIMITS TO THE USE OF TRANSFER-PRICES

There are in general two types of limits to the extent that transfer prices can be moved freely round to suit the overall objective of the MNE, set, first, by the firms themselves (which we may term internal), and, second, by the authorities (external).

Internal Limits
The cohesion, adaptability and structure of the MNE may themselves impose certain constraints on the use of transfer-prices. It may be noted that the 'motivation' of the firm, in the sense of whether it wants to maximise its dividends at the expense of growth or vice versa, or of whether it wants to maximise its stock market valuation or some other objective of the management, is irrelevant to the question of transfer-pricing, which simply aims to *minimise taxes on and threats to profits which have already been earned, regardless of whether they are paid out in dividends or re-invested.*[14] A 'rational' use of transfer-prices by an MNE is therefore compatible with different objectives concerning growth, dividends or even philanthropy.

While an MNE with local equity participation faces obvious internal checks to the use of transfer-prices (subject to qualifications mentioned elsewhere) even an MNE with no local equity participation may face internal constraints at any of the following stages in the manipulation of transfer-prices:

 i. the realisation at the level of the subsidiary's management that what is to be maximised is the profit of the MNE as a whole, perhaps at a cost to the subsidiary;
 ii. the communication of requisite knowledge (on taxes, tariffs, controls, policy) from subsidiary to parent;
 iii. the capacity in the parent firm to process the vast quantity of information on different subsidiaries and to arrive at a determinate set of transfer prices;
 iv. the capacity to implement the transfer prices, in terms of persuading the appropriate subsidiaries to put up with showing losses or low profits.

These constraints boil down to two: the degree of integration and central control in the MNE, and the psychological effects of requiring subsidiaries to conform to the profit declaration targets. As far as the first is concerned, it would appear that transfer-pricing can be used most effectively by very large corporations with tightly exercised central control, sophisticated computational facilities and a wide experience of world conditions and of dealing with governments, and not by investors with limited overseas operations and a great deal of autonomy between different units. The evolving structure of management in the largest firms has in fact tended to increasing rather than decreasing control from the centre (Williamson, 1971; Wells, 1971), with the crucial decisions regarding investment, pricing and research kept to the head office and minor production decisions delegated to individual units.[15] Moreover, as the great bulk of intra-firm trade is concentrated in the largest MNEs (see next section), the purely organisational constraint applicable to small firms cannot be very important from a quantitative point of view.

Firms make a great deal of the psychological constraint. One of their main arguments for retaining flexible transfer-pricing is to enable new subsidiaries to break into markets without showing large losses; some firms seem to operate on the concept of 'profit centres', with each centre required to show its true profitability for the sake of morale as well as more effective control from the centre. It is difficult to take these arguments very seriously.[16] They revolve round the assumption that a local manager takes his performance as reported to the tax authorities or to local shareholders more seriously than his performance as judged by the parent firm. After all, his financial rewards come from the latter, and his loyalties may safely be presumed to lie more with his firm than with his tax authority. All that is required is that the MNE keep two sets of accounts, one showing 'real' profits and the other taxable profits; keeping two account books is one of the oldest business practices in the world and certainly not beyond the capacity of MNEs.

We have assumed till now that the firm knows the 'right' prices for all commodities involved in intra-firm trade, and is able to work the pricing mechanism with precision to achieve its objectives. In fact a large number of such commodities do not have a free-market reference price at all, because they are not traded on open markets or because they are the monopoly of the firm concerned and subject to discriminatory pricing in different markets. It is, moreover, very difficult in many such cases to assign a correct arm's length price due to the existence of joint overhead (especially R and D) costs, and any particular price used by the firms, or assigned by a host government, may be criticised for being arbitrary. This does not reduce the usefulness of the transfer-pricing mechanism: on the contrary, it makes it easier for the MNE to maximise its overall profit without having to keep double sets of accounts, while rendering it more difficult for host governments to calculate costs and profits for individual subsidiaries.[17] Let us now consider the problems faced by the authorities in checking the use of transfer-prices.

External Limits

There are two sets of authorities in the countries of MNE operations which are immediately concerned with transfer prices: the customs and the tax authorities. The former are chiefly concerned to see that shipments are not obviously underpriced, so that they receive a fair amount of tariff revenue. They are not particularly well-equipped to check in a routine manner whether the prices charged are correct or not; the task of checking transfer-prices is a complex and difficult one, and requires specialised technical knowledge over a broad range of commodities. Customs officials may get suspicious if prices are changed very often and in large amount, but the Colombian experience shows that individual items may be marked at 3,000 per cent above prices charged in world markets or by other firms and escape routine notice (Vaitsos, 1974), while the Roche Products case in the UK shows that a highly developed country is equally vulnerable. Though many countries do question customs valuations of firms, the procedure is unsystematic, arbitrary and inadequate.[18]

Tax authorities face similar difficulties. They do not, with the exception of the US, normally enquire into transfer prices directly, and, like customs officials, are not equipped to do so. They may question a firm which is declaring 'too little' profits, and even assign an arbitrarily higher figure, but this is hardly an effective check to a clever manipulation of prices and profits. Such procedures may also be unfair to firms which are making genuine losses, and while permitting firms which show reasonable profits to remit large sums undetected.

While it is very likely that the day-to-day workings of the tax-customs administration will not show up any but the most blatant or careless use of transfer prices, even closer direct checks such as those exercised by the US tax authorities, and the relatively isolated ones by other governments, are fraught with difficulties. We have mentioned above that it is inherently problematical to assign arm's length prices to goods with joint costs which are not traded openly: there are no easy reference prices and marginal cost pricing will not be accepted as 'fair' where heavy R and D expenditures are involved. Many commodities in intra-firm trade do not fall into this category, but for those which do the host governments must negotiate a fair rate of profit with the MNEs concerned after taking into account all the direct and indirect costs of production. As long as some such task is not undertaken, however, and transfer-prices are left to the discretion of the MNEs, it is clear that the latter will have the upper hand and deliberately use the mechanism to their own advantage.

III EVIDENCE ON INTRA-FIRM TRADE AND TRANSFER-PRICING

As most countries do not collect data on intra-firm trade as distinct from inter-firm trade, and transfer-prices are rarely checked, we have to rely for evidence on some surveys carried out in the USA and the UK for the former and on an investigation by the Colombian government for the latter.

US AND UK INTRA-FIRM TRADE

The US Government's Department of Commerce has conducted surveys and published figures on intra-firm trade by a sample of US-owned MNEs. The figures cover the period 1962 to 1970,[19] though the years 1967–69 are missing; details are given in the appendix, which cites the sources and defines the samples and terms used. The Department of Commerce also carried out a comprehensive survey of *all* US firms with foreign investments for the year 1966, the so-called 'benchmark' survey, which enables us to judge the size of the sample coverage in that year; the benchmark-survey figures are also shown in the appendix. Unfortunately, I was unable to get a copy of the original benchmark survey and had to rely on secondary sources (Foster, 1972).

The following points must be noted about the US data:

i. There is no evidence on the amount of US trade accounted for by non-US MNEs; private direct manufacturing investment in the US by foreigners is quite substantial, and came to $3.0 billion in 1963, rising to over $5.3 billion in 1969 (over 18 per cent of US manufacturing investment abroad).

ii. The definition of 'affiliated firms' was changed for the 1966–70 sample, with the requirement raised from 25 per cent US shareholding to 51 per cent US shareholding.

iii. The 1962–64 figures were for a sample (256 MNEs and 25,000 affiliates) extrapolated to represent total MNE trade; later years were not adjusted in this way.

iv. The 1965 sample included 271 manufacturing firms of which 257 reported exports (1,869 affiliates); the 1966–70 sample covered 223 firms and 3,752 majority-owned affiliates.

v. Earnings (dividends, interest, royalties and fees) figures for sample firms were not given, so that the tables show earnings of all US foreign manufacturing investment.

The data are thus neither complete nor fully comparable between different years. Despite this, the facts that emerge about the magnitude of intra-firm trade are extremely interesting, and we may make some very rough adjustments to see the overall impact of such trade. Table 5.1 shows various relationships derived from the Appendix table.

Intra-firm exports of sample firms rose from 18 per cent of US manufactured exports in 1962 to 24 per cent in 1970; if we inflate the 1970 figure by the same extent that the 1966 benchmark figure exceeds the 1966 survey figure, we get a ratio of 35 per cent. If we add another 6 per cent non-US MNE's (18 per cent on the basis of book-value of investments) we get a figure of over 40 per cent. Similarly, for intra-firm imports we arrive at a final figure of over 25 per cent, and for total affiliate trade as a percentage of total US manufactured trade we get approximately 34 per cent. In other words, about *one-third of total US trade in manufactured trade was intra-firm in 1970*, and the general trend seemed to rise over time.

The value of declared earnings on foreign manufacturing investment was far exceeded by the value of intra-firm trade, and a mere 12 per cent change in transfer-prices in 1970 would have equalled the entire dividends and interest earned abroad. If we included royalties and management fees, an 18 per cent change in prices would (ignoring tax-tariff problems) suffice to exceed the total sum of earnings abroad.

Intra-firm exports in the samples grew by 178 per cent (total US manufactured exports by 112 per cent), imports by 261 per cent (234 per cent), and total trade by 204 per cent (155 per cent) during 1962–70. At the same time, the book value of US manufacturing investments grew by 144 per cent, and dividends and interest by 151 per cent. In absolute sums, the value of total affiliate trade for the 1970 sample came to $11 billion, and to approximately $16 billion on a blown-up basis.

The 1965 sample survey reveals a *very high degree of concentration* between the 251 manufacturing firms in terms of their intra-firm exports: 18 parent firms (7 per cent) accounted for 65 per cent of the exports, while at the other end 150 firms (60 per cent) accounted for only 6 per cent.[20] It is very likely, though evidence is not at hand to prove it,

TABLE 5.1 United States: intra-firm manufacturing trade by US MNEs 1962–70 (percentages)

	Sample Data						1966 Benchmark Survey	1970 Blown up (1966 basis)
	1962 (1)	1963 (2)	1964 (3)	1965 (4)	1966 (5)	1970 (6)	(7)	(8)
Exports to Affiliates/Total US manufactured Exports	17.9	19.7	20.3	22.5	21.1	23.5	31.6	35.1
Imports from Aff./Total US manufactured Imports	14.4	15.5	18.5	15.9	14.5	15.6	20.1[a]	21.6[a]
Total Aff. Trade/Total US manufactured Trade	16.6	18.2	19.7	19.9	18.3	19.8	26.7[a]	28.8[a]
Dividends and Interest/Total Aff. Trade	20.0	15.5	17.4	18.5	17.5	16.6	12.0[a]	11.4[a]
Dividends and Interest + Royalties and Fees/Total Aff. Trade	28.2	24.3	26.7	27.9	27.1	25.5	18.5[a]	17.5[a]

NOTE
[a] Based on approximate figure for affiliated imports for 1966 benchmark survey.

that the degree of concentration has increased over time with the increasing importance of large MNEs (Wells, 1971). In any case, if about 50 US MNEs and a similar number of non-US MNEs controlled between them all but a minor proportion of world intra-firm trade, these 100 or so firms would be the ones controlling not only an immense quantity of resources but also the means to move its rewards around practically at will.

Let us consider the UK data, which cover only 1966 but include both British and foreign MNEs.[21] A survey of 1,466 manufacturing firms showed that of their total exports of £3360 million, exports to 'related' firms accounted for £1030 million, or 30 per cent. Total British manufactured exports for 1966 came to £4272 million; thus intra-firm exports came to 24 per cent of the total.[22]

The intra-firm exports of US owned firms in the sample accounted for a much higher proportion of their total exports (56 per cent) than of non-US foreign firms (37 per cent) or British firms (27 per cent). The point frequently made that US affiliates in the UK export a larger proportion of their output than British firms should be accompanied by the point that a far higher proportion of such exports are within those firms themselves.

There are no figures available for the amount of intra-firm imports into the UK, but the picture shown by exports seems rather similar to that of the US. The degree of concentration in the UK is even higher than that of the US: 32 (less than 2 per cent) of the firms account for 52 per cent of intra-firm exports, while the last 1499 (76 per cent) account only for 6 per cent.

It may plausibly be argued that the pattern of intra-firm trade as shown in these two countries is roughly representative of the pattern among the developed countries as a whole. Thus, a quarter to a third of their trade in manufactured products takes place within MNEs: the exact figure does not matter for present purposes, but it is clear that the magnitudes involved are vast, and cannot continue to be disregarded as they have been in the literature.

As far as less-developed countries are concerned, there are no figures on the extent of intra-firm trade. It is probably much more important for their imports than for their exports; the bulk of manufacturing investment in these areas, especially by MNEs, is heavily dependent on imported components, and to a large extent these imports are from related firms. Given that many developing countries control the foreign sector, however, it is likely that the incidence of MNE trade is smaller as a percentage of their total imports of manufactures than in developed

124   *The Multinational Corporation*

countries. Similarly, MNE exports are a relatively new phenomenon, and, though expanding rapidly (Helleiner, 1973), still account for a small portion of total manufactured exports. This is not, however, to argue that such trade is insignificant and its implications inconsequential for less-developed countries. The absolute magnitude of intra-firm trade may still be very large, and the implications of transfer-pricing far more serious, than for the developed world, first because there are many more reasons why this mechanism should be operated against the interests of less-developed countries, and, second, because they can afford far less to lose resources (in foreign exchange) in this way. We shall return to the implications of transfer-pricing in section IV; let us first look at the evidence from Colombia.

TRANSFER-PRICING IN COLOMBIA

The evidence on the use of transfer-pricing in Colombia is especially valuable because of the extreme scarcity of information on this practice in almost all the countries in which MNEs operate. Without such evidence arguments about the dangers of transfer-pricing could simply be dismissed as unfounded or propagandist,[23] even the selective and limited investigations as conducted by the Colombian government provide some proof of its potentialities.

After the Colombian government passed Decree 444 in 1967, imposing various exchange controls and restrictions on the flows of exchange by foreign investors, an examination of the transfer-pricing mechanism was undertaken in the belief that it was pointless to control dividends and royalties when such a wide channel as intra-firm trade was left open. The main sector studied was pharmaceuticals, the industry with the largest number of foreign firms in the country: the rubber, chemical and electrical industries were also investigated, but much less intensively. The research, carried out for 1968 by the Planning Office (Planeación) and for 1967–70 by the Import Control Board (INCOMEX), employed qualified chemists and technicians, and compared the prices actually charged on imports with prices paid for comparable commodities by locally owned firms, by other Latin American countries, and in world markets generally. The objective was to discover the extent of overpricing,[24] and to reduce its incidence by legal action, including the imposition of heavy fines.

In arriving at the world market price, the investigators took the average of available quotations rather than the lowest one, and allowed for transportation costs and a 20 per cent margin for error. Thus, the calculations were, if anything, unduly generous to the foreign firms. Planeación discovered a weighted average of overpricing for a wide range of pharmaceutical imports of 155 per cent (for 1968)[25] and INCOMEX of 87 per cent (for 1967–70), the difference in findings being accounted for by differences in coverage over time and products, with the latter being more comprehensive. The savings achieved by the government's action came to US $3.3 million annually in the pharmaceutical sector, out of a total import bill of $15 million.

It was also found that some rubber imports had been overpriced by 44 per cent, some chemical imports by 25 per cent and electrical components by 54 per cent. Moreover, studies on transfer-pricing undertaken in other neighbouring countries, especially Chile, showed that the pattern was similar (UNCTAD, 1971). The scope of the investigations was more limited, but the tenor of the results was unmistakable. It is clear that unless the mechanism were attacked directly, there are few inbuilt constraints, of the nature discussed previously, to its use.

It may be of interest to consider the evidence for 14 foreign firms in Colombia in rather more detail; these firms are part of a sample studied by the present author in the course of research conducted for UNCTAD. Using the evidence uncovered by Planeación and INCOMEX, and combining it with balance-sheet figures for these firms (which must, of course, remain anonymous), we can see the effect that overpricing has had on their profitability in Table 5.2. The figures pertain to the period before the government's legal action against overpricing took effect. There are 11 pharmaceutical, 1 rubber and 2 electrical firms, and the period covered is 1966–70, and the figures express averages for these years. There are 12 wholly foreign-owned firms (marked A) and 2 foreign majority-owned firms (marked B).

Column 2 shows that the weighted average of overpricing ranged from 33 per cent to over 300 per cent for the imports investigated in the pharmaceutical sector, and from 24 per cent to 81 per cent in the other sectors. The difference made to profitability from proved overpricing (column 4) ranges from 2 per cent to 112 per cent of net worth in the former, and from 0.3 per cent to 6 per cent in the latter, industries; such profits exceed the value of declared profits for 9 of the 14 firms. If we impute the proved level of overpricing to total imports of the firms, including the imports not investigated, we find that profits on overpricing rise substantially in pharmaceuticals, but not so dramatically in the other industries. Imputed overpricing profits exceed declared profits for 11 of the 14 firms.[26]

TABLE 5.2 Overpricing by and profitability of 14 foreign firms in Colombia (1966–70)

Industries and Firms	(1) % Imports Investigated	(2) % Proved Overpricing	(3) Declared Profits as % net Worth	(4) Profits on Proved Overpricing as % Net Worth	(5) Profits on Overpricing Total Imports % N.W. (Imputed)	(6) (3) + (5)
Pharmaceutical						
1 (A)	52.1	158.3	7.6	41.5	79.6	87.2
2 (B)	20.1	39.5	11.2	2.0	10.0	21.2
3 (A)	100.0	56.6	16.5	19.6	19.6	36.1
4 (A)	28.1	81.0	6.3	5.6	19.9	26.2
5 (A)	32.4	288.9	6.3	19.2	59.3	65.6
6 (A)	39.1	33.5	0.1	2.5	63.9	64.0
7 (A)	35.2	33.7	12.4	3.1	8.8	21.2
8 (A)	54.1	95.4	−7.4	17.9	33.1	26.1
9 (A)	48.6	83.7	42.8	111.7	229.8	272.6
10 (A)	44.2	313.8	27.5	39.6	89.6	117.1
11 (A)	30.9	138.9	5.9	9.9	32.0	37.9
Rubber						
12 (B)	60.0	40.0	8.3	6.1	10.2	18.5
Electrical						
13 (A)	22.3	24.1	8.1	0.3	1.3	9.4
14 (A)	30.4	81.1	0.7	1.8	5.9	6.6

NOTES
1. (A) indicates that the firm is wholly foreign owned, and (B) that foreign investors hold 51–99 per cent of the equity.
2. Per cent of overpricing is defined as in footnote 24, and is for the weighted average of all imports investigated (shown in column 1).
3. Declared profits comprises after-tax profits net of depreciation and interest. Minus shows loss.
4. Net worth calculated in terms of constant US dollars.
5. Column (4) shows profits from proved, and column (5) from imputed, overpricing.

Transfer-Pricing 127

It is impossible to generalise from a sample of such a small size and with such variability. Clearly, different foreign firms have different attitudes to transfer-pricing as opposed to declaring profits openly. The inducements to use transfer-pricing in Colombia are obvious enough: there are quantitative limits on profit remittances abroad as well as price controls on pharmaceutical and rubber products; duties on imports of intermediate products are quite low, especially in pharmaceuticals (a nominal 1–2 per cent); there is considerable suspicion of foreign enterprise and restriction on their activities; and some of the foreign firms are exceptionally profitable. Colombia seems to have been almost a laboratory case for the exercise of transfer-pricing. Many other less-developed host countries are in a similar situation, but have not started to react to it effectively.

To reiterate the main points of this section: first, intra-firm trade in manufactures today accounts for a substantial part of world trade, and will account for a larger proportion in the future if MNEs continue to grow; second, such trade is highly concentrated within a relatively few MNEs which also control an immense quantity of world resources and production; third, the declared earnings of MNEs are very much smaller than the value of intra-firm trade, so that a relatively minor change in transfer-prices can cause a very large change in MNE's profitability; and, fourth, the available evidence indicates that transfer-pricing *is* deliberately used to transfer profits from less desirable to more desirable areas, and the existing inbuilt constraints to its use are ineffective. Let us now consider some of the implications of this situation.

IV IMPLICATIONS OF TRANSFER-PRICING

This section is divided into three parts, dealing with the implications of transfer-pricing for trade theory, for the welfare of host economies and for government policy.

TRANSFER-PRICING AND TRADE THEORY

The size and growth of international investment in the modern world has important effects on the determination of trade patterns, both in the traditional Hecksher-Ohlin framework (by altering relative factor endowments) as well as in the more recent technological/oligopolistic theories of comparative advantage (by transmitting technology, changing skills and tastes, extending product differentiation, using various market imperfections and economies of scale).[27] In fact, many of these new theories, of which the product cycle model is a good example, use the MNE as a central agent of dynamic comparative advantage (Johnson, 1969). Moreover, the proponents of the free flow of capital see the MNE ushering in a new era of world-wide efficiency in the allocation of resources and even an international equalisation of factor prices (Kindleberger, 1969).

The assumption implicit in all such reasoning, and its accompanying recommendations for policy, is that trade controlled by MNEs is governed by the same principles of valuation as other forms of trade. Thus, the value of intra-firm trade is taken to be determined by the same factors as inter-firm trade, and the gains arising from the former are assumed to accrue to the various trading countries in the same way as from the latter. If our argument about intra-firm trade and transfer-pricing has any validity, however, it is clear that this sort of assumption is not tenable. In fact, a strong attack may be mounted on both the positive and normative aspects of trade theory for that part of trade which is intra-firm.

As far as its *positive aspects* are concerned, the existence of transfer-pricing introduces a divergence between the explanation of the *quantities* of goods involved in intra-firm trade as distinct from their stated *values*, and thus renders the existing comparative cost doctrines, of both the traditional Hecksher-Ohlin and the modern technological/oligopolistic types, all of which are couched in terms of market values of trade, inapplicable to such trade. The quantities of goods in intra-firm trade may well be determined on considerations of comparative cost, at least from the MNE's point of view, but the values stated may be quite different from those in open-market conditions. Since positive trade theory seeks to explain stated values, however, and assumes some sort of competitive market framework to establish a determinate relationship between market prices and quantities, it cannot hope to explain trade which takes place essentially outside any market.

It is true that in quantitative terms the validity of the comparative cost doctrine remains unimpaired. Its empirical testing, however, become practically impossible for intra-firm trade, and undoubtedly the theory loses a great deal of its interest and significance by being unable to deal with its valuation. What is needed now is for economists to construct an adjunct to traditional theories of trade to encompass intra-firm trade. This would attempt to assess the 'trade creating' and 'trade diverting' effects of transfer-pricing, to stipulate when and how a country becomes a favourable place for profit declaration and thus enjoys a relatively stronger current visible trade account, and to investigate whether commodities specialised in by MNEs (say, those which are technologically advanced or heavily differentiated) are more prone to intra-firm rather than inter-firm trade over time. It may also be worth discovering whether MNEs try to protect or expand intra-firm trade more between countries which differ considerably, as opposed to those which are similar, in their relative attractiveness as centres for profit declaration; and, more basically, to know how MNEs judge such attractiveness, and how individual assessments differ. Certainly, existing trade theory needs new direction if it is to be fully relevant.

The implications for the *normative aspects* of trade theory may be considered more serious. Most economists recommend more and freer trade in the implicit belief that all the trading partners receive due benefits from such trade when their goods are sold in world markets. Clearly, the potential benefits of trade are considerably diminished if the traded products are not priced in competitive markets, but valued in such a way that one factor of production, foreign capital, is able to deprive a country of part of its due share and remit it abroad. Intra-firm trade makes it quite likely that *the benefits of trading are distributed haphazardly between trading partners*, with some countries (the home bases of MNEs in particular) gaining at the expense of others (especially the developing host countries) in such trade.

Furthermore, it may be argued that when the use of transfer-pricing enables the MNE to extract more protection from the government, the host economy is not only deprived of its share in 'fair' profits (including allowances for risk and oligopoly), but the profits made are themselves too high. If the MNE is a dynamic agent of comparative advantage, therefore, it also has the power to extract a high price for its services, to conceal this price and to send its rewards to places of its own choosing.

WELFARE OF HOST ECONOMIES AND TRANSFER-PRICING

If a host country cannot be sure of capturing a fair share of the benefits from the resources used by foreign investors, and from the induced changes in patterns of trade and production, the conventional arguments about welfare gains from foreign investment need considerable modification. Regardless of whether the MNE has been induced to invest for defensive purposes in protected and inefficient facilities or has come in for reasons of efficient resource allocation, *the use of transfer-*

pricing means that the net gains from foreign investment are less, or losses more, than they otherwise would have been.

The loss caused by transfer-pricing may be borne by various groups in the host economy: the government (loss of taxes), local shareholders (loss of legitimate share of profits), trade unions (if it deprives them of higher wages), consumers (from higher prices, if it enables firms to get more protection), and even other producers (if by worsening the foreign exchange situation it causes a shortage of maintenance imports).[28] This is only the immediate impact. Over the long run, it deprives the economy of the benefits of investment foregone, and may distort the pattern of investment (or worsen the existing distortions) by raising levels of real effective protection. At the same time, if the low level of declared profits deters prospective local competitors, it perpetuates the economy's dependence on foreigners.

It is clear that the welfare implications are more serious for less-developed than for developed host countries. Insofar as the terms on which MNEs enter less-developed countries, and their effect on welfare, is the result of a bargaining process, the existence of intra-firm trade acts as a *powerful bargaining counter in the MNE's favour*, enabling it to conceal from the government a crucial item of information. And the advantage is a permanent one, at least as long as intra-firm trade exists.

IMPLICATIONS FOR HOST GOVERNMENT POLICY

The preceding argument has assumed that host governments do nothing special to check the transfer-pricing mechanism. This is indeed the case with most host countries, which act in the belief that world prices in the manufacturing sector are somehow determined by objective market forces, or which have trust in the intentions of MNEs. Neither may be justified. Certainly the concern shown in recent literature with the control of MNEs shows that even some proponents of MNEs are worried about the amount of power wielded by them (e.g. Vernon, 1971). The existence and growth of intra-firm trade increases this power and correspondingly diminishes the ability of governments to regulate and control them. The exercise of effective government regulation must include methods of monitoring intra-firm trade and enforcing reasonable transfer-prices.

We shall not enter into a detailed discussion here of the methods available of countering transfer-pricing, but it may be useful to mention the main alternatives. The presumption is that governments are not willing to adapt their policies in such a way as to make them attractive to MNEs for declaring profits.

First, the government may set tariffs and tax rates at the same levels, so that it realises the same amount of revenue whichever way funds are remitted. This has the drawbacks that it would not stop transfer-pricing in cases where its main inducement is not tax differentials but other factors, and that it would limit tariffs to use as tax instruments rather than for a flexible protectionist policy.

Second, it may try to break the link between imports and parent companies by channelling all imports through an independent (possibly state) agency or forcing firms to buy elsewhere. This would involve a large administrative commitment and the risk of red-tapism and inefficiency.

Third, the tax authority may try to judge the profits of MNEs on evidence other than declared accounts, say, by their profitability abroad, or their sales, or some such measure. This may become extremely arbitrary, contentious and liable to corruption.

Fourth, the government may decide to check transfer-prices directly and compare them with world prices. This would be a difficult task, and, as the US experience shows, subject to some dispute and arbitrariness when items not openly traded on world markets are being assessed. The use of consultants or international agencies may be of great help here.

Fifth, all the governments playing host to MNEs may get together and tax them jointly, rendering the whole process of profit transfer irrelevant. This may be the ideal solution – meeting international threats with international action – but it seems highly impracticable.

Sixth, the government may encourage internal checks to the use of transfer-pricing by enlarging the share of local equity in MNEs. This would be effective only if local shareholders had the technical and business capacity to check transfer-prices, and if they did not themselves collude with their foreign partners. If requirements were too stringent, some MNEs would be deterred from investing at all.

Thus, all such policies face difficulties. The most practicable one at present seems to be direct official checks of the sort started in Colombia; its effectiveness can be increased by inter-government cooperation and exchange of information (as in the Andean Pact). If the transfer-pricing mechanism is really important to MNEs, it may be expected that they would resist any encroachment upon it, especially from less-developed countries where it is most useful. *Some* control seems to be essential, however, if MNEs are to be allowed to expand and benefit the host countries; unfortunately, the existing body of trade and investment

132   The Multinational Corporation

theory is at best inadequate, and, at worst, completely misleading, as a guide to forming policies in this field.

APPENDIX

TABLE A.5.1 US intra-firm manufacturing trade and total trade in manufactures: 1962–70 (in US $ millions) MNE data based on samples[1]

	1962	1963	1964	1965		1966		1970		1966[2]	
				Total by MNEs	With Affiliates	Total	With Aff.	Total	With Aff.	Benchmark Survey Total	With Aff.
A. Data on US Mfg. MNEs											
1. Exports	2549	2945	3490	7866	4057	9975	4208	16139	7079	12600	6300
2. Industry:											
a. Food				381	79	307	124	363	144		
b. Chemicals and Allied				1468	756	1560	679	2075	981		
c. Metals				873	285	768	180	1471	204		
d. Machinery				1956	1121	2965	1153	4762	2270		
e. Transport Equipment				2214	3093	3093	1508	5376	2588		
f. Other				974	435	1290	565	2092	892		
3. Imports	1150	1301	1636		1856	5707	2161	9393	4153		3000
4. Total Trade	3699	4246	5126		5913	15682	6369	25532	11232		9300
B. Data on Total US Mfg. Trade and Remittances											
5. Total US Exports[3]	14265	14928	17188	18043		19940		30177			
6. " " Imports	7970	8415	8851	11671		14943		26627			
7. Dividends and Interest Earned[4]	741	660	893	1094		1116		1859			
8. Royalties and Fees Earned	303	371	479	568		609		1002			
9. Total Earnings (8 + 9)	1044	1031	1372	1652		1725		2861			

NOTES
1. Sample coverages, which vary from time to time, are as follows: a. 1962–64: sample of 256 parent MNEs and about 2,500 affiliates, with 'affiliates' defined to cover firms with 25 per cent or more US equity. The sample figures were 'blown up' to represent all foreign investors. b. 1965: sample of 271 manufacturing firms, of which 257 reported exports to 1869 affiliates (defined as before). There was no blowing up of sample figures. c. 1966–70: sample of 223 manufacturing firms with 3,752 affiliates, which were redefined to cover only 'majority owned' foreign affiliates. There was no blowing up of sample figures.
2. Based on Foster, (1972), because original survey, US Direct Investments Abroad 1966, Part II, was not available here. The figures are rounded, and import figures are approximations, probably too low. This survey covered all foreign investors—3,300 parent companies about 23,000 affiliates, which were defined as 1962–5 above.
3. Total US exports and imports include: tobacco manufactures and cigarettes, alcohol, chemicals, machinery, transport equipment and other manufactured goods. Military shipments are excluded. Figures are from various Statistical Abstracts.
4. Earnings are on all manufacturing investments abroad, since data on sample MNEs are not available separately. They include branch earnings but exclude reinvested profits.

SOURCES
Foster, (1972); Hufbauer and Adler (1968).
Statistical Abstracts (various years), US Department of Commerce.
Survey of Current Business (Dec. 1965); (May 1969); (Nov. 1972) and (Dec. 1972).
US Department of Commerce, Special Survey of US Multinational Companies 1970, (Washington, D.C., 1972).

NOTES

1. The author is grateful for comments to Max Corden, Eprime Eshag, Ken Mayhew, George Richardson, Frances Stewart and Paul Streeten, and for discussions to Avigdor Meroz. I would also like to thank the New York office of UNCTAD for letting me use some data obtained in the course of research conducted for them, and Constantine Vaitsos for his help in getting access to these data and for stimulating an initial interest in this subject.
2. A major exception is Vaitsos (1974).
3. The limits are discussed below in section IIb.

Transfer-Pricing 133

4. The terms 'over-' and 'under-invoicing' may also be used, but these are sometimes used to denote the invoicing of trade between unrelated parties who act in collusion to transfer funds across national boundaries, Bhagwati (1967), Winston, (1970), and we shall keep this distinction.
5. I have refrained from using the term 'misuse', because there is a very fine distinction to be drawn between tax 'avoidance', which is by convention legal and acceptable, and tax 'evasion', which is not. Transfer-pricing may be regarded as avoidance by the firms, and evasion by the host governments, concerned. On the firms' attitudes, see Green and Duerr (1968).
6. This is intuitively obvious, but is established at greater length by Copithorne (1971).
7. Copithorne (1971) has argued that a 'national corporation with foreign operations', as opposed to a truly multinational corporation, would have the objective of maximising profits in A subject to some (arbitrary) profit target in B, and thus would use transfer-prices to ship the rest to A even in these conditions. It is not clear why this should happen, since the amount of profits sent back to A would be the same whether or not transfer-prices were used; some threat to profit declaration in B has to be introduced if the preference for declaring them in A is not to be completely irrational.
8. It may be argued that the cost of interest on losses in A would induce firms to minimise them, even if tax-offsets were available. Whether or not an MNE decides to use its profits in B to reduce interest payments in A depends, however, on the alternative returns available to the use of that money. It is only if the firm cannot invest it in more profitable ways in B or elsewhere that it would prefer to reduce its interest liabilities in A.
9. The case of 'underinvoicing' imports to avoid duty has been noted by Bhagwati (1964, 1967), and that of overinvoicing by Winston (1970). Independent importers have to buy foreign exchange on the black market to make up the difference, and the profit calculation, like the one MNEs have to make for tax differentials and tariffs, is based on a comparison of black market premiums and tariffs. If the primary aim of the trader is to accumulate foreign exchange abroad, however, tariffs may not prove a substantial deterrent to overinvoicing. This is identical to the case where there are quantitative restrictions on remissions by MNEs, and transfer-pricing is used to ship funds abroad regardless of the tariff burden.
10. The argument would apply even if the MNE wanted to re-invest profits in B. As long as tax rates on re-invested profits are the same as on remitted dividends it would pay the MNE to use transfer prices to minimise the tax burden, and re-invest in B by openly sending in addition to equity capital from A. If, as is often the case, the taxes on remissions were higher than on re-investments, the calculation would have to take into account the need for dividends versus re-investments and the appropriate tax differentials. The general effect would be to reduce the inducement to use the pricing channel.
11. The limit in Colombia and other Andean Pact countries, for instance, is 14 per cent of net worth per annum, and includes re-invested profits which may be considered additions to foreign net worth. Excess profits may be held over for a less profitable future year, but not be remitted or added to net worth in that year.
12. The temptation for such collusion would be particularly strong in countries

where the government laid down strict requirements for local equity participation, which were fulfilled by the MNE selling shares to locals who were affluent nominees (traders, landowners, officials) rather than industrialists in their own right. While many leading MNEs may claim to be above this sort of behaviour, there is nothing unusual or surprising about it – the case of under or overinvoiced trade (loc. cit.) involves similar collusion between the local and foreign trading partners.
13. It is important to note that the country which has taken most official action to control the use of transfer-pricing is the United States – the home of the largest MNEs – under section 482 of its Internal Revenue Code. The MNEs have reacted strongly against such interference, implying that the mechanism *is* valuable to them. See Keegan (1969); Greene and Duerr (1968); Duerr (1972). Such action by capital exporting countries to raise their 'fair' share of taxes implies, of course, that less-developed host countries have even less chance of gaining fortuitously from transfer-pricing.
14. This argument would have to be modified if the countries concerned did not have doubletax agreements. Thus, if the parent firm wanted to declare dividends in A, but taxes were lower in B, it would be useless to transfer profits to B via intra-firm trade, declare them there and bring them back to A, since A's government would levy additional tax to bring the overall tax up to its own level. To this extent, motivation would counteract the natural inducement to use transfer-prices.
15. The lack of freedom of subsidiaries in determining transfer-prices is noted in a Ph.D. thesis by J. Shulman, quoted in Tugendhat (1971), ch. 10.
16. The recent investigation of Hoffman-La Roche, the Swiss pharmaceutical firm, by the British Monopolies Commission (1973) reveals an absolutely unconstrained use of transfer-prices. In the Company's own words, transfer prices are determined by 'what is reasonable for tax purposes' (para. 138).
17. On the problems faced by the US tax authorities in assigning correct transfer-prices, and the various rules-of-thumb used, see Keegan (1969) and Duerr (1972). See also the Monopolies Commission (1973) reports on similar problems for Roche Products in the UK.
18. It is possible that intra-firm trade in finished goods is easier to check, and thus less subjected to misuse, than trade in intermediate and capital goods. However, we have no evidence on this.
19. There are no data on intra-firm trade before 1962.
20. Bradshaw (1969). The industrial composition of US intra-firm trade also reflects the pattern of MNE investment, with the sectors having over 50 per cent of their exports going to affiliates being the ones with most rapid expansion of MNEs, e.g. pharmaceuticals, rubber, transport equipment, non-electrical machinery, office equipment. Traditional industries (like food, paper, metal products) have a relatively small incidence of intra-firm exports from the US.
21. *Board of Trade Journal* (1968).
22. Unfortunately, there are no figures available for the earnings of the sample firms, or even of UK manufacturing investments abroad as distinct from total overseas investments.
23. Perhaps some indirect support for our case could be adduced from the evidence on tied aid, which is believed to raise the cost of imports by 20 per

cent to the aid recipients (Pearson Commission, 1969). Since intra-firm trade is simply an extreme form of tying of purchases, it is easy to imagine how much more prices can be pushed up.

24. Overpricing is defined as $(P_c - P_w)/P_w \times 100$, where P_c stands for the price actually paid in Colombia and P_w the comparable world market price. For details of the findings see Vaitsos (1974) and DANE (1971).
25. Overpricing on individual products was sometimes as high as 3000 per cent (Vaitsos, 1974). When brought to court, the firms were unable to justify the prices charged (*El Tiempo*, 1971).
26. In this context, it is interesting to note the Monopolies Commission (1973) findings on Roche Products that profits from transfer-pricing accounted for 76 per cent of total profits in 1966–72, and came to over six times the amount of declared profits (Para. 164). The calculation of arm's length prices of the two relevant products made ample allowance for overhead and R and D costs; the extent of overpricing came to 123 per cent for Librium and 161 per cent for Valium in 1970.
27. For a summary and preliminary empirical testing of various theories, see Hufbauer (1970).
28. The gains from transfer-pricing would accrue similarly to the other country's government, shareholders in the firm, and possibly trade unions. There would also be numerous favourable dynamic effects, on investment, innovation, and growth.

REFERENCES

Barker, B. L. (1972), 'US Foreign Trade Associated with US Multinational Companies', *Survey of Current Business* (Dec.).
Bhagwati, J. (1964), 'On the Underinvoicing of Imports' (*BOUIES*).
—— (1967), 'Fiscal Policies, the Faking of Foreign Exchange Declarations and the Balance of Payments' (*BOUIES*).
Board of Trade Journal (1968), 'Overseas Transactions in 1966–Trade Credits and Exports' (London, HMSO).
Bradshaw, M. T. (1969), 'US Exports to Foreign Affiliates of US Firms', *Survey of Current Business* (May).
Brooke, M. Z., and Remmers, H. L. (1970), *The Strategy of Multinational Enterprise* (London: Longman).
Brooke, M. Z. and Remmers, H. L. (1972), *The Multinational Company in Europe* (London: Longman).
Copithorne, L. W. (1971), 'International Corporate Transfer Prices and Government Policy', *Canadian Journal of Economics*, vol. IV.
DANE (Departmento Administrativo Nacional de Estadistica) (1971), 'Survey of Foreign Investment in Colombia' (in Spanish), *Boletín Mensual de Estadística*, no. 239 (Bogota: June).
Duerr, M. G. (1972), *Tax Allocations and International Business* (New York: The Conference Board).
Dunning, J. F. (1972), Introduction to *International Investment* (Harmondsworth: Penguin).
El Tiempo (1971), 'Incomex Rebajá Precios' newspaper (Bogota: 15 Sept.).

Foster, S. B. (1972), 'Impact of Direct Investment Abroad by US Multinational Companies on the Balance of Payments', *Federal Reserve Bank of New York Monthly Review* (July).
Greene, J. and Duerr, M. G. (1968), *Intercompany Transfers in Multinational Firms* (New York: The Conference Board).
Helleiner, G. K. (1973), 'Manufactured Exports from Less-Developed Countries and Multinational Firms', *Economic Journal* (Mar.).
Horst, T. (1971), 'The Theory of the Multinational Firm: Optimal Behaviour under Different Tariff and Tax Rates', *Journal of Political Economy*, vol. 79.
Hufbauer, G. C. and Adler, F. M. (1968), *Overseas Manufacturing Investment and the Balance of Payments* (US Treasury Department, Washington, DC).
Hufbauer, G. C. (1970), 'The Impact of National Characteristics and Technology on the Commodity Composition of Trade in Manufactured Goods', in R. Vernon (ed.), *The Technology Factor in International Trade* (New York: National Bureau of Economic Research).
Johnson, H. G. (1969), 'The Theory of International Trade', in P. A. Samuelson (ed.), *International Economic Relations* (New York: Macmillan).
Keegan, W. J. (1969), 'Multinational Pricing: How Far is Arm's Length?', *Columbia Journal of World Business*, vol. IV, no. 3.
Kindleberger, C. P. (1969), *American Business Abroad* (New Haven: Yale University Press).
—— (1970), (ed.), *The International Corporation* (Cambridge, Mass.: MIT Press).
Monopolies Commission (1973), *Chlordiazepoxide and Diazepam* (London: HMSO).
Pearson Commission (1969), *Partners in Development* (New York: Praeger).
Reddaway, W. B., et al. (1967), *Effects of UK Direct Investment Overseas, An Interim Report* (Cambridge University Press).
Tugendhat, C. (1971), *The Multinationals* (London: Eyre and Spottiswoode).
UNCTAD (1971), *Policies Relating to Technology in the Countries of the Andean Pact: Their Foundations* (Santiago, TD/107).
US Department of Commerce (1972), *Special Survey of US Multinational Companies 1970* (Bureau of Economic Analysis, Washington, DC).
Vaitsos, C. V. (1974), *Inter-Country Income Distribution and Transnational Corporations* (OXFORD: CLARENDON PRESS).
Vernon, R. (1971), *Sovereignty at Bay* (London: Longman).
Wells, L. T. (1971), 'The Multinational Business Enterprise: What Kind of International Organisation?', *International Organization* (Summer).
Williamson, O. E. (1971), 'Managerial Discretion, Organisation Form and the Multi-Division Hypothesis', in R. Marris and A. Wood (ed.), *The Corporate Economy* (London: Macmillan).
Winston, G. C. (1970), 'Overinvoicing, Underutilisation and Distorted Industrial Growth', *Pakistan Development Review*.

6 Transfer-Pricing and LDCs: Some Problems of Investigation[1]

I INTRODUCTION

This paper intends to review some of the main problems which arise for developing host countries in the investigation of transfer-pricing of commodity trade by transnational corporations (TNCs) in manufacturing industry. It concentrates on the pricing of intra-firm trade (i.e. trade between associated units of a company operating in several countries), but part of the analysis will also be relevant to the pricing of inter-firm trade (between unrelated parties) by TNCs in developing countries.

While the general factors affecting the use of the transfer-pricing mechanism by TNCs, and the losses this may entail for host LDCs, have been amply discussed in the literature,[2] remarkably little seems to have been done since the early days of the Andean Pact to investigate the incidence, extent and distribution of transfer-pricing.[3] Thus, academic work on the phenomenon has languished, and official efforts to discover and control it have been generally confined to some developed countries[4] and a very few developing ones which still maintain a 'tough' line on TNC entry. In part the problem is political – a lax policy on taxation and transfer-pricing is taken to show a liberal and welcoming attitude to foreign investment, and change to a strict policy may betoken a hostile switch. In part, however, the problem is practical: there are enormous difficulties facing host governments wishing to investigate transfer-pricing by large, monopolistic, multi-product transnationals. These difficulties arise from three different factors:

1. an uneven incidence of transfer-pricing across different industries and by different firms;
2. internal and external problems in collecting data relevant to checking intra-firm pricing; and
3. conceptual issues in defining correct transfer-prices.

In the following sections, we shall consider these in turn: Section II deals with the problems raised by the fact that the extent of intra-firm trade, and the potential for manipulating transfer prices, differs from case to case; Section III describes the main handicaps that host governments of developing countries face in collecting data on transfer pricing; Section IV discusses some very difficult conceptual issues that arise in defining the correct reference prices by which transfer-prices may be judged; and Section V draws the main conclusions.

II INCIDENCE OF TRANSFER-PRICING

The available evidence indicates, as we shall see, that the 'effectiveness' of transfer-pricing for TNCs (the extent to which profits can be clandestinely moved by changing intra-firm prices as compared to declaring profits) varies widely from industry to industry and from one firm to another. This is worth taking into account for policy purposes: on the one hand, it makes it more difficult for host governments to formulate general rules and procedures for checking price manipulation, but, on the other, it provides an opportunity to narrow the field which they need to monitor in order to check the largest potential abuse. For governments with limited administrative resources, this is clearly an important consideration.

Three sets of factors acccount for the uneven incidence of transfer-pricing. First, the trade component of TNC production itself varies according to industry. Second, the extent of intra-firm as a proportion of total trade by TNCs differs widely, both according to industry, and also possibly according to the national origin of the firms involved. Third, the possibilities of manipulating intra-firm prices to shift revenues also vary from case to case. The first is obvious and needs little explanation. Let us take the other two in turn.

INTRA-FIRM TRADE

As far as the extent of intra-firm trade (as opposed to trade with unrelated parties) is concerned, we can think of several economic reasons why trading relationships between TNCs and affiliates would vary by industry and by the nature of the markets faced by each.

If a TNC is exporting finished products, it will choose to channel them through an affiliate, rather than through independent buyers or agents, if certain marketing factors make it cheaper or more efficient to use facilities directly owned and controlled by it. Such factors may be the requirements of sophisticated after-sales service (e.g. the 'software' component of computers), the aggressive promotion of brand image or a close coordination between marketing and production, specialised forms of distribution networks, and so on. The size of the market in question, and the availability of local marketing or advertising channels, would also affect the choice: if local facilities were adequate, or the size of the market too small to justify investment, it would often be cheaper for the firm to engage in inter- rather than intra-firm dealings.

For a TNC subsidiary importing intermediate products for local processing or assembly, the choice between buying from the parent company, from other foreign suppliers or from domestic suppliers would depend upon their relative cost, performance and reliability, and on host government policy regarding imports and local purchase. When the product required is highly specialised (because of the nature of the technology, design or the skills required), when it enjoys economies of scale (and the parent company reaps these economies), when production is closely integrated in an international production structure (as with electronic products for 'offshore' assembly, or with IBM computer production in different parts of Europe), and when transport costs (plus tariffs) are favourable, it would pay the subsidiary to buy from the parent company. On the other hand, when the product is standardised, its technology is well diffused, or transport costs are unfavourable, it may be cheaper for the subsidiary – and, by implication, for the TNC as a whole[5] – to buy from unrelated parties.

In general, and at the cost of some simplification, it may be said that the main factors which dispose TNCs to engage in intra-firm trade are 'high' technology (including large R and D requirements, a high level of skills, and firm-specific products, designs and know-how), 'high' marketing (calling for a close coordination between production and selling or for tightly organised promotion, retailing and distribution), and risk or uncertainty attached to open market transactions. The greater the significance of these factors for particular industries or TNCs, the greater the benefits of trading within an enterprise than outside it: not only can outside parties not compete with the parent enterprise on price, quality or service, but the enterprise as a whole maximises the profitability of possessing special monopolistic advantages by internalising trade. It follows, by the same logic, that in industries and for products which are standardised and so do not afford any monopolistic advantage, open market transactions will tend to predominate over intra-firm transactions. TNCs may well dominate the production of such commodities because they possess other sources of monopolistic advantage – for example, they are powerful in several areas of food processing, but food inputs, being standardised, are generally purchased locally or imported on open markets; or, in industrial chemicals and electrical products, the existence of intense competition in technologically well-diffused products makes markets fairly open – but they may opt for external trade in order to achieve profit maximisation.

Data for 1970 on intra-firm exports by US TNCs provide impressionistic support for our reasoning. These data, shown in Table 6.1 for the parent companies and their affiliates separately, do not cover intra-firm trade with minority-owned firms, or with licensees which may have contractual obligations to buy from the TNCs; moreover, they do not provide an indication of the proportion of the affiliates' *imports* that are intra-firm. Nevertheless, they are useful in illustrating some characteristics of US intra-firm trade: their statistical exploration has been undertaken in another paper (see Chapter 4).

The affiliates of US TNCs are on average far more dependent on intra-firm trade for their exports than are their parent companies. For manufacturing as a whole, 66 per cent of the MOFA's exports are intra-firm as compared to only 35 per cent for their parents. This seems to reflect a greater need for the affiliates to use the world-wide network of the parent – perhaps a reflection of the relative specialisations of the parents and affiliates in products of different specifications. In general, however, industries with relatively high levels of intra-firm trade (office machines, plastics, computers, instruments, transport equipment) are all high technology sectors (in terms of high levels of R and D spending, or of requirements of skills and know-how), with some high marketing requirements.[6] Some intermediate intra-firm trade industries are low technology but have high marketing requirements (textiles and apparel and household appliances) or are high technology and marketing, but subject to special regulation (drugs), or medium technology but low marketing (paper). The low intra-firm trade industries are either very low technology (metals, stone and glass) or of medium but well-diffused technology and low marketing (industrial chemicals).

While industrial characteristics may explain much of the variation in intra-firm trade, the national origins of the TNCs concerned may also be a relevant factor. Some data collected by Vaitsos on a sample of 240 TNCs operating in different Latin American countries indicate a marked difference in the propensity to engage in intra-firm trade between TNCs of different origins.[7] (While the figures relate to the

TABLE 6.1 US: Intra-firm exports[a] of US TNCs and their majority-owned affiliates as percentages of their total exports, 1970 (%)

Industry	Intra-firm exports of parent TNCs	Intra-firm exports of MOFAs	Total
All manufacturing	35	66	49
Food products	34	34	34
Grain mill products	47	–	–
Beverages	19	28	24
Combinations	23	26	34
Other	32	42	35
Paper and allied products	25	63	46
Chemicals and allied products	36	45	40
Drugs	38	44	41
Soaps and cosmetics	54	32	41
Industrial chemicals	15	30	20
Plastic materials	88	59	70
Combinations	100	38	57
Other	29	74	48
Rubber	39	65	50
Primary and fabricated metals	12	22	15
Primary	5	21	8
Fabricated, excluding aluminum, copper and brass	24	23	23
Primary and fabricated aluminum	9	–	–
Other	50	20	15
Machinery, except electrical	44	62	52
Farm machinery and equipment	49	88	68
Industrial machinery and equipment	27	37	31
Office machines	75	83	77
Electronic computing equipment	75	–	–
Other	40	75	64
Electrical machinery	28	73	45
Household appliances	25	101	63
Electrical equipment and apparatus	15	71	28
Electronic components, radio, and TV	29	76	49
Other	92	52	56
Transportation equipment	41	84	61
Textiles and apparel	40	63	52
Lumber, wood, and furniture	11	27	20
Printing and publishing	25	55	41
Stone, clay and glass products	32	18	25
Instruments	62	63	62
Other manufacturing	23	63	36

NOTE
(–) implies not available.
[a] Intra-Firm refers to trade between majority-owned affiliates only, it does not cover minority-owned affiliates or firms tied to the TNCs in any other way.

SOURCE
US Tariff Commission (1973) p. 367, table a-14.

proportion of imports from the home country of the TNC rather than to intra-firm imports proper, it may reasonably be assumed that most of these are in fact intra-firm). Thus, while the overall average for imports from home countries as a percentage of total imports is 57 per cent, four countries have figures very much higher (Japan 93 per cent, West Germany 80 per cent, Sweden 72 per cent and Holland 69 per cent), while others, viz. the US (59 per cent), the UK (49 per cent), Canada (38 per cent), France (46 per cent), have much lower figures.

Vaitsos notes that while the host country where subsidiaries are located and the size of the TNCs concerned affect the extent of intra-firm imports, the home country of the TNC seems to exercise the greatest influence. He offers the explanation that, for TNCs from small home countries (Holland and Sweden), the dependence on intra-firm trade reflects the inability to recoup fixed expenditures at the head office on domestic sales: thus, 'tied inter-affiliate trade flows and transfer-pricing become a key element so as to remit earnings from abroad *before* they are taxed in the *host* countries to cover the costs incurred in their *home* countries'.[8]

The fact that some large home countries have high intra-firm imports into Latin America (Japan and West Germany), or that some small ones have low intra-firm trade (Belgium at 18 per cent and Switzerland at 51 per cent) does not, however, support this particular explanation. The main problem about generalising from this set of data is that the *industrial* distribution of the TNCs from different countries is not given, so that we are unable to judge whether the differences lie in national origins or in industrial characteristics. A similar problem affects calculations by Buckley and Pearce (1977), who survey data provided directly by 156 TNCs to examine, among other things, the extent to which parent companies indulge in intra-firm exports. There are considerable nationality variations: the average is 41 per cent, with 59 per cent for Swedish, 55 per cent for US, 8 per cent for Japanese and 13 per cent for French firms (and some of these differences are statistically significant). The results for the non-US firms, however, differ markedly from those shown by Vaitsos' Latin American data, leading us to suspect that the industrial compositions of the two samples, and differences in the host countries where subsidiaries are located, are more important than the national origins of TNCs. This is strengthened by the finding of Buckley and Pearce that research-intensive industries have much higher intra-firm exports (57 percent) than non-research-intensive industries (18 per cent), a finding that is confirmed in my own

Transfer-Pricing and Developing Countries 143

(chapter 4) more extensive statistical work on the pattern of intra-firm exports of US parent companies.

Such evidence as exists does not, however, contradict Vaitsos' hypothesis: it is possible that, given the industry, TNCs from small home countries indulge in more intra-firm trade than large ones. However, it is equally possible that national origins exercise no independent influence. Until both hypotheses are properly tested, we must remain agnostic.

MANIPULATION OF TRANSFER-PRICES

Let us now consider differences in the potential manipulation of transfer-prices given the existence of intra-firm trade. Here, again, variations are likely, depending on the nature of the traded product and the identity of the firm concerned.

The nature of the traded product affects the use of transfer-pricing (as a deliberate profit-shifting device) essentially by its 'specificity' to the TNC concerned. The more generally traded, and so less specific, a product, the greater will be the danger that a transfer-price differing from its open market prices is discovered by the authorities. 'Specificity' in this sense has several aspects:

i. A product may be specific *in the highest degree* when it is an intermediate traded *only* within a particular TNC. Here there are no open market prices available for reference, and the potential for arbitrary pricing is at its maximum.

ii. A product may be *highly specific* when it is produced only by one TNC, but is sold both to affiliates and to third parties. Here arm's length prices may be established by a host government with references to prices charged to unrelated buyers, but with two problems: first, the prices charged to buyers in different countries may be secret; and, second, these prices may incorporate a high degree of monopoly rent, and they may vary from case to case, so that a particular reference price may be misleading or unsatisfactory. This raises problems of monopoly power in trade more generally, and cannot be discussed here; but we shall touch on these issues again in Section IV.

iii. A product which is sold on a discontinuous basis (like tailor-made capital equipment) will be *highly specific*, because prices of identical products elsewhere would be very difficult, or impossible, to obtain.

iv. A product which is made up of large numbers of component parts (an extreme example being a turnkey plant) would be *fairly specific*, unless such products required a standardised and well-diffused technology.

v. A product which was highly differentiated from its competitors, because of promotion (for consumer goods), or because of performance, quality, specifications and delivery times (for producer goods), would be *fairly specific*.

In general, the more advanced and firm-specific the level of technology embodied in a product, and the more discontinuous its supply, the greater the scope for transfer-pricing. Since the technological intensity of a product also to a large extent determines the incidence of intra-firm trade itself, and also influences the degree of monopoly power in the pricing of products in open markets, the cases in which the potential abuse of transfer-pricing is greatest are also those in which intra-firm trade and the existence of monopoly powers are likely to be high. The correspondence is not exact, of course; there are several high marketing industries where intra-firm trade is significant but the potential for profit shifting is low (e.g. textiles). And there are some high technology industries where intra-firm trade is high but the products are sold in a finished form (e.g. computers) rendering comparisons with open markets rather easier.[9] These narrow the task of checking transfer-pricing for host governments, but the 'area of danger', where all the difficult problems converge, is still quite large.

The scattered evidence that exists on transfer-pricing[10] confirms that its 'abuse' (defined as the difference between intra-firm and arm's length prices)[11] is higher in industries with highly specific products than in those with standardised products. The industry with the highest incidence of enormous price differentials between transfer and arm's length prices is pharmaceuticals, where evidence from Latin America, Iran, Sri Lanka and elsewhere (including the UK)[12] shows a potential for 'abuse' so far unmatched by any other manufacturing industry. The intermediates which account for most of intra-firm trade in this industry are usually specific in the highest degree. In contrast, differentials in other sectors, like rubber or (simple) electrical products, with standardised products, have been found to be much smaller.

If further research bears out the line of reasoning, it follows, from the point of view of policy, that governments should concentrate on what has been termed the 'area of danger', where there is advanced technology, a great deal of intra-firm trade, the products are highly specific and there is considerable monopoly power in the relevant markets. Other industries should not be completely neglected, but for these an occasional check, with a very small investment of resources, would probably suffice.

The 'area of danger' may perhaps be further narrowed if the nature of the TNCs involved is itself studied. In an earlier paper (see Chapter 5), I had shown that there was a very high degree of concentration in the firms which accounted for US and UK intra-firm exports. Of the 25 TNCs in the US on which such data were available (and these accounted for the bulk of US foreign investment), only 18 accounted for 65 per cent of intra-firm exports. In the UK, similarly, 32 firms out of 1466 accounted for 52 per cent of intra-firm exports. Both figures are for the mid-1960s, and it is likely in view of the continued growth of TNC dominance that this concentration has increased. Governments need, therefore, to devote most of their attention to the biggest firms; the small fry can be dealt with cursorily.

It seems that there is, even within the select group of large TNCs, considerable variation between firms as far as their policies regarding transfer-pricing are concerned.[13] Such differences have been found to lead to several TNCs being 'sub-optimal' (from the corporations profit-maximising objective) in their use of intra-firm links, causing business specialists to recommend a more positive and rational use of transfer-pricing to minimise tax payments.[14] There are several possible reasons for these variations:

i. Firms of different nationalities may have different corporate philosophies and 'styles'.[15] This sort of difference may be expected to diminish in significance over time as 'styles' get more similar and TNCs grow even more international.

ii. Firms with different histories and with different balances of size between parents and affiliates may have different attitudes to central direction (necessary for extensive use of transfer-pricing) as opposed to autonomy.

iii. Firms with different control and accounting structures will have different abilities to manipulate transfer-pricing. Those, for example, that use a 'profit centre' system (with several centres autonomously maximising their own profits) cannot use transfer-pricing as well as those with centralised control.

iv. Firms with tightly-knit, hierarchical systems of control (as is becoming increasingly common with multi-divisional structures) can use transfer-pricing much better than those with looser structures.

Thus, both attitude and ability will differ from case to case and canny host governments may use this fact to their own advantage. We should not, however, be too hopeful on this score. First, organisational structures and financial strategies are in a constant process of evolution, and commercial logic clearly dictates that TNCs become more 'rational' in their use of transfer-pricing (unless governments constantly apply countervailing measures to reduce the danger). Second, the firms in which organisational structures are most hierarchical and centralised, and so which can best use transfer-pricing, are precisely those in high technology and high marketing industries[16] which have the greatest incidence of intra-firm trade. On this count, therefore, the 'area of danger' is not to be further diminished significantly.

To end this section, we may point out that the existing literature on transfer-pricing has tended to ignore the great differences in the effectiveness with which TNCs can use transfer-pricing in different cases. It has given the impression that there exists a vast and complex problem in the taxation and regulation of TNCs which applies with equal force to the whole area of foreign investment. We have tried to demonstrate here that in fact the problem differs greatly in scope and intensity between different industries and (to a lesser extent) between different TNCs. There are several interesting academic issues here that need explanation, but the policy implication is clear: attention must be focused on the real 'area of danger' where the extent of intra-firm trade and scope for price manipulation are maximum and where the monopoly power of TNCs is greatest. This area is, by and large, defined by the high technology fields of international investment.

III DATA ON TRANSFER-PRICING

An extensive check on the use of transfer-pricing requires the collection of a large quantity of data, some of which can be got within a host country, and some of which has to be sought abroad. The need for such a large amount of information does not arise in every instance, but in cases where the problem is most pressing the checking of transfer-prices becomes (as we shall see) tantamount to assessing a TNC's total operations, evaluating its technological contribution and deciding upon the correct balance between market power and technical process. The problems in collecting data may be separately discussed for those arising within a host country (internal) and those arising abroad (external). Since cases in which the products involved in intra-firm trade are standardised, and their open market prices well known, are not difficult to handle, let us ignore them and concentrate on the 'area of danger': firms with specific products, usually in a high technology industry and with no easily accessible reference price.

INTERNAL PROBLEMS

Since the main objective of official policy on transfer-pricing is to ensure that the host country gets a proper share of profits earned within it, information collected internally has to provide a complete picture to the government on a subsidiary's operations (sales, growth, assets, use of capacity, labour relations and so on) as well as on all its financial links with the parent company (declared profits, royalty payments, service and other fees, interest on foreign loans and intra-firm trade). Only when all this information is collected and evaluated can the authorities have a realistic estimate of how well the subsidiary is doing and how much it is paying its parent.

The first barrier to the collection of such information is a simple but effective one. In most countries, data on different aspects of a subsidiary's operations are collected by different ministries or departments (e.g. customs collect data on import and export prices, tax authorities on declared profits, statistics departments on costs, capacity utilisation, and employment, the central bank on various exchange dealings, and so on). Yet firm-level information is normally confidential to each department, and there is no legal way (at least under normal laws) by which it can be centralised.[17] Tax authorities can ask for specific information from firms which they suspect of under-declaring profits, but they are not equipped to conduct a regular and comprehensive monitoring of a subsidiary's operations. What is needed is a special unit to deal with TNCs, which routinely collects all relevant information, analyses it to assess subsidiaries' performance, and compares the result to what the firms report for tax purposes.

While a relatively minor legal change may dispose of this problem, a second, and very important, barrier prevents many governments from initiating such a measure: the *political* one. As noted in the introduction (and as repeatedly stressed to me in Malaysia) any overt move to tighten the laws and conditions governing foreign investment may be interpreted by TNCs as a hostile act – or at least the host government might fear that it will be so interpreted. Where political stability is an important consideration (as it often is in LDCs) and the attraction of foreign capital is an important policy objective, the need to maintain a 'good image' might consequently prevent host governments from undertaking even minor policies to remove lacunae in the system of regulation.

It should be noted that it is the political and psychological elements which are predominant. The fact that tighter control of transfer-pricing would also raise the effective tax rate, and so may restrict capital inflow, is also a consideration, but, in my view, a secondary one as far as LDCs are concerned. There are several reasons for this view. First, tax rates in most developing countries are equal to or lower than in developed ones, and improving their realisation should not by itself affect TNC's investment plans. Second, there is little evidence that foreign investment (sourcing investments apart since these may be quite sensitive to tax rates) is very responsive to fiscal incentives – so that what is in effect the tightening of control on one incentive should not restrict capital inflows. Third, the theoretical models[18] which predict a fall in TNC investment in response to higher taxes, based on neo-classical assumptions about profit-maximisation in competitive markets, ignore important elements of uncertainty, monopoly rent and oligopolistic reaction characteristic of TNC-dominated industries. And finally, it is the larger recipients of capital inflows, those which have favourable political climates, which have been able to impose the tightest controls on transfer-pricing (the US, UK, France, Holland, and West Germany among developed countries, Mexico among less developed countries) without greatly altering their attractiveness to TNCs.[19] In other words, host governments which can tighten controls while maintaining an otherwise welcoming posture (and of course, attractive economic conditions) can go much further in this respect than those which are politically unstable, economically unattractive or otherwise hostile to foreign capital.

The third problem in internal data collection is the administrative one. An effective collection and evaluation of information on TNCs may require a large, costly and sophisticated unit which many LDCs cannot provide or afford. The potential benefits of collecting more taxes may well be outweighed, at least in the smaller and powerful LDCs by the cost of financing the operation.

EXTERNAL PROBLEMS

Even if a host government collects and analyses all relevant data on the operations of a TNC subsidiary, it needs a certain amount of data on the operations of the TNC as a whole in order to assess the correctness of profit declarations and transfer prices of the subsidiary. The minimum requirements are information, first, on the profitability of the TNC as a

Transfer-Pricing and Developing Countries 149

whole, and, second, on comparable open market prices where these are available. The maximum requirements, where arm's-length prices have to be assigned or negotiated, can be much greater. They may encompass detailed cost data on the production and fixed expenses relevant to the commodities involved, the interpretation of which raises issues which we come to in the following section.

The knowledge of a TNC's overall profitability may be useful because it provides a yardstick – albeit a crude one – of what sort of performance a particular host country may expect in the industry in which the firm operates. It creates, in other words, a presumption about the firm's profitability, departures from which (especially in a downward direction) can be questioned. There may of course be several causes for departures: excess capacity, high costs, labour problems, local market conditions, and so on. If these are taken into account, and allowance made for higher profitability due, say, to tariff protection and dominant market position (both common to TNCs in LDCs), the host government can get an approximate idea of what to expect. It is, however, a very rough approximation, and further analysis will generally be required in fairness to both parties.

As far as the problem of collecting available data on market prices is concerned, it is surprising how limited the resources and capabilities of some LDC administrations are, even in situations where modest research would yield large dividends. The fact that tax authorities are simply not geared to collecting such information and doing detective work on prices abroad means that they are far more dependent on what TNCs tell them than they need to be. An example, based again on my Malaysia experience, will be illustrative.

In Malaysia there are 5 assembly plants for passenger cars, all foreign controlled. Officials complained that the CIF prices charged by TNCs for the completely knocked down (CKD) packs for local assembly were higher than the CIF prices for the same cars fully built-up (FBU). They felt that something was obviously wrong with this structure of prices, but could find no concrete evidence to counter the TNCs' argument that the cost of packaging and freighting the CKD packs was greater than the cost of assembling and freighting the FBU units. It was possible that the economies of very large-scale assembly reduced its cost sufficiently below the cost of packaging the several components that go into a CKD pack – this was explained to me by a TNC subsidiary – that the CIF prices of two favoured the finished product. This price structure persists, as far as I know, to this day.

Yet in England I came, quite accidentally, upon a study by Rose

(1971) which deals with just this question for the New Zealand car assembly industry. His data contradicts the case advanced by the TNCs, on two grounds:

i. Freight charges for CKD packs are lower than for FBU units, since the former require less space (body panels, for example, can be nested into small crates, and crates can be piled together): this is contrary to the impression given by the firms in Malaysia. The difference in cost per car for New Zealand is nearly 200 per cent on shipments from Japan, 458 per cent from the east coast of the US and 308 per cent from North Europe.[20]

ii. The cost of FBU units, for New Zealand purchasers, is 26 per cent on average (for 12 cars from 7 companies) higher than for CKD packs.

The total difference in CIF values of CKD and FBU units is 43 per cent *of the cost of the CKD pack* for New Zealand. Rose's data are for the late 1960s: unless the relative cost ratios have changed dramatically in 6–7 years, Malaysia affiliates are being grossly overcharged by TNCs.

The point of the example is that in some cases LDC administrations, faced with a situation where their own knowledge is insufficient, are not equipped (or perhaps not willing) to undertake the sort of investigation which would correct the deficiency. In this case, clearly the requisite data were available: if not from Rose's study, then from the sources used by Rose, or from other specialists in the industry. Perhaps intergovernmental exchange of information would have sufficed; perhaps some detective work on freight rates and prices in the home countries of TNCs would have been necessary. In any case, none of these measures were undertaken, and the TNCs were able to exploit the situation with great ease.

The automobile industry is not, however, a particularly difficult case to tackle as far as transfer-pricing is concerned. It is not a high technology industry. There is a substantial amount of inter-firm trade.[21] Costs of production are easy to discover and fixed costs are not particularly difficult to allocate since there is little R and D, components are fairly standardised and produced by large numbers of subcontractors, and innovation is not particularly risky. This is not to say that TNCs cannot manipulate transfer-prices in the absence of special regulatory measures, only that there are few problems *in principle* for a government which is determined to control the practice. The case falls into the group where remedies are possible mainly by the collection of information. It is not one where, as we shall see in a moment, information collection by itself is insufficient.

The actual collection of price, cost and profitability information is by no means an easy matter for LDC governments. A certain amount of balance-sheet data are published by public limited corporations in their home and host countries, which can provide a starting point for investigations. There are also publications like *Who Owns Whom* which list affiliated companies: again a basic piece of information often not possessed by tax authorities in LDCs. Several industry and trade journals provide price data, financial analysis, and the like. Specialised consultancy services (like the Swiss General Superintendence Company which operates a world-wide network to check the quality and market price of traded commodities) may provide further information.

After all these sources have been tapped, there may still remain cases where the requisite data can only be provided by the TNC itself (say, when costs of production of firm-specific commodities are necessary) or by governments of other countries involved in that TNC's infra-firm trade. The extent to which TNCs can be forced to divulge information depends on the bargaining power of the country concerned and on the political factors mentioned above. Clearly the developed countries and the larger LDCs can extract more than small host governments in the developing world.

As for the exchange of firm-level data between governments, there are obvious legal as well as political barriers. The recent experience of countries in the developed world shows, however, that legal barriers are not insuperable when information exchange is clearly of mutual benefit. The customs authorities of several European countries exchange price data, especially on pharmaceuticals, where suspicious TNC transactions are involved.[22] The US and Canadian authorities have gone further. They are arranging to have *joint tax audits* of TNCs with the prime aim of investigating transfer-pricing, starting with 3 enterprises (in pharmaceuticals, chemicals and primary commodities) but contemplating the study of 1200 firms.[23] This is clearly the logical next step in the control of TNC transactions, and may well establish a precedent for other developed nations. What it promises for LDCs is not obvious. On the one hand, LDCs would benefit greatly from having access to the data collected by customs and tax authorities in developed countries; on the other, the fact that they have less useful information to offer in return (because the bulk of TNC activity is in developed countries), and certainly have less political and economic weight, may keep them out of the emerging 'club' of governments implementing more effective controls on TNCs.

IV DEFINING CORRECT TRANSFER-PRICES

Let us assume that a host government in a less developed country has access to all the production cost, fixed cost, intra-firm prices and profit data it wants on a TNC with operations in its jurisdiction. Let us assume also that the firm concerned is in a high technology industry, with heavy R and D expenses, a lot of intra-firm trade in firm-specific products and with considerable market power in final product markets. Can it then proceed in a straightforward manner to assign 'correct' transfer-prices on the goods which enter or leave its country?

Unfortunately not. A 'correct' transfer-price must be one which is fair in some sense to both the government and the TNC concerned, and it must be compatible with the continuation of desirable technical progress in that industry. It must, in other words, be a price which provides a just reward for investments in R and D by that TNC, bearing in mind the riskiness of innovation in the industry, but not one which permits unjustified monopoly profits or socially wasteful expenditures on building up monopoly power. The complexities of the issues can be illustrated with the example of the pharmaceutical industry, the prime target of transfer-pricing investigations.

The transnational pharmaceutical industry is heavily dependent for its success on innovation and brand-name promotion. TNCs in this industry indulge in a great deal of intra-firm trade, and it is well known that the prices charged for intermediates, in developed and developing countries, are very much higher than the direct costs of production. The fact that TNCs can maintain a dominant position in world markets despite charging prices, in intermediate and final markets, much higher than smaller firms which imitate their products depends partly on their technological leadership (legally maintained for certain periods by the institution of the patent system) and partly on brand preference created by extensive promotion.[24]

The bulk of investigations of the pharmaceutical industry in LDCs have defined the correct transfer-price as the price at which they can obtain the chemical from another supplier: its 'opportunity cost' to the country. For new drugs, the alternative supplier is an imitator from a non-patent observing country; for older drugs, it may be competitors (of all sizes, but generally small firms which sell unbranded, or generic, drugs) from developed and less developed countries. The TNCs concerned defend their admittedly higher prices by referring to the expense and riskiness of the R and D involved (for new drugs) and by the better quality (and also contribution to the R and D effort) of older drugs.

It is clear that both sides have a point. The TNCs are right in that the price charged by an imitator does not represent a correct transfer-price for an innovating firm: if this price were charged on a large enough scale, the drug itself would not be brought into existence. It is not a price which is compatible with (presumably socially desirable) innovation. The LDCs are right to the extent that the transfer-price set by the TNCs may be much higher than is required to provide a just return to innovation: it may incorporate returns to market power created by promotion and the abuse of patent protection. The matter is further complicated by such factors as: (a) particular successful drugs must bear the burden of financing R and D on hundreds of others which fail; (b) particular host countries may be interested only in some of the innovations of a TNC, and so may not wish to contribute to R and D on others; (c) LDCs may wish to contribute at a lower rate than developed countries for drugs (like psychotropic or cancer drugs) which are intended primarily for rich markets; and (d) LDCs may feel that a large part of the promotional expenditure (which usually ranges from 15–25 per cent of the price of drugs) that is required to commercialise innovations is wasteful, and serves only to perpetuate barriers to entry of competition.

It should be clear that, in such a situation, it is impossible to define a transfer-price which is correct in an objective sense. Reference to prices charged by the TNC in other markets, or by other firms which do not innovate, are not solutions: *the correct transfer-price must represent society's view of how to finance risky innovation*, in an oligopoly situation with indivisible R and D costs that have to spread over a number of products, with strong elements of market power, and complicated socio-political considerations at stake. This aspect of the problem of investigating transfer-pricing – which has ramifications much wider than simply collecting a fair share of taxes – has been unduly neglected in the literature (by myself, among others). Yet it is of crucial significance as far as the 'area of danger' in intra-firm trade is concerned. No solutions are proposed here, since there cannot be a correct theoretical or practical solution for high technology, high risk, innovative industries. What is proposed is that, in such cases, the issue of transfer-pricing be taken out of the restrictive and misleading context of tax realisation and placed in the broader, more complex, but more relevant context of paying for innovation in the framework of TNC dominated international oligopoly. The emphasis should then be on negotiation and detailed evaluation (and, inevitably, some trial and error) rather than on detecting tax evasion. Negotiation and evaluation must, in turn, be based on information, but the information by itself cannot yield a set of objectively correct transfer-prices.

Negotiation on the right rate of return on risky innovation is not a task we may recommend lightly to any administration, certainly not to the overburdened officials in LDCs. Even the sophisticated and experienced office of the US International Revenue Service which deals with the TNCs resorts to a large number of arbitrary decisions or 'horse-trading' in cases where difficult problems of the sort mentioned above arise.[25] LDCs may do well in the longer run to pool their resources in order to negotiate from a stronger and better informed base, but, as matters stand, they are faced with an immensely difficult task which needs to be continuously faced. Leaving transfer-prices to be decided freely by TNCs is one easy way out, but it probably gives too much away.[26] Assigning transfer-prices with reference to alternative prices is another easy way out, and may indeed have no effect on innovation if a small number of LDCs practise it. As prices charged in different countries get increasingly linked to each other, especially in pharmaceuticals, this is not an ideal long-term solution. But no realistic long-term solution seems to be in sight at this time.

V CONCLUDING REMARKS

In this paper we have discussed some of the important problems which arise in the investigation of transfer-pricing in commodity trade from the point of view of less developed host countries. The precise relationships between the structure and nature of particular industries, the growth of intra-firm trade, the sorts of commodities that enter into such trade, and the scope for price manipulation, are matters which still require much more study, from the viewpoint of policy formulation as well as because of their intrinsic theoretical interest. We have tried to make a distinction between cases where the problems raised by transfer-pricing may be satisfactorily tackled with more information and those where satisfactory solutions are very difficult. The main difference between these cases lies in the nature of technological innovation: in industries with rapid and risky innovation, oligopolistic structures and considerable market power in final markets, the determination of 'correct' transfer-prices is almost impossible, since it cannot be undertaken independently of the determination of the right rate of return to innovation as such. In less innovative industries, where the goods that enter into intra-firm trade are fairly standardised, it is easier to come to grips with the problem, although many LDCs have practical difficulties in collecting and assessing the information necessary to do so. The most hopeful line of action seems to lie in cooperation between countries, for problems which *can* be solved this could be the cheapest and most efficient solution.

NOTES

1. This article is substantially revised from a paper presented at an IDS/UNCTAD seminar on 'Intra-Firm Transactions and their Impact on Trade and Development', held at the Institute of Development Studies, Sussex, 7-11 November 1977. I am grateful to the participants of the seminar for comments.
2. See Chapter 5 above, Vaitsos (1974) and UNCTAD (1977).
3. For a recent survey of empirical work see Kopits (1976). Roumeliotis and Golemis (1977) provide an extension of research on transfer-pricing by their work on Greece.
4. Reviewed in depth by Verlage (1975).
5. Unless the parent company has excess capacity, or it does not, for political reasons, wish to rely on other suppliers. In more theoretical terms, the choice between external and internal trade for the TNC as a whole can be posed as one of the advantages of internalising external transactions, based on scale, market imperfection and risk considerations of the two sorts of markets. For a simple exposition, though not related to TNCs specifically, see Jacquemin and de Jong (1977), pp. 61-3, 79-81.
6. This would also apply to the recent rapid growth of 'sourcing' exports from developing countries, much of which is intra-firm. See the US Tariff Commission (1970), Helleiner (1973) and Finger (1975).
7. Vaitsos (1977), pp. 50-1. I am grateful to Constantine Vaitsos for permission to quote from this paper, which forms part of a forthcoming report by UNCTAD.
8. Ibid., p. 50. Italics in the original.
9. Figures for intra-firm manufactured exports by US TNCs for 1970 show that 40 per cent of the total were finished products for resale, 5 per cent were capital goods and 55 per cent were intermediates. See UNCTAD (1977), Table 1.
10. See, in particular Chapter 5 and Vaitsos (1974).
11. Inverted commas are used because there are conceptual difficulties in defining the reference (arm's length) price, discussed in Section IV of this chapter.
12. See Lall (1975), Vaitsos (1974), UNCTAD (1977) and Chapter 9.
13. An early survey of US TNCs shows marked differences in corporate policies and attitudes towards inter-affiliate pricing. See Greene and Duerr (1968).

A more recent description of such differences is by Barrett (1977).
14. See Robbins and Stobaugh (1973).
15. Arpan (1972).
16. Stopford and Wells (1972). Robbins and Stobaugh (1973) argue, however, that the very largest TNCs find it more difficult (because of the sheer size of the task) to rationally·manipulate transfer-prices than do medium-sized TNCs. It is difficult to believe that, if this were so, the firms concerned would not find methods of solving the problems over the long term with the help of the enormous data-processing facilities now available.
17. This was brought home to me forcefully in Malaysia, where, despite an official invitation to study transfer-pricing, I was unable to get access to existing data. The same problem faced individual government departments there (see Lall (1977)). Some developed country governments face similar problems, as is described for France by Graham and Tron (1974).
18. See for instance, Booth and Jensen (1977). For a review of empirical work on taxation and TNC investment see Kopits (1976); he notes the dubious nature of the relationship as far as LDCs are concerned.
19. In this context the experience of the Andean group, which had gone the furthest in instituting transfer-pricing controls and imposing a (rather unrealistic) permissible return on foreign capital of 14 per cent per annum, is instructive. The tightening of controls accompanied a generally hostile change in policy towards foreign investment, and succeeded in so restricting its flow and provoking political pressures internally and abroad that by 1975–6 most of the strict controls were dropped. See *Business Week* (1976).
20. Rose (1971) table 15.
21. The figure of 61 per cent for intra-firm trade in transportation equipment shown in Table 1 is misleading in that a very large part of intra-firm trade by US firms takes place under a special agreement between Canada and the US.
22. See Strobl (1974). A case has been reported recently where a product (Metroclopramide) is made in France and exported by a TNC for 100 Fr. a kilo. It passes through various subsidiaries in Belgium and Switzerland, and is reimported into France (unchanged in form) at Fr. 4000 a kilo (see *Scrip* 1977a). Customs cooperation should prevent this kind of manipulation.
23. *Scrip* (1977b).
24. For a more detailed discussion see Lall (1975) and Chapter 8.
25. See Verlage (1975) and Adams and Whalley (1977).
26. This is based on the premise that most LDCs are unlikely to be desirable places to which TNCs will shift profits for declaration. There are exceptions, of course, like tax havens, but most other LDC governments continue to express grave concern about the transfer-pricing problem.

REFERENCES

Adams, J. D. R. and J. Whalley (1977), *The International Taxation of Multinational Enterprises* (London: Institute for Fiscal Studies).
Arpan, J. S. (1972), *International Intracorporate Pricing: Non-American Systems and Views* (New York: Praeger).

Barrett, M. E. (1977), 'Case of the tangled transfer-price', *Harvard Business Review* (May–June), pp. 20–38.

Booth, E. J. R. and O. W. Jensen (1977), 'Transfer-prices in the global corporation under internal and external constraints', *Canadian Journal of Economics*, pp. 434–46.

Buckley, P. J. and R. D. Pearce (1977), 'Overseas production and exporting by the world's largest enterprises – a study in sourcing policy', University of Reading, Discussion Papers in International Investment and Business Studies, no. 37.

Business Week (1976), 'Reversal of policy: Latin America opens the door to foreign investment again' (9 Aug.) pp. 34–50.

Finger, J. M. (1975), 'Tariff provisions for offshore assembly and the exports of developing countries', *Economic Journal*, pp. 365–71.

Graham, P. and J. M. Tron (1974), 'Tax treatment in France of international transactions between affiliated companies', *British Tax Review*, no. 6, pp. 368–77.

Greene, J. and M. Duerr (1968), *Intercompany Transfers in Multinational Firms* (New York: The Conference Board).

Helleiner, G. K. (1973), 'Manufactured exports from less developed countries and multinational firms', *Economic Journal*, pp. 21–47.

Jacquemin, A. and H. W. de Jong (1977), *European Industrial Organisation* (London: Macmillan).

Kopits, F. G. (1976), 'Taxation and multinational firm behaviour: a critical survey', *IMF Staff Papers*, pp. 624–73.

Lall, S. (1975), 'Major issues in transfer of technology to developing countries: a case study of the pharmaceutical industry' (Geneva: UNCTAD, TD/B/C.6/4).

—— (1977), 'Transfer-pricing in assembly industries: a preliminary analysis of the issues in Malaysia and Singapore' (London: Commonwealth Secretariat) mimeo.

Robbins, S. M. and R. B. Stobaugh (1973), *Money in the Multinational Enterprise* (New York: Basic Books).

Rose, W. D. (1971), *Development Options in the New Zealand Motor Car Assembly Industry* (Wellington: New Zealand Institute of Economic Research, Research Paper no. 16).

Roumeliotis, P. V. and C. P. Golemis (1977), 'Transfer-pricing and the power of transnational enterprise in Greece' (mimeo). Paper presented to IDS/UNCTAD conference on Intra-firm Transactions, Nov. 1977, University of Sussex.

Scrip, 'World news in brief' (15 Oct. 1977a) p. 19.

Scrip, 'EEC Commission to investigate metro-clopramide pricing by Delagrange' (19 November 1977b) p. 2.

Stopford, J. M. and L. T. Wells (1972), *Managing the Multinational Enterprise* (New York: Basic Books).

Strobl, J. (1974), 'Tax treatment in the Federal Republic of Germany of international transactions between affiliated companies' *British Tax Review*, no. 5, pp. 3312–23.

Tariff Commission (1970), *Economic Factors Affecting the Use of Items 807.00 and 806.30 of the Tariff Schedules of the United States* (Washington, DC:

Government Printing Office).
Tariff Commission (1973), *Implications of Multinational Firms for World Trade and Investment and for US Trade and Labour* (Washington, DC: Government Printing Office).
UNCTAD (1977), 'Dominant positions of market power of transnational corporations: use of the transfer pricing mechanism' (Geneva: UNCTAD/ST/MD/6).
Vaitsos, C. V. (1974), *Intercountry Income Distribution and Transnational Enterprises* (Oxford: Clarendon Press).
Vaitsos, C. V. (1977), 'The integration of Latin America with the rest of the world in view of the operations of subsidiaries of TNCs' (mimeo), paper presented to IDS/UNCTAD Conference on Intra-Firm Transactions, Nov., University of Sussex.
Verlage, H. C. (1975), *Transfer-Pricing for Multinational Enterprises* (Rotterdam: Rotterdam University Press).

Part Three

The International Pharmaceutical Industry

7 The International Pharmaceutical Industry and Less-Developed Countries[1]

I INTRODUCTION

The pharmaceutical industry is today one of the most 'multinational' of modern manufacturing industries, and the firms which dominate it in the developed countries are present, in some capacity, in almost every less-developed country outside the Socialist bloc. It is a dynamic and important industry: indeed, the social importance of its products is such that in recent years it has been subjected to increasing enquiry and criticism in several countries, and it is a tribute to its strength that few of these criticisms have led to reforms in its basic structure.

Section II of this paper examines the main characteristics of the international pharmaceutical industry as it functions in the developed world, paying special attention to the anomalies and distortions which exist because of the peculiar structure of the drug market[2] and of the great oligopolistic power exercised by the leading firms. The implications of this industry for developing countries, to which many of its less desirable features are transferred wholesale, are discussed in section III; the additional social costs imposed on these countries by playing host to the drug multinationals are described, using the Indian case as an example. The options open to the governments of developing countries to reduce the cost of obtaining drugs are considered in section IV.

We shall draw heavily on research into the pharmaceutical industry in the USA and the UK, where official enquiries have uncovered a great deal of information on its performance and practices not normally available to outsiders. We shall devote special attention to the Swiss pharmaceutical firm, Hoffman-La Roche, which is now the largest drug company in the world, because of the detailed work done on it by the British Monopolies Commission and because of pieces of information available on its operation in the US, Colombia and India.

II THE PHARMACEUTICAL INDUSTRY IN DEVELOPED COUNTRIES

THE BACKGROUND

The modern pharmaceutical industry is a relatively recent phenomenon, and may trace its present research-based, rapid-product-change, synthetic-process characteristics to the 1920s and 1930s. By 1969 the total market for pharmaceutical products exceeded US $10 billion for the OECD area; this market was served by some 4–5 thousand companies, ranging from tiny establishments and off-shoots of chemical concerns to enormous specialised manufacturers with turnovers of over $1000 million per annum.[3] The vast majority of these firms are, however, very small, and production in each country has been dominated by a relatively few firms which are truly 'multinational' in their operations, though their ownership tends to remain closely held in their countries of origin. A recent report lists 38 firms with turnovers of over $50 million in 1970, led by Roche, and comprising 18 firms from the US, 4 from the UK, 4 from Germany, 3 from Switzerland, 2 each from France, Italy and Japan, and 3 from other countries.[4]

The British pharmaceutical market is fairly representative of the general structure: the Sainsbury Committee (1967) reported that of total sales by 53 firms of NHS (National Health Service) products of £161 million in 1965, over 60 per cent was supplied by 11 firms, and over 80 per cent by 20 firms. Of these largest 20 firms, only 5 were British; the rest were composed of 11 American, 3 Swiss and 1 other European firm. The 53 firms in the Committee's sample accounted for about 90 per cent of the total value of prescription medicines in the UK, with several hundred smaller firms sharing the remainder of the pharmaceutical market. Similarly, of some 500–700 pharmaceutical firms in the US, the largest 35 accounted for 80–95 per cent sales in 1961,[5] and included most of the large European international concerns. This pattern is, according to the OECD study, common to all the developed countries.

Little was known about the peculiar characteristics of the industry before 1959, when the Kefauver Committee undertook to examine 'Administered Prices in the Drug Industry' in the US.[6] Senator

The International Pharmaceutical Industry and LDCs 163

Kefauver was responsible for introducing legislation to remedy some of the least desirable practices of the drug industry, but later Senate hearings, under G. P. Nelson and then under E. Kennedy, show clearly that the basic economic and social problems were left unresolved. Investigations in the UK revealed similar problems, and, again, recommendations for reform were left largely unimplemented. The official enquiries stimulated a strong and penetrating academic response, especially in the US, and several works critical of the industry appeared in the early and mid sixties by Harris, Steele, Schifrin and others. Academic interest appears, with the exception of Walker (1971), to have flagged since, despite the fact that the industry continued to expand strongly in the developed countries and elsewhere, with its worrying features left intact. Social concern has, on the other hand, grown greatly, and many countries are continuing to study the sector closely with a view to tighter control over its operations.

So much for the background. Let us now briefly consider some of the characteristics of the drug industry, to see the causes of the concern felt, and to gauge whether its social costs have been higher than can be justified with reference to the risks, expenses and responsibilities of the industry.

MAIN CHARACTERISTICS OF THE INDUSTRY

The salient features of the pharmaceutical industry in developed countries may conveniently be grouped under four headings: production structure, technology, marketing practices, and profitability.

i. Production Structure
We have already noted that the pharmaceutical industry in each country consists of a large number of small, locally-owned firms supplying a marginal proportion (say 10–15 per cent) of medical preparations, and a small number of large, mainly international, firms controlling the remainder. The reasons for such a structure lie in the concentration and nature of technology and in the marketing practices of large firms, which we discuss below; here we need only make two points.

First, it has been argued that despite the overwhelming presence of large firms, the degree of concentration is 'slight' because 'the maximum share of the market held by any one company rarely exceeds 7 per cent . . . 2 to 5 per cent are common for the larger companies, whether they are locally owned or international subsidiaries'.[7] Such an argument is misleading, because the pharmaceutical market is extremely heterogeneous, and comprises a number of sub-markets within which firms have tended to specialise.[8] This has led to *concentration within product classes which is high both 'in degree and stability'*,[9] and which spreads over both products protected by patents as well as older products. Thus, in each of the 13 major groups, the four largest firms accounted for 60–80 per cent of sales, sometimes even more.[10] In tranquillisers, for instance, Roche's two main products, Librium and Valium, accounted for almost 70 per cent of the value of British NHS prescriptions in this area; these two products are also claimed to hold over a third of the entire world tranquillizer market.[11]

Second, in marked contrast to most other manufacturing industries, especially those dominated by multinationals, the pharmaceutical industry enjoys practically *no economies of scale* in production (Steele, 1962 and OECD, 1969). The active ingredients are normally manufactured in relatively small volumes, and in many cases an increase in production merely requires the addition of fermentation vessels of standard size. As far as production technology is concerned, therefore, large firms have no special advantage over small firms, and there is no economic benefit to be gained in terms of production costs from encouraging bigness; the fact that bigness has succeeded is due to an entirely different set of reasons.

ii. **Technology**

The pharmaceutical industry is highly research intensive; indeed, of all non-military industries in the US, it recorded the highest proportion of research expenditure to sales in the mid-1960s, and devoted the largest part of its R & D expenditures to 'basic' research as opposed to other kinds of research and product development.[12] Total R & D expenditure in the UK on NHS products came to £18.5 million in 1965 (Sainsbury Committee), and to £20.2 million in 1968[13] while in the US it was over 10 times higher in 1965 and approached $431 million in 1967.[14] The US was by far the largest spender on pharmaceutical R & D, and also accounted for the bulk of new drugs marketed in the post-War period. Switzerland and West Germany, followed by the UK and France, were also responsible for a number of new discoveries, though in the US market they each accounted for 7 per cent or less on the new drugs introduced in 1941–64, while US firms accounted for 61 per cent.[15]

In general, large pharmaceutical firms spent about 10 per cent of their turnover on R & D in the USA and UK in the mid-1960s.[16] Roche currently claims to be spending almost 15 per cent on R & D,[17] which is

The International Pharmaceutical Industry and LDCs 165

high but by no means unusual in this industry. There is no doubt that the pharmaceutical industry spends a lot on R & D and has produced a number of valuable new medicines. However, this admission tells us little about whether the expenditures have been *efficient from a social point of view*, whether or not the same number of effective new drugs could, in other words, have been developed at a smaller cost to society. It is, by the very nature of the problem, difficult to pass any definite judgement on this score, since no alternative complete system of conducting pharmaceutical research exists in the West. The firms themselves stress the long gestation period (up to 7 years) and high (and rising costs) involved in developing, testing and marketing drugs, and point out that the element of risk in such R & D is extremely high. Critics have to rely on more circumstantial evidence, which suggests that the firms' claims, while true to some extent, conceal a number of factors which contribute to their R & D costs without conferring much benefit on society. Let us consider these.

(a) First, R & D expenditure is very highly concentrated among large firms: in the US, for instance, the four largest firms accounted for 40 per cent, the eight largest for 63 per cent and the twenty largest for 95 per cent of total R & D in the industry.[18] In the UK, the Sainsbury Committee found that the four largest firms spent over 70 per cent of the total, the higher concentration being partly explained by the fact that foreign firms did relatively little R & D in this country. Such concentration would be desirable if there existed economies of scale in conducting pharmaceutical research. The empirical work which has been done in this subject is not conclusive, but it does suggest that there are economies of scale (measured in terms of innovations resulting from R & D expenditures) up to a certain size of firm, after which research productivity tends to decline.[19] Most of the big drug firms have establishments much larger than the 'optimum' size, which indicates that the present allocation of R & D resources is not the most efficient possible.

It is not clear why such diseconomies of scale in R & D should come into play for very large establishments; perhaps the problems of coordination and administration rise sharply after a certain level, or perhaps the nature of research activity is such that a certain amount of decentralisation and freedom is essential. If diseconomies do exist, however, why do firms maintain such large facilities? The explanation may be that diseconomies of scale in R & D are *not incompatible* with high expenditures being profitable for the firms concerned, since the

private benefits yielded by innovations from extra R & D may continue to exceed the costs involved for substantial increases in size. Profitability in this industry depends greatly on individual firms' hold over patents as one source of market power (see below), and R & D costs and benefits are necessarily difficult to compute in advance; thus, it is not surprising that the largest firms should finance vast laboratories.
(b) Even if diseconomies of scale in research did not exist, it could be argued that the basic *nature* of private R & D in this industry, aiming at patentable products and processes, leads to the misallocation of research expenditures. The vital role of patents in the drug industry is well known, and we discuss some implications of the patent system below; the point to note here is that a great deal of R & D, which is generally treated as a current tax-deductible expense, is devoted to squeezing out the maximum possible amount of profits from the patent system. Thus, for a firm which produces a new drug, patents can serve not only to protect the initial discovery, but can, with judicious timing and some careful changes, help to introduce related 'new' products and so prolong patent protection for periods long after the initial patent has expired. For rival firms, it may prove very profitable to imitate the innovation by 'molecule manipulation' and thus secure a marketable product.[20]

The common practice of imitative patenting leads to a great deal of socially worthless but privately profitable research. Though a certain amount of imitative research leads to useful new compounds of existing chemicals, it is arguable that the same improvements could be achieved at a much lower overall cost at non-competitive research establishments. Naturally, there are problems in evaluating the real contribution of 'molecule manipulation', which enable drug firms to make claims that are difficult to challenge. The consensus of opinion among economists is, however, that the present system is wasteful and inefficient, and that an appropriate change in the direction of R & D would be beneficial.
(c) Though the industry claims to do a large amount of 'basic' research, and though the claim is, if not the full extent stated, justifiable, there has evolved a certain division of research labour between the private sector and government/academic institutions. Comanor (1966), and the Sainsbury Committee argue that there is a necessary complementarity between the more fundamental and non-profit orientated work done in the latter and the market-orientated work of the former. It is not, however, clear that such a division of labour is 'natural' or 'necessary'; on the contrary, it has evolved precisely *because* marketing and production have been left to a profit-maximising private sector, and

because the public sector researchers are not geared to producing finished drugs. If the research structure had been different, it is easy to imagine that a less wasteful form of R & D would have been undertaken without any loss in the quality and quantity of drugs produced.

This case can be strengthened by two points. First, the amount of state-sponsored research is very large, coming to about £20 million in the UK and £440 million in the US in 1965, and exceeding private research in this field by 200–300 per cent.[21] Since the results of such research are published (and so provided free) or sold for nominal licence fees to the private drug firms for further development, it serves, where appropriate, to provide a valuable input to the latter without their paying the due cost to society. Since the profit on new drugs tends to be higher than on old ones, moreover, it also serves to raise the overall rate of profit of the firms concerned. Second, where official agencies, such as the Medical Research Council in the UK, *have* tried their hand at producing marketable drugs, they have been extremely successful.[22] There does not seem to be any intrinsic disadvantage in public research in this field, and the fact that private firms conduct most of the final R & D is not because private efforts are necessarily more productive but because public R & D is rigidly accorded second place.

(d) The problem of *drug patents* has been a vexed one, and much has been written on both sides of the debate,[23] without a clear answer emerging on the optimal form of legal protection to be granted to private innovators. In most developed countries patent protection is granted for periods of 16–20 years (16 years in the UK and 17 in the US); in the pharmaceutical field a distinction is drawn between processes and products, with many countries (e.g. Switzerland) permitting only process-patents and some permitting both (the UK with some restrictions, and the US with none).[24] The US lies at one extreme with very liberal patent laws (which include normally unpatentable 'naturally occurring' substances), and Italy and Finland at the other with no pharmaceutical product or process patents permitted at all.

The essential case for the granting of patent protection is similar to that for granting any form of protection against competition – the recipient of the privilege is given a monopolistic position which enables him to charge higher prices than he otherwise could, and the short-term welfare loss due to these higher prices is supposed to be offset in the long run by a higher rate of innovative output and a decline in the price of the protected product after the recoupment of a 'fair' return on the R & D investment. The original conception of such protection was of course to encourage small innovating firms or individual inventors, though it is very likely that large private research-based firms need this protection just as much as if they are to survive the rigours of oligopolistic competition.

The pharmaceutical industry has often been accused of 'abusing' the patent privilege granted it. What constitutes 'abuse' in this context? There may be several forms:

(a) We have already noted how the system encourages a great deal of wasteful expenditure on imitative R & D and patenting, by directing research primarily at the production of marketable rather than therapeutically new products.

(b) The complexity of patent laws and high cost of litigation works strongly in favour of large firms; small firms often find it easier to sell their innovations to their giant competitors for a lump sum rather than to contest infringements in protracted court cases.[25] To this extent, patents limit rather than promote competition in research.

(c) A substantial portion of allegedly R & D expenditure in fact goes into buying international patents. For instance, the cost of international patenting to three large US drug companies in 1972–3 came to £15 million, and was charged as a research expense.[26] Such measures are purely for extending the monopoly position of firms from domestic to international markets, and it is misleading, for the purpose of evaluating research effort, to place them in this category.

(d) The main abuse of patent-protected monopoly is, however, that it permits '*excessive*' *profits* to be earned by pharmaceutical firms. We shall return to the profitability of the industry later, but it should be noted that the granting of a long period of virtual monopoly in a product which faces very inelastic demand and which is heavily promoted (these market characteristics are described in the following section) violates the main economic justification of patenting, i.e. that the returns earned are 'fair' in some sense of the word.[27] The returns in fact earned by the pharmaceutical industry are high by any standards, and cannot, as is argued below, be justified by the riskiness of the R & D effort. Moreover, the pricing policies of the large drug firms are based on purely monopolistic principles of 'what the market can bear' rather than on the socially responsible one of lowering them after recovering research costs. Roche, for instance, had not lowered the price of Librium at all in the UK since its introduction in 1960, until the government forced a price reduction on the firm in 1973; the case is now being hotly contested.

To summarise this section, the structure of private research and development in the pharmaceutical industry, and its supporting framework of patent laws, lead to heavy and not necessarily efficient concentration of R & D in large firms, to a great deal of wasteful expenditure on competitive patenting, and to granting patent protection which can lead to 'excessive' profits.

iii. Marketing Practices

The technological structure of the pharmaceutical industry provides only one explanation, probably the minor one, of its oligopolistic market power and ability to earn high profits. The other lies in the peculiar market structure, and the resulting marketing practices, of the industry, which lead it to have practically the highest ratio of promotion and advertising costs to sales, ranging, in the US, from *three to four times its R & D expenditures*, and accounting for about *one-third of the value of the sales*.[28] In many cases the promotion costs have actually exceeded the cost of goods sold, though on the figures available the cost of promotion in the UK has been much lower than in the US.[29]

There are three reasons for this state of affairs: first, there is a complete separation of identity between the purchaser (the patient) and the choice-maker (the doctor) in the pharmaceutical market. In countries which have nationalised health services, the patient also becomes separated from the purchaser, the state; in either case, the person who pays for the drugs is totally divorced from the one who actually chooses them. There is, therefore, no *direct* pressure on the effective buyer, the doctor, to economise, though he may, *if* he had full knowledge of prices and no brand preference, prescribe drugs according to the income of the patient; the patient is, of course, obliged to obey the doctor's orders and his demand curve is likely to be fairly inelastic, to the extent that he can reduce other expenses under his control. In fact, there is little evidence that doctors are very price-conscious, as figures on price differentials given below show.

Second, there is a sharp distinction between products marketed under generic names and those sold under brand names.[30] The bulk of the promotion effort goes into persuading doctors to prescribe by brand names, introducing what is in many cases a completely spurious product-differentiation between drugs with identical pharmacological properties. In cases where there is patent protection, advertising helps to promote the brand image and secure it for periods long after the protection has expired; in other cases, it introduces a strong monopolistic element into what would otherwise be a more competitive market.

Third, the very speed of introduction of new products and the profusion of brands (there are, for instance, about 700 drugs sold under 20,000 names in the US), coupled with a virtual absence of official provision of systematic information in the field, has made the medical profession heavily dependent on the firms themselves for information about new treatments.[31] The industry can therefore claim to be serving a social function by its promotion, when in fact the purely informational content is low relative to the commercial content but can be most profitably blended with it.

These factors, combined with the fact that this is the one aspect of drug manufacture where there *do* exist considerable economies of scale,[32] have led to the evolution of marketing practices which rely heavily on free samples, frequent visits by representatives, voluminous and glossy mail literature, banquets on the introduction of 'new' products, free trips and expensive presents, and Madison Avenue-style magazine and journal advertising, and which cost over $750 million in the US in 1958, and about £41 million in the UK in 1970. The effects of such promotion have been extensively discussed, especially in the US Senate hearings; the main ones are:

(a) The use of brand as opposed to generic names is actively promoted by large firms, in that they themselves, subject to approval, can choose generic names upon the patenting of new products and deliberately choose complicated ones; brand names are always simpler and more catchy in comparison. Furthermore, in the layout of drug advertisements, brand names are invariably more prominently displayed than generic names.

(b) It is very difficult, if not practically impossible, for prescribing doctors to have immediate access to information which would enable them to compare prices of identical drugs, despite the amount of promotion undertaken. Advertisements hardly ever mention prices – ignoring one of the basic precepts of 'socially responsible' marketing – while representatives are trained to promote their wares on non-price grounds. In fact, in the US it is even *illegal* for generic name catalogues to compare their prices with those of branded equivalents, or even to mention brand name equivalents of generic name products.[33] This state of affairs, combined with the effects of patent protection, has led to price anomalies which would be difficult to imagine in almost any other industry:

i. Differences in the price of the same brand between different parts of a country or to different purchasers: for instance, Roche's Librium was being sold, in the US in 1965, at $45 (for 500 capsules of 25 mg each) in Des Moines, at $18.50 in Philadelphia, and at $21.75 to the Veterans' Administration, the difference between the lowest and highest city prices being 243 per cent.[34]

ii. Differences in the price of the same brand between different countries: to take Roche again, Librium cost the pharmacist (before the compulsory price cuts) $2.40 in England (for 100 tablets of 10 mg) and $6.82 in the US, in 1973,[35] while Valium cost twice as much in Australia, and over 6 times as much in Switzerland, as it did in this country.[36]

iii. Most surprising of all, differences in the price of the same drug between brand names and generic equivalents, or between heavily promoted brand names and those of small firms in the same market. There are innumerable examples (especially in Kefauver, 1966 and Steele, 1964) of branded products being sold at prices ranging up to over 1000 per cent higher than others, with no effect on the large market shares held by them. In Roche's case, a small British firm, D.D.S.A., supplies its equivalent of Librium under a compulsory licence at prices 25 per cent lower than Roche yet had not been able to capture even 3 per cent of the market for this drug by 1970.[37] Furthermore, to illustrate the importance of promotion as opposed to patent protection: in Italy, where no patents are allowed on pharmaceuticals, there are a number of copiers of Librium. Seven firms sell at prices 30 per cent lower than Roche, yet have 'failed to make any headway in the market', with Roche holding 80 per cent of the market.[38] It is important to note that such differences apply to drugs whose patents have expired as well as to patent drugs manufactured under compulsory licence; in other words, there is no relationship at all between the price differential and the returns 'legitimately' earned on R & D – promotion serves simply to create and maintain an artificial monopoly position.

(c) Pharmaceutical marketing does not gain its ends only by a repetition of the scientifically established virtues of its products. Many instances have been reported of excessive claims, suppression of information about side-effects, or incomplete reporting of results; as is only to be expected in circumstances where profitability depends on such promotion, firms take their claims to the limits of scientific acceptability, and often exceed them.[39] Roche, among many other firms, has also been accused of unfair advertising tactics; to quote evidence given before the US Senate:

The advertisement (for Valium) did not mention some important qualifications . . . background information and qualifications which might appear in a scientific article (were) omitted and the results exaggerated beyond what the authors intended. This particular advertisement has now been withdrawn but . . . it was the subject of the most extensive advertising campaign which I have ever seen for a psychotropic drug.[40]

The role of representatives ('detailmen' in America) is of particular importance in such promotion. Not only do their visits save doctors the trouble of having to read, their conversations are unrecorded, they use such tactics as 'gifts and fast-talk gimmicks' to win over nurses and receptionists, they sometimes gain access to confidential files to discover doctors' prescribing practices, and they subject recalcitrant doctors to 'concentrated sales assaults' to win them over to their products.[41] Evidence now being presented before Senator Kennedy's Committee in Washington has led him to consider very strong measures to control and reform the marketing system there.

(d) A similar problem to that of the 'hard sell' arises from the promotion and sale of *ineffective* drugs. Recent reports in the *Guardian* (13 May 1974) have claimed that US and Swiss firms are selling in the UK over 100 drugs, costing several million pounds each year, which have been withdrawn from the American market after being found to 'lack evidence of effectiveness' by the Food and Drug Administration. There is no official body in Britain which evaluates the effectiveness of drugs now on the market – the Committee on Safety of Medicines does not compare the effectiveness of existing drugs and is primarily concerned with safety[42] – and the only body competent to do so (the Macgregor Committee) was disbanded in 1970, allegedly under pressure from the industry.[43] While there do exist difficulties in testing the effectiveness of drugs, which have caused the drug firms' representative body (the Association of British Pharmaceutical Industries) to call the US official rating 'relatively useless', this problem cannot be dismissed casually, and all serious investigators have recommended urgent reform of a system so patently liable to abuse.

(e) Finally, a great deal of advertising by large pharmaceutical concerns is intended to disparage the lower-price products of small competitors, especially by the unwritten means of representative persuasion. 'There is probably no other industry in existence where the disparagement of the quality of lower priced products can so completely substitute for actual price competition.[44] Detailed surveys of the evidence in the US give no reason to believe that the generic equivalents of branded drugs are inferior in quality or checked less intensively for a quality-control: if there exists any basis for hesitation, a small diversion of the present advertising expenses of the large firms would be enough to strengthen official drug inspection sufficiently to remove it.[45]

The case against the existing structure of private drug marketing – a peculiar configuration of private profitability, doctors' convenience and official inaction – is thus very strong. There is no doubt that the drug companies' promotion serves the useful social function of bringing new discoveries to doctors' notice; there is, however, also no doubt that this promotion creates powerful monopoly positions, confuses the flow of correct information, may induce inappropriate prescribing, and generally leads to considerable social waste. The problem is a greater one than that raised by private R & D, and has been recognised for many years.[46] *Yet nothing has been done to effectively remedy it*: a triumph for the economic and political power of the drug industry,[47] which has enabled it to maintain its profit earning capacity over long periods. We turn now to this aspect.

iv. Profitability

It is hardly surprising, in view of the extent of market control exercised through the factors discussed above, that the pharmaceutical industry is one of the most profitable industries in the developed world. It has since the mid-fifties consistently recorded profits substantially higher than the average for all industry in both the US and the UK;[48] in 1966, the industry earned 21 per cent on capital employed in the US as compared to 13 per cent for all manufacturing, and in the UK a survey of 110 pharmaceutical companies showed a return of 26 per cent for 1967–69 as compared to 12.6 per cent for all manufacturing.[49] A recent publication reveals that the returns on capital employed for the three leading British drug companies in 1972 were: Beecham Group, 41 percent, Glaxo 22 per cent, and Boots 45 per cent; Beecham and Boots were beaten by only one firm, Rank Xerox, in the top 100 British firms in that year.[50] The Sainsbury Committee report, while expressing reservations about the declared profits of foreign drug firms, shows that of the 27 largest firms in the UK, 23 had returns on capital employed of over 10 per cent, 8 of over 30 per cent, and 3 of over 50 per cent.[51]

Stated profitability figures are, of course, rather difficult to interpret, partly because of the existence of hidden profits in the form of transfer prices and various charges (discussed below), and partly because of the unreliability of the book value of assets as a measure of the real value of investment. Inflation (particularly in recent years) has rendered the book value of fixed capital a very unrealistic gauge of their present worth, and it may be argued that the denominator in the profitability ratio should include 'investments' in good will, brand names, marketing channels and patents. While such adjustments would certainly bring down the rates now seen to be earned, we should bear in mind that inflation affects all industries, and should not bias a *comparison* of inter-industry profits, and that expenditures on patents and marketing are all charged as current costs, and may not be seen as 'investments' by firms allocating capital resources. Thus, it still seems valid to assert that the pharmaceutical industry is as a whole exceptionally profitable relative to other industries, and that this position has been maintained by virtue of its great market power over a very long period.[52]

The defenders of the drug industry, while admitting to its high profitability, have sought to counter the charge that it is 'excessive' by pointing to the *exceptional risk* attached to research-based operations. If the claim of exceptional risk were valid, we would expect an analysis of the data to show that risk and uncertainty, as opposed to other factors, exercised a significant influence on the profitability of drug firms; furthermore, we would expect the industry to show considerable fluctuations in its earnings relative to less risky industries and we would expect to find drug firms which were exceptionally unproductive of innovations to show relatively low returns. None of these factors are supported by the evidence: econometric analysis of the determinants of profits *does not* show that risk is a very significant variable;[53] the industry has *consistently* earned profits higher than the average; and firms producing few innovations have nevertheless shown very high profits.[54]

It is, therefore, difficult to accept that the drug industry faces *exceptional* risks which can justify its abnormally high profits; indeed the evidence at hand leads one to believe that profits derive mainly from a monopolistic situation which seems to be very secure rather than very vulnerable. Risk would be a more convincing bogey if the stranglehold exercised by patents and marketing were not so tight: in present conditions it is hardly surprising that the industry has been so often accused of charging 'excessive prices', in relation to costs of production and permissible profits, by people who have made a close study of its costs and practices.[55]

We must at this point consider an aspect of profitability which is directly related to the international operations of pharmaceutical firms.

The International Pharmaceutical Industry and LDCs 175

There is a close integration of operations, via the trade of intermediate chemicals, between different branches of international pharmaceutical firms, which offers ample opportunities for the misuse of *transfer-pricing* (on the commodities so traded) to ship profits clandestinely from one country to another. There are many reasons why firms may wish to declare profits in one country rather than another, the main ones being tax differentials, restrictions on repatriation, and some threat to profitability if it is seen to be too high.[56] The drug industry is especially vulnerable to threats because of its social importance, especially in less-developed countries, but it is also exceptionally profitable and offers exceptional facilities to use this channel, because intra-firm trade is quite large and chemical prices are very difficult to check.

The Roche case in the UK offers a clear illustration of the possibilities. This firm has always declared very low profits in England, generally below 5 per cent on capital employed. Yet the Monopolies Commission found, on very careful and conservative estimates, that its real profitability was *over 70 per cent* on capital employed (£25 million) for the period 1966–72, and declared profits comprised only 12 per cent of this total.[57] The Sainsbury Committee also remarked (paragraph 301) on the possible use of transfer-prices by foreign firms;[58] no doubt the profitability of the firms as reported would have been much higher if such prices could have been checked.[59]

This concludes our survey of the main characteristics of the pharmaceutical industry in the developed world; let us now sum up its main social costs as shown in the above discussion.

THE SOCIAL COSTS OF THE INDUSTRY

The social costs of the pharmaceutical industry may be defined very broadly as the costs of providing its products over and above the costs of the next best alternative. The alternative posited here, for illustrative purposes, is a completely socially-owned industry, with publicly financed research and a central non-competitive information service, and earning acceptable (whatever that may be for public services) or zero profits.[60] It would be foolish to attempt to put figures on any such estimate; a mere indication of the factors involved will have to suffice.

The costs of the present structure exceed the costs of the alternative in the following respects:

i. The same amount of useful *research and development* results could probably be achieved at a much lower cost; the industry wastes a lot of money at present in imitative and misdirected R & D in buying up international patents, in inefficient concentration, and in unnecessary litigation.[61]

ii. There is even greater wastage involved in the *promotion activities* of pharmaceutical firms: these involve the creation of monopoly privilege which permits enormous and unjustified price differentials, the confusion of necessary market information, the wastage of doctors' time in meeting representatives and the denigration of cheaper products which prevents effective competition.[62]

iii. The level of *profits* is much higher than private capital earns elsewhere in the economy, and cannot be justified by the existence of any special degree of risk.[63]

These costs are borne either directly by the patient or indirectly by the taxpayer. In the first case, where medicines are privately purchased, the hardship created is much greater than in the second because many ill people (probably disproportionately more than income distribution figures would indicate) are poor, and must either divert resources from other necessary uses or must do without the medicines altogether. In the second case, though everyone is able to receive medication, it is likely that the state allocates a certain total sum to social expenditure, and a high medical bill diverts resources from other social activities.

III THE PHARMACEUTICAL INDUSTRY IN LESS-DEVELOPED COUNTRIES

THE BACKGROUND OF LDCs

The pharmaceutical industry in LDCs embodies all the essential features of the industry in the West. Most of the large international concerns operate in those LDCs which actively promote import substitution in drug manufacturing, though in most cases the manufacturing operation consists simply of formulating and packaging imported chemicals.[64] In a few relatively industrialised countries, such as India, Mexico, Argentina, Brazil and the UAR, the industry has managed, behind protective barriers, to achieve considerable backward integration with the growth of an indigenous fine chemicals sector; in others, however, import dependence remains very heavy.

The technology of drug manufacture is, of course, almost entirely imported from developed countries, and the system of patenting, the marketing methods, and the levels of profitability, are all very similar to those described in the previous sections. As in developed countries, the more industrialised LDCs have large numbers of local firms which supply very small proportions of total pharmaceutical sales, with the foreign multinational firms possessing overwhelmingly dominant positions in their markets.[65] Given the profitability of their own manufacturing investments, the multinationals are naturally unwilling, unless forced to do so by local laws, to license indigenous firms to manufacture their patented products; and, given the existence of patent protection as well as the entire paraphernalia of drug marketing backed by the prestige of established foreign brand and company names, the multinationals can – and have done so far – easily maintain their dominant positions in perpetuity.

The social costs of this structure as noted for the developed countries apply even more strongly to the LDCs, in that there are certain special factors in the latter which further raise the burden on the host economies:

i. Though there is little original R & D done in LDCs by the pharmaceutical multinationals, beyond relatively minor adaptive research, their control over *patents* is even more complete than in developed countries.[66] In many LDCs, including the more industrialised ones (with the rather odd exception of Brazil), the percentage of total patents, including non-pharmaceutical ones, owned by foreigners borders on or exceeds 90 per cent;[67] of the 10 per cent owned by nationals, there is reason to suspect that a large proportion is of little commercial importance.[68] Though figures are not generally available on pharmaceutical patents as such, some data from Chile indicate that foreign ownership in this industry was the second highest of 10 industrial groupings in 1967,[69] while information from the UK, where only 6 per cent of pharmaceutical patents filed in the mid-1960s were nationally owned as opposed to 14 per cent some twelve years previously,[70] suggests that there is an increasing tendency in all countries with multinational drugs firms to have foreign owned patents.

What are the implications of this trend for LDCs? Do they have reason to dislike it any more than, say, the UK? Recent analysts of the patent system in LDCs agree that the rationale of its existence there is not so much to provide an inducement to innovative activity – since the innovating firms invest in R & D primarily with a view to their main markets in developed countries[71] – as to stimulate the inflow of foreign direct investment and the transfer of new technology. These analysts, especially Vaitsos,[72] also express grave doubts about the acceptability of this rationale, on the ground that the patent system serves primarily to increase the monopoly power of foreign investors, and thus enables them to restrict technological transfers, raise import prices and indulge in various other restrictive practices.

There is little reason to doubt, on the basis of the experience of developed countries, that the patent system does increase the monopoly power of multinational firms in this particular industry, though it would be incorrect to put the entire blame for monopolistic practices in LDCs on patents as distinct from other sources of market power, especially marketing practices. It is, however, impossible to envisage what the structure of the industry would be if the entire international patenting system were scrapped; patents may be only one of the supports of the present system, but they may be vital to its existence.

If we accept, then, that patents are of some value in enhancing monopoly in the pharmaceutical industry – as indeed they are intended to be – the charges which can be levelled against them are: (a) they allow multinationals to buy up most of the patents in LDCs and *not use the vast majority of them*, thus providing a captive market for exports for the producers in developed countries, while preventing the emergence of indigenous enterprise or the purchase of cheaper imports;[73] (b) they stifle local research efforts; and (c) they allow foreign sellers of technology to impose restrictive conditions in contracts or to charge excessive prices for the technology transferred. The most balanced review of these criticisms is by Penrose (1973), who argues that many of these effects would exist even without the patent system, that there may be valid economic reasons for the non-working of patents, and that more stringent official checks could counter most of these abuses. However, she ends by saying that there is a strong, but not conclusive, presumption that LDCs 'gain little or nothing, and may even lose, from granting patents on inventions developed, published, and primarily worked abroad'.[74]

The reason why the case against patents is not conclusive is that they may 'in some industries and in some circumstances . . . promote technological transfer and its implantation in the local economy'.[75] The circumstances where this is particularly true is where a lot of technological backing is required beyond the mere sale of patented know-how, and where, consequently, the willing support of foreign firms is valuable. This is *not*, however, true of the pharmaceutical industry: the production technology is relatively simple, and, while the multinational drug firms do invest and produce the whole array of modern medicines,

The International Pharmaceutical Industry and LDCs 179

the concomitant monopolistic costs of foreign control are particularly heavy. Thus, while an abolition of patents may not by itself remove the existence of foreign monopoly in drugs, in particular LDCs today, to the extent that the international patent system permits or enhances monopoly in this industry the system does appear to have more costs than benefits.

ii. These costs (which are attributed to the overall structure of the industry and not simply to patents) are of two general kinds – financial and social. The *financial costs* of the multinational dominance of this industry are particularly important for those LDCs which are extremely short of foreign currency, since they all accrue in foreign exchange and benefit the foreign investors or their home governments.[76] They arise from various factors, the most important being the use of transfer pricing (which we have noted above, but which, for reasons discussed elsewhere,[77] tends to work particularly against the welfare of LDCs), the charging of excessive royalties even on technology purchases from within the same firm, and the imposition of export restrictions. All these have been discussed in recent literature on multinational corporations and LDCs and need not be elaborated on here; it need only be pointed out that most of the evidence on transfer-pricing has been based on investigations of the pharmaceutical industry, and that the incidence of export-restrictive clauses has been particularly common here. To return for a moment to Roche, investigations in Colombia for the late 1960s showed that this firm was overcharging its subsidiary (as a percentage of world market prices) by 94 per cent for Atelor, by 96 per cent for Trimatoprium,[78] by over 6,000 per cent for Diazepam and by over 5,000 per cent for Chlordiazepoxide.[79]

iii. The *social costs* of the present pharmaceutical industry in LDCs arise from an unfortunate combination of circumstances in such countries where extreme poverty, the lack of effective social welfare systems, the high incidence of disease, and the absence of modern medical treatment in rural areas are exacerbated by the unreasonably high prices of medicines charged by the multinational drug companies. We have already remarked on the social costs of excessive drug prices in developed countries; in poor countries their welfare cost is immeasurably greater. Not only do expensive pharmaceuticals put a great deal of medication out of the reach of vast sections of the population and reduce proper treatment to an élite preserve, they also prevent a more rapid spread of medication to non-urban areas where most of the people live and where illness is rife.

These are the special problems which the modern drug industry creates for LDCs, quite apart from the ones which were described in the previous section. While the general structure of the industry is similar in developed and less-developed areas, however, there is one major difference: the developed countries produce the technology and will continue to do so, the less-developed ones import it and may expect to do so in the future. Since the operation of multinationals ensures that the latter also pay in full for the proliferation of products and for international brand-names, the problem of policy in the two areas is quite different. Both are concerned with minimising the cost of medicines, but *for developed countries the problem is to maintain or improve research while cutting out its present wasteful elements*, while *for LDCs the problem is to obtain the results of research done abroad as cheaply as possible*. We shall return to this when we discuss policy options for LDCs; let us first consider the position of the industry in India.

THE PHARMACEUTICAL INDUSTRY IN INDIA

In 1970–71 the total production of pharmaceuticals in India was approximately Rs. 2500 million ($333 million at the current exchange rate of Rs. 7.5 = $1); of this 80–90 per cent was accounted for by some 100 large units, and about 70 per cent by the 30 largest firms.[80] Approximately 2300 smaller units supplied the remainder of the market. The total consumption of pharmaceuticals in India in 1966–67, when comparable figures are available for other countries, was about $250–300 million, while it was $4667 million in the US, $640 million in Italy, and $71 million in Belgium (the smallest consumer in the OECD).[81]

There are several plants in the public sector in India which produce both basic chemicals for use by the pharmaceutical industry as well as some finished pharmaceutical products. However, the bulk of pharmaceutical production still lies in the private sector, and here foreign firms are in a dominant position. Of the top 15 firms, ranked by sales in 1966, only 4 were wholly Indian owned;[82] of the 39 'medium and large' public limited pharmaceutical companies (which include nearly all firms of moderate size), 33 were foreign controlled in 1968–70.[83]

The 33 foreign controlled drug firms accounted, in 1969–70, for 93 per cent of the value of sales of the 39 medium and large drug companies, for 96 per cent of their net fixed assets, and for 109 per cent of their profits before tax. If these 39 large companies are assumed to

The International Pharmaceutical Industry and LDCs 181

have provided 70–80 per cent of total pharmaceutical demand in the country, the 33 foreign controlled firms supplied about 65–75 per cent of the total market.[84]

These 33 firms, exactly 10 per cent in number of the 330 total 'foreign controlled rupee companies' surveyed by the Reserve Bank for 1969–70, accounted for 9 per cent of the value of net sales of the total sample, and for 8 per cent of net worth. An earlier survey of India's international investment position (*R.B.I. Bulletin*, 1971) as at the end of March 1968 shows that total foreign direct investment in branches and foreign controlled firms in the pharmaceutical sector (Rs. 381 million) came to 11 per cent of total such foreign manufacturing investment in the country.

Though the 33 foreign controlled pharmaceutical firms accounted for less than 10 per cent of sales and net worth of the 330 foreign controlled firms in 1969–70, they accounted for nearly 18 per cent of their total profits before tax. The percentages of profits before tax on total capital employed came to 15 per cent for the 330 firms and 30 per cent for the 33 drug firms, as compared to 8 per cent for 1,926 Indian public limited companies in the same period. Furthermore, medium and large drug firms recorded profits before tax on capital employed of *over 20 per cent in every single year* from 1965 to 1971 when the average for the total of 1,501 medium and large firms was always 10 per cent or less. The drug industry was consistently the most profitable of all 23 sectors (including non-manufacturing) covered for the 6-year period, with one exception in 1970–71 when mineral oils achieved somewhat higher profits. The foreign companies in the pharmaceutical industry were always more profitable than the local ones; in fact, the latter 6 firms recorded net losses in the years 1968–70 when the former were earning extremely high profits. Thus, the foreign drug companies in India are *not only the most profitable among manufacturing firms in the country generally but also among all types of foreign controlled enterprises, including those in non-manufacturing sectors.*

Of the foreign firms in the pharmaceutical sector, Roche is one of the most profitable. In 1968, for instance, when the 33 foreign controlled drug firms earned profits before tax of 24 per cent on capital employed, Roche recorded profits of 57 per cent, and its weighted average profit for the period 1965–68 was 45 per cent.[85] Similarly, the firm's ratio of profits before tax (net of depreciation) to sales was 37 per cent in 1968, as compared to 18 per cent for the 33 foreign companies, and to only 8 per cent for the total 1,501 medium and large public limited companies.

The existence of transfer-pricing, of course, reduces the reliability of declared profits as indicators of true profitability. India is less vulnerable to this particular practice than most other countries, if only because the Government's strenuous efforts at import-substitution have forced down imports to a relatively low level. The fall in imports as a percentage of production from 25 per cent in 1960–61 to 10 per cent in 1963–64 for foreign subsidiaries, and its further reduction to about 8 per cent for the industry as a whole by 1972,[86] shows that the industry has managed to achieve a fair degree of self-sufficiency. With the planned increase in production of chemicals by public sector plants, the extent of import dependence will probably continue to fall in the next few years.

This is not to argue, however, that transfer-pricing is not used by foreign firms, nor that it does not make a substantial difference to the profitability of the firms concerned. There are few data on the use of transfer-pricing in India, though plenty of impressionistic and indirect evidence exists that it is widely used.[87] Certainly there are many inducements to use it – high tax rates, price controls, political pressures, and so on – and there are few effective deterrents, such as the direct checks exercised by the Colombian Government. In Roche's case, for instance, imported chemicals came to 19 per cent of the value of production in 1968; if 90 per cent of the value of imports were simply the transfer of profits (a conservative estimate, on evidence from the UK and Colombia), the real profits after tax of the firm would be almost exactly *double* the declared profits. The figures are pure conjecture, of course, but there is little reason to doubt the real dangers inherent in the system.

India is well-known for having relatively high drug prices.[88] Part of the fault lies with the Government for its general policy of heavy import substitution, which has led to manufactured products in general being expensively produced in the country, and which has, in this case, obliged firms to buy costly chemicals from local sources. However, the cost of chemicals does not tell the whole story, since they comprise a small part of the value of sales (see below). With the obvious exception of heavy R & D expenditures, all the usual costs of producing and marketing pharmaceuticals are present in India: there are heavy promotion expenditures (though the exact cost breakdown is not available), there are high profits, royalty payments, and a proliferation of branded products, and there are vast differences between brand name and generic name products. Roche's Librium was sold in 1972 for Rs. 16 (per 100 tablets of 10 mg each) when generic name equivalents were available from small units for prices as low as Rs. 1.50.[89] Similarly, public sector units were supplying Phenobarbitone at 1 paisa per tablet and Diethyl Carbamazine Citrate at 3 paise per tablet, when brand name foreign equivalents were being sold at 3 paise and 8 paise respectively.[90] Many such cases have been recorded for a wide range of products, with the price differentials being very large indeed, but this is hardly surprising in view of comparable differences observed in developed countries.

The position of foreign brand name products is, if anything, stronger in a country like India than in developed countries. Not only is there a long-standing prejudice against local products in every industry, 'medical practitioners and consumers have a rigid faith in the quality of the high-priced drugs from foreign companies'.[91] Two special factors must, however, be noted about the Indian industry which are relevant to this discussion. First, the cost of intermediate chemicals supplied by public sector plants is high relative to international prices, and foreign firms often blame high retail drug prices on the high cost of their raw materials. Second, quality control by the authorities is neither comprehensive nor very efficient, and a number of cases of drug adulteration by small producers have been recorded.

These points may seem to support the case for promoting foreign drug firms and reducing public sector production. The first, however, is not very convincing because the retail prices charged by these firms is very much higher than can be justified with reference to raw material prices. Generic equivalents are marketed much more cheaply by smaller firms which use the same chemicals as raw materials. Even in cases where the public sector prices are over three times import costs, as with Phenobarbitone, or Vitamin B, the prices of competing foreign brand name equivalents are much higher (about 50 per cent and 300 per cent respectively).[92] The cost of raw materials is always such a small proportion of selling prices in this industry that it is in any case difficult to accept this argument at its face value. Of course the public sector should be made more efficient, but *even an inefficient one provides cheaper drugs than the multinationals.*[93]

The second point is more serious. The enforcement of quality control varies greatly from state to state, with Bihar and Madhya Pradesh lacking drug control staff altogether.[94] The incidence of damage caused by drug adulteration and poor quality drugs is rising, and, given the enormous profit margins, the inducement for small producers to enter the industry without proper controls is very high. To the extent that the foreign firms enforce rigid quality control, certainly a strong plea can be entered in their favour; the situation is now, however, one which calls so much for extending the scope of foreign manufacturers as for *enforcing better quality control*, or, as argued below, for *extending public sector production*. After all, there *are* good generic equivalents available from many small producers and from public sector firms, and at much lower prices than foreign branded products; the obvious solution is to promote low priced products with adequate quality safeguards.

The Indian Government's policy towards the pharmaceutical industry has been a combination of extreme stringency in some respects with gross inadequacy in others. Let us briefly consider the salient aspects of its policy:

i. Prices
In 1970 the Government issued a Drug Price Control Order, based on recommendations of a Tariff Commission study, to determine the prices of 18 basic drugs and their 69 formulations.[95] A formula, giving a 15 per cent pre-tax return on net capital employed for manufacturers, and another 15 per cent for formulators, was used; the implementation of the Order eventually led to a reduction in the prices of the controlled drugs, though we do not possess information on the exact magnitude of savings achieved. These 18 drugs accounted, however, only 9 per cent of the total value of drugs marketed in India; the Order had the perverse effect of inducing firms to increase their other prices, leading to a rise in the overall drug price index of 12 points in 1970–71, the highest annual increase recorded since 1960.[96] The pace of increase in drug prices quickened in fact, after 1966, when the Tariff Commission investigation of prices was instituted. Whatever the merits or faults of the Order within its context of 18 drugs, therefore, it certainly did not provide a means of checking overall pharmaceutical prices in the country.

ii. Patents
We have already noted the Indian Government's early objections to the effects of the patent system. After a great deal of prolonged debate a Patents Bill was passed in 1970 reducing the period of patent protection from 16 to 7 years, ruling out product patents and providing for compulsory licensing after 3 years for a royalty not exceeding 5 per cent of the value of production.[97] These measures put India among the countries with the strictest of patenting provisions, though clearly not in the class of Italy which allows no drug patents at all.

iii. Public Sector Production
While the Government is, in line with its general industrial policy,

continuing to expand public sector production of drugs and related chemicals (in various plants of Hindustan Antibiotics Limited and Indian Drugs and Pharmaceuticals Limited), far more would have been achieved by now had the private sector not interfered in early stages of negotiations with the Soviet bloc for technical assistance. Kidron cites this as one of the instances of political pressure wielded by the foreign investors in collaboration with their Indian counterparts; in this case a Russian offer was rejected in favour of more expensive private deals. [98] The main present problem is one of high costs of production; this may be a 'teething' problem which is resolved with time. There seems to be no inherent reason why in this industry indigenous production should not be efficient by world standards, since economies of scale or production technology are not particularly important or sophisticated. Of course, there may be political pressures on public sector firms which prevent their efficient running, and this can be solved only by political action. To repeat an earlier point, however, even an inefficient public sector markets drugs at lower prices than an efficient private foreign sector.

iv. Transfer Prices

The Government has shown a complete lack of interest in this aspect of the drug companies' operations, despite many indications that foreign firms in this and other sectors use arbitrary pricing to remit profits abroad. The growing canalisation of imports through the State Trading Corporation may have alleviated the risks, along with the reduction in the degree of import dependence, but a substantial amount of foreign exchange is still spent on imports bought directly by the private companies. Given the inherent arbitrariness in pricing in the international pharmaceutical industry, therefore, the neglect of this phenomenon (even in calculating costs for the 18 price controlled drugs) is unfortunate.

v. Marketing

As with most other countries, the marketing of drugs is left entirely to the devices of the private manfacturers, and so involves all the wastages already noted. This aspect of the industry is so fundamental to its present structure and functioning that it is difficult to envisage reforms which leave it out of consideration; yet the Government has shown little awareness of the issues involved even in its bravest attempts to cut pharmaceutical prices. Not only has it not considered the setting up of a nationalised drug marketing system, it has not even implemented measures to sell drugs by generic rather than brand names (which other countries, like Pakistan, have done).

In all these respects – plus those of quality control and the removal of export restrictive clauses[99] – there are gaps and defects in official policy. However, piecemeal measures to remedy one aspect or another of the drug industry will not result in the elimination of social waste and the lowering of drug prices; only a comprehensive approach can resolve the basic anomalies in the industry. Let us now consider the policies open to LDCs, and especially to the Indian government, to achieve a practical solution.

IV POLICY OPTIONS FOR LDCs

Let us restate the fundamental problem: LDCs want the benefit of having the best drugs available to modern medicine; they want to import or produce them at the lowest possible cost, using the results of research which is generally conducted in developed countries;[100] they want to bring them to consumers with the lowest possible expenditure on marketing, and, at the same time, provide adequate and honest information on new preparations and their prices to prescribing doctors; and they want to eliminate monopolistic elements in pricing of brand name products and every possibility of drug adulteration.

How is all this to be best achieved? One solution, perhaps the best from a global point of view, would be a thorough reform of the pharmaceutical industry in the developed capitalist countries, along the lines mentioned at the end of Section II. If the undertaking of pharmaceutical research, production and marketing were socialised, and the products (finished or intermediate) made available to LDCs at prices approximately the real costs of production, most of the undesirable elements in the present international structure of the industry would disappear. The LDCs would still be faced with the problems of internally processing and marketing the drugs, but any sensible distribution system would be able to deliver the goods at prices far below present ones.

This is hardly a policy which is open to LDCs. Despite the occasional outbursts of protest, the pharmaceutical industry is likely to continue undisturbed in its present form in developed countries; if the LDCs want to lower its costs, they will have to do so on their own, within the given structure of the industry in the West.

The policies which a particular LDC can adopt are determined, of

The International Pharmaceutical Industry and LDCs 187

course, by its industrial capacity and the abilities of its domestic entrepreneurs and administrators. There are crucial differences on the production side between those countries which possess developed chemical industries and can therefore produce most pharmaceuticals entirely on their own, and those which have to import the finished drugs or the intermediates in an almost finished form. On the distribution side, similarly, there are crucial differences between countries which are capable of managing an information and marketing system on a nationalised basis (with no help from the international drug firms) and those which are not.

Countries which have simple processing facilities but possess neither developed chemical industries nor an administration capable of handling sophisticated information and marketing systems can choose between the following alternative 'packages' in ascending order of desirability:

i. an industry dominated, as at present, by multinationals, which performs all the requisite functions but at very high cost, and against whose brand names and patents local enterprises have little chance to compete;

ii. similar to the first, but with patents eliminated, in which case local enterprises can legally copy the multinationals' products, but may still find it impossible to compete against their brand names;

iii. the next stage, the substitution of generic for brand names, which may still be ineffective because the multinationals can, as they do now in Pakistan, continue to persuade doctors that their products are superior, and so still create a monopolistic privilege by inducing consumers to buy drugs made by particular companies;

iv. the elimination of foreign enterprise altogether, with local manufacturers buying intermediate products from the lowest-priced world sources – from small firms selling under generic names in developed countries, or from producers which copy new technology cheaply (Italy), or from the Socialist bloc[101] – which may save a great deal of the foreign exchange cost of multinational profits but may not prevent the social wastage inherent in private marketing of drugs.

Thus, a nationally-owned but private drug processing industry would be able to take advantage of price differentials and non-patent-observing producers in world markets, but it would continue to be dependent on imports and it would not resolve the basic contradictions involved in the private selling of nicdieines. Local firms would probable end up using tactics of advertising and promotion similar to those used by large firms in developed countries – this would occur even if brand names were banned, as long as the manufacturer's name was identifiable – and so raise the final price to consumers. The social costs would remain internal rather than flowing abroad in the form of foreign profits, but the most important aim of reform would not be achieved. Furthermore, the dangers of inadequate quality control may be higher if local firms are less stringent than foreign ones, and if the government is incapable of implementing proper controls. The ultimate advantages of reform may still be substantial, however, if this particular risk is averted, and if the local oligopolists are able to sell at prices lower than present ones.

The options open to LDCs such as India, which have sophisticated public sector production units, advanced chemical industries and well-developed administrations, are much broader. To continue from the fourth 'package', therefore:

v. a more or less complete self-reliance in the production of intermediate chemicals, in either the public or private sectors, copying technology from abroad whenever necessary without paying royalties and importing chemicals from cheap sources where technology is especially difficult, and completely locally owned production of pharmaceuticals (again without eliminating private marketing costs), with strict quality control measures by the government;

vi. a continued reliance on private pharmaceutical production but with a national purchasing service which determines individual drug prices on a fair basis, markets drugs purely by generic names, and provides doctors with the requisite information on drug uses and innovations; and

vii. a complete socialisation of drug production as well as marketing, thus minimising the extent of private profit and, if so desired, running the industry as a non-profit making public utility.

It is obvious that the seventh package can, if it were practicable, provide medicines at the lowest possible cost both to the country as well as to the consumer. That it is in principle practicable to have a public sector drug industry in LDCs is illustrated by the Egyptian example (and by the more limited one of India); that international patents can be disallowed in this sector is shown by Italy; and that socialised distribution can be introduced is proved by the socialist countries. Whether the actual costs will reach the optimum level envisaged or not will depend on whether public sector units can be run efficiently, whether quality control can be enforced, whether a government distribution and information system operates smoothly and, of course, whether the political situation of the country will permit such a radical change to be introduced.

In the particular case of India, while there is bound to be considerable political opposition to a complete public takeover of the pharmaceutical industry, matters have changed greatly from the 1950s when the private sector could actually hinder determined moves in this direction. The problem of quality control is, if anything, worse under the present system of thousands of small producers than it would be with a few large public sector units; the elimination of the small units would by itself rule out many of the present abuses. The provision of regular and up-to-date information on drugs to doctors should not prove very difficult, especially if the government uses the results of clinical tests and official checks done in the developed countries. Since the technology of drug production is basically not very complex, the copying of foreign products should be fairly straightforward; in the few cases that there are lags or difficulties, the drugs could always be imported from cheap sources abroad. The only remaining question concerns efficiency; however, as long as one accepts that there is no *intrinsic* reason why public sector units should be less productive than private ones, experience and effort should resolve it with time.

We conclude, therefore, that in the long-run the best way to deal with the various and complex problems of the present international pharmaceutical industry as it operates in LDCs is to move in appropriate stages towards a socially-owned indigenous pharmaceutical industry which copies foreign technology, bans brand names and markets the products through official agencies. Given the social importance of this industry, moreover, and the human costs involved in the present high-price structure, it is vital that reform be undertaken as a matter of urgency. Prevarication can only serve to worsen the dependence on multinational firms and increase the social costs of their operation.

NOTES

1. I am grateful to a number of people who discussed an earlier draft of this paper; I would, in particular, like to thank Michael Ashfield, Angus Hone, Deepak Nayyar, Edith Penrose, Frances Stewart and Raymond Vernon for comments and criticisms. I retain full responsibility for the views expressed here.
2. The analysis applies mainly to 'ethical drugs, medicines sold under brand names on prescription, but many characteristics of such drugs are also

common to 'household' medicines sold directly to the consumer.
3. See the survey by OECD (1969).
4. Appendix 5, Monopolies Commission (1972). Of the *first* 10 firms by size of drug sales, 3 were Swiss, 1 German and 6 American. The 4 British firms were considerably smaller, and their combined drug sales came to only about one-third of the sales of the Swiss firms.
5. The exact number of pharmaceutical firms and value of their production is not known for the US, but estimates by Schifrin (1967) and Walker (1971) put the figures in the broad range mentioned above.
6. For a summary of this Committee's findings, see Kefauver (1966).
7. OECD (1969), p. 49. The report by NEDO (1972) makes a similar point.
8. See OECD, p. 69, for a breakdown of different products in 5 European countries: of the 13 groups, 'other' accounts for *33–44 per cent of the total*.
9. Schifrin (1967).
10. Ibid.
11. *Financial Times* (1973). This estimate is given by the firm itself and may, in view of the pressures put on Roche in several countries, be highly conservative.
12. Schifrin (1967). The Sainsbury Committee notes that 'fundamental' research accounted for 57 per cent of the total R & D expenditures in the UK in 1963–5, though it expresses grave reservations about the definition of the term as used by the firms. The comparable US figure is 17 per cent, which seems more realistic (see Walker).
13. *Trade and Industry* (1974). The figure is for 'Pharmaceuticals and Toilet Preparations'; in terms of ranking, this industry came fourth for R & D as a percentage of turnover and fifth for R & D as a percentage of net output and value added.
14. Wortzel (1971), Table 5.
15. Ibid. See also the OECD study for a comparative description of R & D in various countries.
16. OECD and Sainsbury Committee.
17. *Financial Times* (1974a).
18. Walker (1971) p. 128.
19. Comanor (1965), and Monopolies Commission (1972), Appendix 6.
20. Schifrin (1967), quotes an official US publication to the effect that of the total number of new products ((5386) introduced in 1949–63, most were duplicates of existing products or new compounds of existing products; only 618 (11 per cent) contained new chemical entities not previously known. *The Economist* (1974), points out that of 1500 patents filed in 1972, only 45 were 'genuine new drugs' and 150 were 'major modifications'; the rest were purely imitative. To some extent, therefore, R & D by drug firms consists simply of 'market research', scouting the industry for copiable products.
21. Cain (1967). Private research is defined to include research undertaken at the firms' cost at universities.
22. Ibid. In some cases the 'skills' of the Medical Research Council are hired to private firms and joint research projects are becoming more common; as with research output, such co-operation redounds mainly to the benefit of the firms.

The International Pharmaceutical Industry and LDCs 191

23. For a brief survey of patent laws in 34 countries see UN, 1964; for a defence of patents as a stimulant to pharmaceutical innovation see Cooper (1967), and for critiques see Schifrin (1967), Scherer (1971), Johnson (1970) and Steele (1964). The effect of patents on less-developed countries is discussed later.
24. Process patents are supposed to stimulate the search for more efficient ways of producing given products rather than simply to imitate existing products.
25. See Steele (1962) and Scherer (1971). Unfortunately no figures are available on the legal expenses of drug firms.
26. *The Economist*, (16 Feb. 1974). The charge made that a large number of patents are bought in less-developed countries and left unused is considered later.
27. Nearly all countries, with a major exception of the US, have legal provisions for compulsory licensing after a few years of granting patent protection in order to stimulate competition. The Roche case (Monopolies Commission, 1973) illustrates the limited effectiveness of this provision. It is worth noting, however, that the US Supreme Court does occasionally grant compulsory licences; for instance it recently forced ICI and Glaxo to give a compulsory and free, unrestricted licence for an antibiotic (*Financial Times* 1974b). It remains to be seen how far this constitutes a basic change in policy towards patenting. On various proposals for reform of the patent system, see Scherer (1971).
28. See Kefauver (1966), Steele (1962) and Schifrin (1967). The most thorough discussion of this topic is in Walker (1971). In 1967 the industry accounted for the highest single share (17 per cent) of advertising of the total for 27 US industries; its sales accounted for less than 5 per cent in that year. See Wilder (1974).
29. OECD (1969), and Sainsbury Committee. It is possible that a part of the expenditures classified under 'administration' are in fact on marketing; even the reported level of promotion expenditures has, however, been severely criticised by the Sainsbury Committee, which concludes (p. 71) that pharmaceutical manufacturers have in their sales promotion efforts failed to measure up to the 'appropriate responsibility'. The Monopolies Commission (1973) shows a steadily rising cost of promotion as a percentage of sales, from 13.9 per cent in 1965 to 14.8 per cent in 1970 (p. 40).
30. Walker (1971, p. 32) estimates that of the total of 696 drugs in use in the US in 1961, 377 (58 per cent) were produced by single firms only; of these 293 (78 per cent of 277) were marketed under brand names by the 33 large firms. Of the 588 drugs marketed by large firms, 450 (77 per cent) were under brand names and only 138 under generic names; of the 384 drugs marketed by small firms, 227 (59 per cent) were under generic and the rest under brand names. In many countries prescriptions using brand names cannot legally be substituted by the pharmacist for cheaper generic products.
31. This state of affairs is also the result partly of inadequate teaching of clinical pharmacology in medical schools and partly of apathy on the part of the doctors who do not take the trouble to read medical journals or other

serious literature. The only guide to the effectiveness and cost of drugs in the UK, Prop List, was stopped three years ago by the Department of Health, allegedly on grounds of economy, but perhaps under pressure from the drug industry. See *New Scientist* and *Guardian* (1974).
32. See Monopolies Commission (1973) p. 40, for a breakdown of sales promotion expenditure by size of firm.
33. Steele (1962). Charges have been levelled recently in the UK that the industry's promotion methods often lead to over-prescribing and mis-prescribing by doctors. Dr Gould in the *New Scientist* (1974), concludes after a survey of the evidence that 'There is thus no existing body in Britain with the responsibility for acquiring the information needed for the intelligent handling of medicines' (p. 471). Raphael in *The Guardian* (13 May 1974), makes a similar point.
34. US Senate, part 5, p. 1745, and Steele (1964).
35. *The Times* (8 Nov. 1973). Librium prices in India are discussed below.
36. *The Financial Times* (22 June 1973 and 20 Feb. 1974). Roche is now under investigation in West Germany, Sweden, Australia, the US, Holland and the EEC Secretariat for its pricing policies.
37. Monopolies Commission (1973), D.D.S.A. advanced a number of reasons why Roche had advantages in marketing from its sheer size and tactics.
38. Cooper (1967). A report in the *Sunday Times* (27 May, 1973), compared the prices of some leading drugs in the UK with the comparable 'free market' price (from non-patent observing countries like Italy and Finland) and found, for instance, that Eaton (US) was charging the NHS *102 times* the alternative price for Nitrofurantoin, ICI (UK) was charging 60 times higher for Propanolol, and Smith Kline (US) was charging 145 times higher for Trifluoperazine. A comparison of the cost of 4 leading drugs in the UK (Aldomet, Penbritin, Intal and Indocid) to the NHS (total US $71.3m, year unspecified) with their free market cost ($18.5m) shows that the NHS could have obtained these drugs for about 25 per cent of their actual cost. These figures are computed from the *Sunday Times* report.
39. See, for instance, Walker (1971) pp. 84–7. Not only are representatives briefed to play down all unfavourable aspects, a great deal of money is spent on financing clinical studies and buying 'testimonials' which are misleading and sometimes bogus, and serve only to promote sales. Walker notes how many of the questionable tactics of selling toothpaste or household medicines, with the backing of spurious 'doctors advice', are also used in drug advertising.
40. US Senate Hearings, part 13 (1969) p. 5417.
41. These findings are reported in the *New Scientist* (1974) p. 491.
42. On the defects in the present system of official scrutiny and subsequent mis-prescribing by doctors, see *New Scientist* (1974). Such is the 'general ignorance about medicines [that] there must be official control over advertisements and other techniques for promoting drug sales, since doctors and patients are normally in no position to judge the validity of claims made by the manufacturer' (p. 471).
43. *The Guardian* (14 May 1974) p. 1. The accusation was made by Labour MPs dealing with health problems.
44. Steele (1962).

The International Pharmaceutical Industry and LDCs

45. Ibid.
46. The Sainsbury Committee, whose recommendations were largely unimplemented, suggested strict control over promotion and a gradual official takeover of the information function from private firms. Various American authors, cited above, have recommended the abolition of brand names and alternative means of providing information: the Bill to be introduced by Senator Kennedy will set up a centre to study, among other things, the possibility of using *independent* representatives to keep doctors informed.
47. On the fascinating political processes by which the British drug industry was able to resist reform see R. W. Lang, *The Politics of Drugs: A Comparative Study of the British and Canadian Pharmaceutical Industries, 1930–1973* (D. C. Heath, Ltd.), may cast light on just this. According to the publisher's advance notice, the author, Director of the Legislation Department of the Canadian Labour Congress, discusses 'why British manufacturers were successful in resisting the Labour government's legislative programme to reduce costs'.
48. See Parker and Kelly (1968), Sainsbury Committee (1967), Schifrin (1967), Smith (1972); and Monopolies Commission, 1972 (appendix 14).
49. NEDO (1972) p. 30. This report notes the higher profitability of the larger firms as compared to smaller ones in the industry.
50. *The Times 1000*. The profits earned are on all the activities of the firms, not only drugs.
51. Sainsbury Committee, p. 110.
52. The figures for 1973/4, reported in the business section of *The Guardian* (11 June, 1974, p. 17), show that 'Profitability is *considerably higher for drugs than most other manufacturing industries* even though the actual level has been falling. The average return on capital is still 18 per cent . . .' (italics added).
53. Parker and Kelly (1968) conducted a comprehensive econometric test of the causes of abnormal profits in the drug industry and concluded 'the high profit experience of the drug industry is related only minimally to risk and uncertainty in a causal way . . . [it is] more closely associated with high barriers to entry of new competition' (p. 165).
54. Schifrin (1967).
55. For instance, by the Kefauver Committee, which found that the actual cost of goods sold was less than one-third the value of sales for the 22 largest drug firms in the US.
56. See Chapter 5 above.
57. Monopolies Commission (1973) pp. 45–9.
58. See Sainsbury Committee, Appendix 1 Table 7.
59. One estimate of transfer-pricing profits is £400 million per annum as a whole, and £35 million for France. See *The Economist* (1974).
60. The alternative of restoring competition in some form by breaking up the large firms into small private firms is not considered as efficient as the alternative of a socially-owned industry because it would not prevent either a misdirection of R & D expenditure or costly and misleading advertising practices; in the long run, therefore, it would be impossible to prevent a re-emergence of the present situation.

194 *The Multinational Corporation*

61. This assertion begs a number of questions about the operation of publicly-financed R & D institutions – their efficiency, their need to buy international patents, their size in relation to the 'optimum' scale – which we cannot enter into here in detail. The experience of public research is very encouraging, as we have argued previously, and it certainly cuts out imitative patenting; a public corporation could, if it wanted, buy foreign patents and sell licences, though this is not recommended below for LDCs; the size of research establishments could of course be adjusted to any desirable scale, given the massive total R & D expenditure involved.
62. This particular feature could presumably be remedied within the present framework of ownership by stricter control over marketing and promotion and the abolition of brand names; however, a really efficient control system would in practice amount to a state selling service, not very different in this respect from our alternative.
63. As with marketing, an efficient state buying service could in theory ensure 'reasonable' profits for private firms, but the Voluntary Price Regulation Scheme in the UK has not been able to achieve this for the NHS, and it is difficult, for political and administrative reasons, to envisage comprehensive negotiation on prices and profits. However, any move in this direction should lead to a lowering of costs.
64. See Wortzel (1971) for a brief description of the pharmaceutical industry in LDCs.
65. The market shares of multinational pharmaceutical firms in the late 60s were as follows in some selected LDCs: Brazil, 78 per cent, Argentina 65 per cent, Peru 95 per cent, Venezuela 90 per cent, the Philippines and Central America, over 80 per cent. See Wortzel (1971), and Vaitsos (1973). See below for details on India.
66. On the effects of patents in LDCs see Penrose (1973), Vaitsos (1973), and UN (1964).
67. UN (1964), pp. 94–5.
68. Vaitsos (1973).
69. Vaitsos (1973) p. 75. The foreign ownership of pharmaceutical patents was 98.4 per cent as compared to 94.5 per cent for all industry.
70. Cooper (1967) p. 40.
71. This is probably even more true of the pharmaceutical industry, in which all the LDCs together account only for about 16 per cent of total non-Soviet Bloc pharmaceutical consumption. See Wortzel (1971) p. 40.
72. Vaitsos (1973). See also the views of the Indian Government as expressed to the UN, in UN (1964) p. 57.
73. Vaitsos (1973) estimates that 98–99 per cent of patents taken out by foreigners in Colombia and Peru were unexploited in 1970, the bulk of them in the pharmaceutical industry. The Indian Government, quoted in UN (1964) levels the same charge, though the exact proportion of unexploited patents is not mentioned.
74. Penrose, loc. cit., p. 783.
75. Ibid., p. 784.
76. Here we are considering costs above the usual ones in developed countries of excessive profits, which also results in foreign exchange drains, and high marketing expenses, which are generally in local currency unless the

advertising firms are also foreign owned.
77. See Chapter 5.
78. These two figures are derived from details of public prosecutions of pharmaceutical firms published by a Bogota newspaper (*El Tiempo*, 1971); the annual savings achieved by reducing the prices of these two chemicals came to almost US $400 thousand.
79. The last two are from Vaitsos (1973) table 7; where Diazepam is mentioned as 'substance of Valium'. These two figures are the highest recorded for overpricing in this table, but are not very startling when compared with the 4000 per cent and 4500 per cent overpricing respectively found by the British Monopolies Commission's investigation of Roche (p. 38).
80. Agarwal et al. (1962) and Ministry of Foreign Trade (1972). A different estimate for 1966 puts the share of the largest 25 firms at 74 per cent of the total market, and claims that this has not changed much over time (Mote and Pathak, 1972).
81. OECD (1969) table 2.
82. Mote and Pathak (1972).
83. *R.B.I. Bulletins* (1972 and 1973). The definition of 'foreign controlled' used by the Reserve Bank of India includes firms with 40 per cent or more foreign equity and other firms which are foreign managed and have 25 per cent of their equity held abroad. As these firms cover only public limited companies, wholly owned branches of foreign firms are not included; these account for 12 per cent of total foreign direct investment in the pharmaceutical industry (*R.B.I. Bulletin*, 1971).
84. This range may be slightly higher if branches of foreign firms are included, bringing it to 70–80 per cent.
85. From Roche's annual accounts. The firm has now been in operation in India for over 25 years with a foreign shareholding of 89 per cent in 1968.
86. See *R.B.I.*, (1968) and Ministry of Foreign Trade, (1972).
87. See, for instance, Kidron (1965) and Agarwal et al. (1972).
88. See Kidron (1965) p. 251.
89. Agarwal, loc. cit. Table 3. Roche's price was slightly lower than the equivalent in the UK (about Rs. 18) before 1973, but is much higher than the price recommended by the Monopolies Commission, and enforced by the British government.
90. Ibid., Table 1. Both these products were introduced over 25 years ago, so they are in no way an embodiment of heavy recent research expenditures.
91. Ibid., p. 2290. Doctors also mention that high priced treatment is considered more effective, and is sometimes treated as a status symbol, by rich patients.
92. Ottuketkal (1970).
93. This has also been noted for Egypt in an unpublished study by Miss Handoussa, mentioned in a footnote on p. 777 of Penrose (1973).
94. Agarwal et al. (1972).
95. For details, see Mote and Pathak (1972).
96. Agarwal (1972).
97. See Gupta (1970).
98. Kidron (1965) pp. 163–5.
99. *R. B. I.* (1968) notes the heavy incidence of restrictive clauses in technical

196   The Multinational Corporation

agreements of foreign subsidiaries in this industry, p. 38. Despite official efforts, restrictive clauses are still present in many agreements.
100. While the following discussion does not go into the role of local R & D in LDCs, clearly indigenous research is not excluded; there is no reason why local efforts should not complement research done abroad, though it is unrealistic to envisage complete self-sufficiency in this field. For reasons explained above, there should be no detrimental effect on the amount of R & D done in developed countries if less-developed ones do not adhere to the present international patent system; this is assumed throughout.
101. The role of 'shopping around' continuously is vital, since total dependence on a single producer (say, in the Socialist bloc) may easily induce them to charge monopolistic prices.

REFERENCES

Agarwal, P. S., Ramachandran, P. K., and Rangarao, B. V. (1972), 'Anomalies in Drug Prices and Quality Control', *Economic and Political Weekly* (18 Nov.) pp. 2285–92.
Cain, J. C. (1967), 'State Support for Research', in G. Teeling-Smith (editor), *Innovation and the Balance of Payments: The Experience of the Pharmaceutical Industry* (London, Office of Health Economics) pp. 84–96.
Comanor, W. S. (1965), 'Research and Technical Change in the Pharmaceutical Industry', *Review of Economics and Statistics*, pp. 182–90.
—— (1966), 'The Drug Industry and Medical Research: The Economics of the Kefauver Committee Investigations', in Part 5 of US Senate's *Competitive Problems in the Drug Industry*, pp. 2086–91.
Cooper, M. H. (1967), 'Patents and Innovation in Britain, India, Italy, Japan and the USA', in G. Teeling-Smith (ref. no. 2) pp. 37–48.
Economist, The (1974), 'Patented Profits' (London: 16 Feb.) p. 88.
El Tiempo (1971), 'Incomex Rebajá Precios' (Bogota: 15 Sep.).
Financial Times, The (1973), 'Roche: What the Lords will be Deciding Today' (London: 22 June).
Financial Times, The (1974a), 'Why Roche is Fighting to the Finish' (London: 20 Feb.).
Financial Times, The (1974b), 'Strained Relations in the Drug World' (London: 9 May).
Guardian, The (1974), Various Articles on the drug industry by A. Raphael (esp. 13 and 14 May).
Gupta, A. (1970), 'Restricted Patents and the Drug Industry', *Economic and Political Weekly* (26 Sep.) pp. 1585–6.
Harris, S. E. (1964), *The Economics of American Medicine* (New York: Macmillan).
Johnson, H. G. (1970), 'The Efficiency and Welfare Implications of the International Corporation', in C. P. Kindleberger (editor), *The International Corporation* (Cambridge, Mass.: MIT Press) pp. 35–56.
Kefauver, E. (1966), *In a Few Hands: Monopoly Power in America* (Harmondsworth:Penguin).

Kidron, M. (1965), *Foreign Investments in India* (London: Oxford University Press).
Ministry of Foreign Trade (1972), *Profile of Indian Industry* (New Delhi: Government of India).
Monopolies Commission, The (1972), *Beecham Group Limited and Glaxo Group Limited, The Boots Company and Glaxo Group Limited* (London: HMSO).
Monopolies Commission, The (1973), *Chlordiazepoxide and Diazepam* (London: HMSO).
Mote, V. L., and Pathak, H. N. (1972), 'Drug Price Control: An Evaluation', *Economic and Political Weekly* (15 July) pp. 1369-79.
NEDO (1972), *Focus on Pharmaceuticals* (London: National Economic Development Office).
New Scientist (1974), 'Can We Handle Modern Drugs?' pp. 460-71; and 'Cleaning up the Drug Trade', p. 491 (25 May).
OECD (1969), *Gaps in Technology: Pharmaceuticals* (Paris: Organisation for Economic Co-operation and Development).
Ottuketkal (1970), 'Facts about Drug Prices', *Economic and Political Weekly* (21 Mar.) pp. 507-8.
Parker, R. C. and Kelly, W. H. (1968), 'Profitability in the Drug Industry: A Result of Monopoly or a Payment for Risk?', in Federal Trade Commission's *Economic Papers, 1966-69* (Washington, DC. US Government) pp. 144-83.
Penrose, E. T. (1973), 'International Patenting and the Less-Developed Countries', *Economic Journal* (Sep.) pp. 768-86.
RBI (1968), *Foreign Collaboration in Indian Industry* (Bombay: Reserve Bank of India).
RBI (1971), 'India's International Investment Position in 1967-68', *Reserve Bank of India Bulletin* (Mar.) pp. 552-93.
RBI (1972), 'Finances of Medium and Large Public Limited Companies', *Reserve Bank of India Bulletin* (Sep.) pp. 1425-584.
RBI (1973), 'Finances of Branches of Foreign Companies and Foreign Controlled Rupee Companies, 1969-70', *Reserve Bank of India Bulletin* (Mar.) pp. 344-68.
Sainsbury Committee (1967), *Report of the Committee of Enquiry into the Relationship of the Pharmaceutical Industry with the National Health Service, 1965-67*, (London: HMSO).
Scherer, F. M. (1971), *Industrial Market Structure and Economic Performance* (Chicago: Rand McNally).
Schifrin, L. G. (1967), 'The Ethical Drug Industry: The Case for Compulsory Patent Licensing', in Part 5 of the US Senate's *Competitive Problems in the Drug Industry*, pp. 1890-1900.
Steele, H. (1962), 'Monopoly and Competition in the Ethical Drugs Market', *Journal of Law and Economics* (Oct.), pp. 131-63, reprinted in US Senate's *Competitive Problems in the Drug Industry*, pp. 1950-70.
—— (1964), 'Patent Restrictions and Price Competition in the Ethical Drugs Industry', *Journal of Industrial Economics* (July), pp. 198-223, reprinted in US Senate's *Competitive Problems in the Drug Industry*, pp. 1973-97.
Sunday Times (1973), 'Do all drugs cost too much?' (London: 27 May) p. 59.
The Times (1973), *The Times 1000, 1973-74* (London).

The Times (1973), 'Americans Pay La Roche "Three Times as Much" for Tranquillizers' (London: 8 Nov.).
Trade and Industry (1974), 'Research and Development by Manufacturing Industry' (2 May) pp. 210–17.
UN (1964), *The Role of Patents in the Transfer of Technology to Developing Countries* (New York: United Nations).
US Senate, (Various) *Competitive Problems in the Drug Industry*, Hearings before the Sub-committee on Monopoly, of the Select Committee on Small Business (Washington, DC: US Government).
Vaitsos, C. V. (1973), 'Patents Revisited: Their Function in Developing Countries', in C. Cooper (editor), *Science, Technology and Development* (London: Frank Cass) pp. 71–98.
Walker, H. D. (1971), *Market Power and Price Levels in the Ethical Drug Industry* (Bloomington: Indiana University Press).
Wilder, R. P. (1974), 'Advertising and Inter-Industry Competition', *Journal of Industrial Economics* (Mar.) pp. 215–26.
Wortzel, L. H. (1971), *Technology Transfer in the Pharmaceutical Industry* (New York: UNITAR) Research Report, no. 14.

8 Price Competition and the International Pharmaceutical Industry[1]

I INTRODUCTION

The issue of the pricing of pharmaceutical products has aroused considerable controversy over the past two decades. Much impassioned debate has ranged around whether the large firms which dominate the industry in developed as well as less-developed countries exercise excessive market power, whether the market power conferred on them legally (by patents) or by commercial practice (advertising of brand names) is abused by charging prices higher than social interest warrants, and what measures (if any) governments should adopt to regulate the pricing and other activities of large firms while maintaining a commercial incentive to invest in innovation.[2] The US leads in the public debate on these problems, with the FDA (Food and Drug Administration) vigorously seeking to lower prices of drugs for its health programmes and to diminish the hold that brand names exercise over the choice of drugs. Several European countries have launched comprehensive schemes of price control, while a large number of LDCs are starting on the difficult path of pharmaceutical regulation and reduction in the cost of medicines to the public.

Supporters and representatives of the industry have not been inactive. The main burden of their defence of the present system of drug provision has rested on the high risk and cost of drug innovation, but several forays have also been made to preserve promotional practices, extend patent life, hasten new drug introduction, strengthen brand names and so on. It is one such foray that this paper is concerned with: the attempt to show that there is sufficient price competition in the industry to eliminate, in due course, the market power initially granted to innovators by the patent system, and that by implication, no official regulation of prices is needed after the innovators have reaped a return on their R & D during the protected period.

If this were indeed true, it would have very important implications for policy. While it would not answer whether or not the prices charged during the patent period yielded the 'right' rate of return for investments in R & D, or whether the promotional methods used and costs incurred to realise the profits on new drugs were socially justified, it would certainly end the need for governments to regulate prices on 'multi-source' drugs (i.e. those available from more than one supplier). If it could be shown that prices of identical products were brought to approximately the same level within reasonably short periods by untrammelled market forces, many of the price-control policies being followed by governments would be redundant or harmful – and many recommendations made to LDCs (by, among others, myself)[3] misguided.

If, on the other hand, the evidence showed that market forces did not by themselves equalise the prices of identical products, that significant differences persisted over time between prices charged by the dominant firms and the small ones without affecting their market shares, a strong case could be made that elements of monopoly power (based on the promotion of the branded products of the former) existed that called for remedial policy.

In this paper, we are not concerned with policy issues as a whole, since these must also tackle the difficult problem of financing innovation and providing information to prescribers, but simply with the effectiveness of price competition in this industry. In section II, we deal with the problem generally, analysing the arguments produced on developed countries by the industry to support its case for *laissez faire*. In section III, we discuss evidence on antibiotic prices in the US, and in section IV, that on pharmaceutical prices from Sri Lanka. The bulk of medicinal requirements in Sri Lanka are purchased on open international markets, and a State Pharmaceuticals Corporation (SPC) was set up in 1972 to handle all imports; the relevance of Sri Lanka's case lies in the fact that the SPC was able to collect detailed prices on drug imports in free markets before its takeover, and to compare these with prices at which other suppliers were prepared to supply identical products. We close with some implications for other LDCs.

II THE DEBATE ON PRICE COMPETITION

It had been accepted for a long time, by supporters of the industry as well as by its critics, that price competition was not the major form of inter-firm rivalry in the pharmaceutical industry.[4] The peculiar nature of the market, with the effective decision maker (the doctor) completely separated from the buyer (the patient or some health scheme), combined with very inelastic demand and the need for effective, absolutely reliable products, was believed to render active price competition a secondary strategy for drug firms. The main strategy was supposed to comprise some appropriate combination of the introduction of innovations, the presentation of existing products in a new and different form, and advertising and direct representation to promote them.[5] Price rivalry, while known to be occasionally practised, was not the 'hidden hand' that kept private enterprise in harmony with social interest: this was believed to be competition in product innovation. Supporters of the industry believed that the system was, despite persistent price anomalies, an efficient method of providing new drugs; critics believed that it was socially wasteful.

The new case on price competition was advanced by George Teeling-Smith, the Director of the Office of Health Economics (the pressure group for the large British drug companies), with the collaboration of Duncan Reekie, in 1975.[6] Named the 'Canberra Hypothesis' and introduced with considerable publicity, it argued that price competition was alive and flourishing in the drug industry. Using data on price declines in broad spectrum antibiotics (from $15 to $5.10) and the introduction of benzodiazepine tranquillisers (the famous 'Librium' and 'Valium' of Roche) at relatively low prices, it made the point that, as far as new drug introductions went, manufacturers set prices according to the cost of existing and relevant therapies on the market. The choice between relatively high or low entry prices showed the influence of actual and expected market competition. Furthermore, the fact that high initial prices were lowered over time showed an awareness, or the actual effect, of increased competition from substitute innovations of rival producers.

The Canberra Hypothesis promised further evidence on competition in drug pricing. This has been subsequently provided by Reekie in two papers, on the UK (1977a) and the US (1977b). Both papers claim that the pricing of new drugs, without exact substitutes, takes existing and potential competition into account – the OHE terms this 'price and performance' competition, as contrasted to the 'common commodity' competition that emerges when a product has perfect substitutes. Evidence on price declines of new drugs, and the pricing of introductions in relation to the therapeutic novelty of the product (major innovations tending to be relatively higher priced, in comparison to

202   *The Multinational Corporation*

older treatments, than minor ones), is presented to show that there is effective competition in the industry. Reekie concludes, in support of Teeling-Smith's argument, that 'There is very little here to encourage sweeping allegations of monopolistic pricing behaviour in the pharmaceutical industry' (1977a, p. 29).

The evidence that some competition existed in the pricing of drugs is taken by Teeling-Smith and Reekie to establish that market forces work satisfactorily in pharmaceutical markets, and that no monopoly power persists over the long run (when 'common commodity' competition emerges) which may necessitate government regulation. Teeling-Smith states explicitly, though without providing any evidence, that, as large firms' products neared patent expiry, these firms would be

> ... gradually lowering the product's price from the effective level under 'price and performance' competition to the level which the company judges to represent a competitive price under the rules of 'common commodity' competition. By doing this, the manufacturer will have created a situation similar to that with any run-of-the-mill minor product when its patent expires. *No competitor will be able to undercut or even to match the originator's price, because his economies of scale in production will give him a decisive advantage.* He cannot, however, unreasonably exploit this happy situation because the rules of 'common commodity' competition will always remain in operation as a safeguard.[7]

Reekie uses the same argument – deducing from the premise that firms take existing and potential competition into account in pricing new drugs the conclusion that competition works satisfactorily to eliminate monopoly power in the long run – to attack those who have argued that considerable market power persists in the hands of large firms. In his US paper (1977b) he singles out my article (chapter 7) for extensive criticism, accusing me of providing 'scant empirical back-up' for my statements on market power, and extracting four points which he believes he refutes with his data:

(i) there are tremendous price anomalies in the industry between identical products offered by large and small firms;
(ii) the price premium charged by large firms bears no relationship to 'legitimate' returns on R & D; and
(iii) prices of large firms reveal considerable market power even after

patent expiry (and, presumably, after the recoupment of R & D costs); and
(iv) doctors do not appear to be very price-conscious.[8]

The arguments of Teeling-Smith and Reekie, and the evidence on drug pricing provided by them, do not, however, establish that competition works to eliminate monopoly power (or refute the points made in my paper). The fallacy is a simple one. The fact that innovators take competition into account in pricing new drugs *merely establishes that they are oligopolists and not absolute monopolists*. It does not show whether or not oligopolistic competition eliminates market power over the long term. If the dominant firms possessed no source of market power other than patent protection, the expiry of patents would lead to the situation described by Teeling-Smith above. If, however, they did possess market power, created by promotion which persuaded doctors that their branded drugs were 'better' than the drugs of smaller-firms which may be clinically equivalent, there is no reason to expect that competition would be fully effective, i.e. that it would equalise the prices of identical products.

Since it has not been argued that drug companies were absolute monopolists who could ignore all competition,[9] Reekie's attack seems to be misguided. The correct method of testing the efficacy of price competition would obviously be to examine prices of multi-source drugs. Evidence on initial pricing strategy is irrelevant: it would be very surprising if oligopolists did *not* take each other's reactions into account. Despite his strictures on 'empirical back-up', however, Reekie does not provide evidence on multi-source markets, and ignores existing evidence on the US (described in the following section) which casts doubt on his case.[10] If evidence on multi-source markets showed that large firms were able to continue charging large premia on their products, then the points made in my paper are vindicated. If, on the other hand, it showed that prices of identical products were equalised, or, as Teeling-Smith argues, that innovators who had been able first to achieve economies of scale charged *lower* prices than all latecomers, the case of the industry would be vindicated. When such evidence exists, it is pointless to confine oneself (as Reekie does) to inferences about effective competition based on new product pricing.

204   *The Multinational Corporation*

III ANTIBIOTIC PRICES IN THE US

Let us turn to the evidence, starting with the antibiotics market in the US. Antibiotics are universally accepted as the leading instance of price competition in the pharmaceutical industry. The OHE paper singles it out to illustrate dramatic price falls, and, if its argument on economies of scale is valid, we should expect to find the larger producers charging significantly lower prices than smaller ones in markets which have been multi-source for some years. A valuable study by Brooke (1975) provides detailed figures on prices and market shares in antibiotics, and illustrates how market forces have worked in the most competitive sector of pharmaceuticals.

Brooke shows (table 2, p. 28) how prices for three major antibiotics have declined since their introduction. Published prices of erythromycin, introduced by Lilly in 1952 and Abbott in 1954, declined from $30.60 and $33.42 (for 100 capsules or tablets of 250 mg.) to $14.84 and $14.99 respectively in 1974. At this time, Upjohn, another major company, was selling the drug for $13.35, and Pfizer, Squibb, Parke Davis, Bristol, SKF and Robins were selling their own branded erythromycins for prices somewhat lower.[11] Similarly, tetracycline hydrochloride and potassium phenoxymethyl penicillin, both introduced in the 1950s, declined from about $30 to around $3 and $9 respectively for the large firms in 1974. Each of these antibiotics had over 30 suppliers, with a good mixture of small and large firms facing a market with prescribing by both brand and generic names. At first, sight therefore, Reekie's inference about near-perfect competition resulting from initial price declines seems to be borne out.

Brooke shows, however, that such an inference would be unjustified. For every multi-source antibiotic product, there were several good quality generic products sold by small firms at prices far below those of the large firms, yet which were unable to capture a significant share of the market. For 1974, for instance, erythromycin was available at $5.70 (62 per cent less than Lilly's price), tetracycline at $1.90 (30–50 per cent less than major firms and 90 per cent less than Pfizer's 'Terramycin' brand of oxytetracycline), and penicillin at $1.85 (80 per cent less than Lilly and Abbott products). Brooke computes market shares for leading products in several antibiotic markets for 1973, and finds that in every case higher-priced branded products dominated the market and in several the highest priced product held the largest share of the market.

Some of Brooke's main findings are displayed in a suitably summarised form in the Appendix in Table A.8.1. The last two columns of this table show the prices of the dominant sellers as percentages of the prices charged by lowest-cost sellers. A comparison of these differences with their respective market shares (the share of the low cost seller was always insignificant) shows the extent of price discrepancies that exist. As Brooke notes, 'In most cases, the branded product that sells at the highest price to the drug stores has the largest share of the market; this market domination held when measured in annual sales volume, number of prescriptions and number of units.' (p. i)[12]

Brooke calculates the social cost entailed in this sort of price structure as the total premium charged by large firms over lowest average price for each drug: for 7 drugs and 11 major firms studied, this premium totalled $90–107 million (depending on the assumptions used) in 1973, or 52–62 per cent of sales to the drug stores. The evidence does not support Reekie's case on the effects of price competition. Competition does exist, as the figures in columns 1 and 4 of Table A.8.1 show, but it is the preserve of the large companies. As Schwartzman, a strong defender of the industry, notes in his study of the US, 'the most effective competition comes from the entry of large firms';[13] this competition is effective because it can be backed up by well-known manufacturers' names and heavy promotion, neither of which can be provided by small manufacturers. The continuing price discrepancies may be taken to indicate the distortion of information exercised by the marketing system, and the recent efforts of the FDA to encourage generic prescribing and to enforce law prices may be regarded as external inputs to restore true competition.

The most common justification given by large firms for their high prices is the better quality of their products and their better 'bioavailability' (i.e. effectiveness on absorption into the body).[14] Brooke reviews the evidence on this detail, and finds the companies' claims to be largely unfounded and misleading. Poor quality *is* a real problem in pharmaceuticals, but its incidence is not significantly higher in small than in large firms in the US, and the very growth of generic prescribing – and the efforts of the FDA – testify to the fact that quality differences between branded and generic drugs are not such as to justify observed price differences. A clear example of the premium that attaches solely to the brand name may be taken from Brooke. He notes that several antibiotics are manufactured up to their final dosage form by firms which do not market them. They are then sold at widely different prices by different firms: Milan Laboratories makes erythromycin for Sherry (a small generic producer) and Squibb (a large multinational): the same product is then sold at $5.70 by the former and at

$11.83 as 'Ethrill' by the latter. Such examples can be multiplied for several drugs, but the point need not be belaboured.

To sum up this section, we have suggested that price competition in pharmaceuticals, while it certainly exists, is largely the preserve of large firms, and does not lead to the elimination of market power exercised by them. Those who attempt to infer that market forces are fully effective, and government regulation unnecessary, have used faulty reasoning and irrelevant data. Reekie's attack on the critics of the industry is misplaced, since he has misconstrued their case; his failure to take account of existing evidence casts grave doubt on his conclusions.

IV PRICE COMPETITION IN SRI LANKA

Let us now turn from evidence on price competition in advanced countries to that in an 'open' less-developed country. We can now examine if the process of international competition has led to a pricing situation which can be termed 'truly competitive'.

The data used are on the prices of imports of pharmaceutical products into Sri Lanka in 1972, divided into two parts. During the first six months of the year, imports were unregulated by the government and were handled by private traders, representatives of drug companies and their local subsidiaries. During the second six months, the newly formed State Pharmaceuticals Corporation (SPC) took over the imports of 52 drugs, and purchased these on the basis of worldwide tenders after careful checking for quality and bioavailability.[15] Since the SPC had recorded the prices charged by private suppliers before the takeover for early 1972, a comparison of these prices with the prices paid by the SPC can show the extent of savings that may be achieved by exploiting the competition latent in pharmaceutical markets.

Table A.8.2 in the Appendix gives detailed figures for 35 drugs, which accounted for 75 per cent in value of the total SPC purchases in 1972, which in turn accounted for one-third of the total purchases previously made by the private sector.[16] Table 8.1 shows the frequency distributions, according to three criteria, of the ratio of the private sector price to the SPC price (as given in the last column of the appendix table). Both tables illustrate the enormous range of differences between the private sector and SPC prices. Of the 35 drugs, over half of have private sector prices more than double SPC prices and 10 have ratios higher than 4.1. There are two factors, which unfortunately we cannot correct for, that may even understate the true extent of price differentials between the large TNCs and SPC suppliers: first, there may have been some increase in prices between the first and second halves of 1972; and, second, the price charged by the TNCs may have been slightly higher than the average private sector price (though not much higher, if they accounted for the bulk of the market). Even as they stand, however, the price reduction achieved by regulatioin are remarkable, and it is worth noting that they are fairly high on such well-established products as aspirin, ampicillin or phenylbutazone.

TABLE 8.1 Frequency distributions of ratio of private sector to SPC prices, Sri Lanka (price ratios)

	Under 1.2	1.2–1.5	1.6–2.0	2.1–4.0	4.1–7.0	Over 7.0	Total
A. By no. of SPC bids							
1–5	–	1	2	1	–	–	4
6–10	–	1	–	1	3	1	6
11–20	2	1	2	4	–	1	10
Over	2	3	3	2	2	3	15
B. By no. of private sector suppliers							
1–3	–	2	3	6	4	3	18
4–8	2	2	2	1	1	–	10
9 and over	2	2	2	1	–	–	7
C. By source of SPC purchase: Developed countries (of	3	3	1	3	1	–	11
which, TNCs)	(3)	(1)	(1)	(2)	–	–	(7)
Eastern Europe	–	2	4	3	1	2	12
Less developed countries	1	1	2	2	3	·3	12
Total	4	6	7	8	5	5	35

SOURCE
See appendix Table A. 8.2.

The total cost of the 35 drugs imported by the SPC was $248 thousand. Had the same quantity of drugs been imported at private sector prices, the cost to Sri Lanka would have come to $472 thousand. The savings achieved by regulation, $224 thousand, were spent partly in increasing the quantity of drugs purchased (imports of the 35 drugs in the first half of 1972 by the private sector had come to $357 thousand) by $115 thousand, and partly in providing foreign exchange for other uses ($109 thousand).

The distributions of price differentials shown in Table 8.1 suggest that the extent of competition in international pharmaceutical markets and the source of purchases affect the savings which regulation can achieve. While the difference between free market oligopolistic prices and truly competitive prices (taking the SPC price to approximate the latter) is mainly determined by brand-name promotion which is not measurable with the data at hand, we would expect to find that competition of two sorts would influence the differential: first, the extent of competition among the private sector suppliers, as measured by their number prior to the SPC take-over; and, second, the extent of competition among SPC suppliers, as measured by the number of bids received. Furthermore, the price differential would also be influenced by the source of SPC purchase: suppliers from Eastern Europe may be expected to be cheaper than those from developed countries, while those from LDCs would be cheaper than both.

These hypotheses are tested by multiple regression analysis, with the ratio of private sector to SPC prices as the dependent variable, and the number of private sector suppliers (PSS), the number of SPC bids (SPC), a dummy variable for SPC purchases from Eastern Europe (EE), and a dummy variable for purchases from LDCs (LDC) as the independent variables. We expect the dependent variable to be negatively related to PSS, and positively to the other factors. The results are set out in Table 8.2.

TABLE 8.2 Influences on ratio of private to SPC prices for 35 drug imports

Equation	Constant	PSS	SPC	EE	LDC	Corrected R^2
1	224.4	−30.2[a]	6.38[c]	139.9[c]	289.8[a]	0.26
	(3.02)	(−2.48)	(1.30)	(1.46)	(3.02)	
2	350.3	−30.7[b]	7.19[c]			0.09
	(1.36)	(−2.29)	(1.36)			
3	426.7	−17.7[b]				0.07
	(1.86)	(−1.86)				
4	282.7	−18.9[b]		164.3[b]	296.9[a]	0.24
	(3.07)	(− 2.19)		(1.73)	(2.07)	

Figures in parentheses give t values.
NOTES
Levels of significance (one-tail test) are indicated: [a] = significant at 1%, [b] = significant at 5%, [c] = significant at 10%.

The results of the regressions serve to confirm expectations. None of the equations has a high R^2, with the best one explaining only 26 per cent of the variation in the dependent. This supports the argument of preceding sections that pharmaceutical markets contain a large element of market power which is not eliminated by competitive forces. Competition does, however, exercise some influence on prices. The variable PSS is always negatively related to price differentials, as expected, and is always significant at the 1 and 5 per cent levels. While its independent explanatory power is rather low, it does testify to the effect of oligopolistic competition in free markets.

The variable SPC has the correct sign and is significant at the 10 per cent level in equations 1 and 2. However, it exhibits some multicollinearity with PSS, and, when tried on its own, shows no significance at all. The number of potential suppliers is not, therefore, a strong influence on the savings that may be achieved by 'shopping around'. This may be because small bidders serve specialised markets at prices fairly near marginal cost, so that the *number* of bidders does not affect their prices significantly. It may also be due to the fact that in 1972 the tendering procedure of the SPC was very new and did not reach a sufficient number of potential suppliers. In subsequent years, as more firms came to learn of the SPC purchases and of each others' prices, the number of bids may have had a stronger effect on the final price. Furthermore, the SPC did not automatically accept the lowest bid submitted. In several cases the cheapest bid was rejected because of the risk of poor quality of the lack of independent information on the supplier's quality control procedures: thus, pure price competition was only one element in determining the SPC's savings, and the effect of the number of bids may have been correspondingly reduced.

The dummy variables for the source of SPC imports also exhibit the expected signs. LDC performs far better than EE, but both variables are significant and quite 'clean'. The coefficients confirm that price differentials are higher when purchases are made from LDCs (in Sri Lanka's case, mainly India) than from Eastern Europe, and also that Eastern Europe is cheaper than developed countries. Since the SPC ensured that its imports met necessary standards of quality and bioavailability, these figures demonstrate the capability of the more industrialised LDCs to supply cheaply a wide range of modern drugs.[17]

It may be noted that while the SPC relied in this early stage on imports of some multi-source drugs from the relatively expensive developed countries, it rapidly reduced these as it collected better data on the quality of other suppliers. By 1975 no such drugs were purchased from developed countries, and imports from TNCs were restricted to those advanced products on which they held an effective monopoly. The savings indicated by the 1972 figures thus only show the effects of the first round of regulation. Subsequent rounds led to even larger savings due to 'learning by doing', though the exact magnitude of these savings are difficult to calculate because of large price changes in 1973.[18]

The lessons of the Sri Lanka experience are clear. The existence of substantial market power in the pricing of drugs by large manufacturers is confirmed, and no support is found for the general case made by Reekie and the OHE that market forces lead, by themselves, to 'workable competition' in this industry. As far as pharmaceutical imports by LDCs are concerned, an unregulated market raises the cost of drug imports enormously over a situation where a buyer collects objective information on prices and qualities of drugs in international markets and economises accordingly. A free market does not seem to provide sufficient information for rational economic choice to be made, though it does exhibit signs of competition among the dominant firms. There appears to be a strong need for regulatory policies to strengthen competitive forces latent in pharmaceutical markets, and LDC governments would do well to study carefully the recent efforts of the FDA (and various European authorities) and the SPC to implement such policies.

APPENDIX

TABLE A.8.1 Price differentials in US antibiotic markets between small and large firms (1972)[a] (prices in US$)

	(1) Price	(2) Dominant Supplier Name	(3) Market Share %	(4) 5 Largest Average Price[b]	(5) Firms Market Share	(6) Lowest Available Price	(7) (1)/(6) %	(8) (4)/(6) %
1. Erythromycin	12.96	Abbott	46	9.91	80	5.70	227	174
2. Pottassium Penicillin	8.36	Squibb	(app. 78)[c]	5.40[d]	(over 90)	1.20	697	475
3. Penicillin VK	8.32	Lilly	52	7.21	88	1.85	450	390
4. Oxytetracycline	18.43	Pfizer	96			1–90	970	
5. Tetracycline	22.70	Squibb	35	22.52	86	4.12	551	547
6. Ampicillin	13.81	Bristol	24	10.62	72	4.40	314	241
7. Chloramphenicol	23.71	Parke-Davis	99			n.a.	app. 300	
8. Sulfoxazole	22.50	Roche	(n.a.)[e]	n.a.	n.a.	8.90	253	

SOURCE
Calculated from Brooke (1975), various tables.

[a] The 'average transaction price' for the main dosage form of the drug is used; the figures on market shares are also calculated for the main dosage form only.
[b] Simple average of transaction prices.
[c] Market share of main dosage form not available, so market share of Squibb for the total potassium penicillin market used.
[d] Two firms only.
[e] Exact market share not available, but Roche is known to be the dominant seller.

TABLE A.8.2 Prices of 35 drugs imported by the private sector (Jan.–June 1972) and by the State Pharmaceuticals Corporation (July–Dec. 1972) Sri Lanka (US$)

Drug	Unit	Private Sector No. of Suppliers'	Private Sector Average Weighted	No. of Bidders	SPC Price	Origin of Supplier[a]	Ratio of Private Sector Price to SPC Price
A. *Antibiotics*							
1. Tetracycline Capsules 250 mg.	1000 Caps.	23	12.02	44	6.62	EE	1.82
2. Tetracycline Syrup	1000 ml.	12	3.72	29	2.02	DC (TNC)	1.84
3. Chloramphenicol Caps. 250 mg.	100 Caps.	12	10.50	41	7.53	EE	1.39
4. Chloramphenicol Syrup	1000 ml.	9	2.65	27	2.60	DC	1.02
5. Benzyl Penicillin 1 mµ.	100 v.	7	6.21	13	5.34	DC (TNC)	1.16
6. Pencillin V 125 mg	1000 Tabs.	4	6.05	21	5.31	DC (TNC)	1.14
7. Penicillin Syrup	1000 ml.	1	11.27	8	5.34	DC (TNC)	1.14
8. Procaine Penicillin (fort.)	100 v.	4	4.71	16	4.22	DC (TNC)	1.12
9. Ampicillin 125 mg.	100 Tabs.	1	7.99	16	2.56	DC (TNC)	3.12
10. Ampicillin 250 mg.	100 Caps.	2	7.52	24	3.43	EE	2.19
11. Benzathine Penicillin	100 v.	1	47.15	7	4.87	EE	9.68
12. Benzathine Penicillin (Fortified)	100 v.	2	28.48	7	5.07	EE	5.62
13. Streptomycin 1 g.	100 v.	7	6.80	14	4.57	EE	1.49
14. Streptomycin 5 g.	100 v.	3	23.79	11	15.22	EE	1.56
15. Erythromycin Suspension	1000 ml.	4	17.02	5	9.22	LDC	1.85
16. Erythromycin Tablets	100 Tabs.	3	11.89	16	3.90	DC (TNC)	3.05
17. Neomycin Tablets	1000 Tabs.	2	128.12	9	24.11	DC	5.31

B. Other Drugs

18. Phenformin Tablets	1000 Tabs.	1	20.88	5	15.93	DC
19. Phthalysulphathiazole Tabs.	1000 Tabs.	4	2.36	33	1.47	EE
20. Prednisolone Tabs.	1000 Tabs.	12	4.58	37	3.70	LDC
21. Diethylcarbamazine Tabs.	1000 Tabs.	10	2.28	22	1.03	LDC
22. Diethylcarbamazine Syrup	1000 ml.	2	3.40	3	1.79	LDC
23. Phenylbutazone 100 mg.	1000 Tabs.	5	6.97	36	0.83	LDC
24. Phenylbutazone 200 mg.	1000 Tabs.	8	12.93	36	1.93	LDC
25. Chloroquin Tabs.	1000 Tabs.	6	6.74	34	4.57	DC (TNC)
26. Metronidazole Tabs.	1000 Tabs.	5	27.51	21	3.58	LDC
27. Aspirin powder	1 kg.	2	1.46	12	0.81	EE
28. Aspirin Tablets	1000 Tabs.	7	1.38	32	0.51	EE
29. Promethazine 25 mg.	1000 Tabs.	3	6.25	21	1.34	LDC
30. Promethazine Syrup	1000 ml.	3	2.08	10	1.61	DC
31. Reserpine 0.1 mg.	1000 Tabs.	1	5.99	11	0.60	LDC
32. Chlorpromazine 25 mg.	1000 Tabs.	2	7.91	29	1.02	EE
33. Chlorpromazine Syrup	1000 ml.	2	3.31	10	0.60	LDC
34. Tolbutamide	1000 Tabs.	1	9.03	19	2.56	EE
35. Guanethidine	1000 Tabs.	1	34.05	4	9.39	LDC

1.31	
1.67	
1.24	
2.21	
1.90	
8.40	
6.70	
1.47	
7.68	
1.80	
2.71	
4.66	
1.29	
9.98	
7.75	
5.52	
3.53	
3.63	

SOURCE
Records of the State Pharmaceuticals Corporation, Sri Lanka.
[a] Shown as EE = Eastern Europe; DC = Developed non-socialist country (TNC indicates supplier is a large transnational company); LDC = Less developed country.

NOTES

1. The author is very grateful to the State Pharmaceutical Corporation of Sri Lanka, and especially to the late Professor S. Bibile, who was its Chairman until early 1977, for providing access to their records on pharmaceutical purchases.
2. The literature is too large to give adequate references here, but see the various US Senate hearings related to the drugs industry, as well as Schwartzman (1976), the Monopolies Commission (1973), Reekie (1975) and Lall (1975) for a representative sample.
3. See Lall (1975). Most of those recommendations were subsequently endorsed by the Non-Aligned Summit in Colombo in 1977, and a joint task force of WHO, UNIDO and UNCTAD is now seeking to implement them.
4. See Cooper (1967) and Slatter (1977).
5. For a clear exposition of these strategies see Slatter (1977).
6. OHE (1975).
7. OHE (1975) p. 26. Emphasis added.
8. Reekie (1977b), page 1. These points are made in Chapter 7.
9. Unfortunately, Reekie chooses to interpret my point about market power to mean that drug prices, once set, remain static, as Lall suggests' (Reekie, 1977b, p. 2). I have not suggested this. To quote, 'the pricing policies of the large drug firms are based on purely monopolistic principles of "what the market can bear"' (Chapter 7), and later, in cases where there is patent protection, advertising helps to promote the brand image and secure it for periods long after the protection has expired; in other words, it introduces a strong monopolistic element into what would otherwise be a more competitive market'.
10. The evidence was available to Reekie, since he quotes Schwartzman (1976) who discusses it in his section on antibiotics.
11. These prices are published prices, and usually differ from actual 'transaction prices' which are generally lower. Brooke discusses these various prices and the problems of estimating them; their differences do not affect the argument about the structure of any given set of prices.
12. For erythromycins, 'a statistically significant relationship was found between weighted transaction price and sales, that is the greater the transaction price, the greater the sales.' Brooke (1975) p. i. The r^2 was 0.63 and the 't' statistic 3.46 for this correlation.
13. Schwartzman (1976) p. 259.
14. On bioavailability see the OTA (1974) study. The latest findings are that bioavailability raises serious problems for only a few of several hundreds of drugs.
15. The Sri Lanka experience and procedures are described in detail in Bibile (1977) and Chapter 9 below.
16. The SPC was able to take over the total of private sector imports only by the end of 1973. Figures are available for drug purchases and prices until 1975, but because of sharp rises in world prices since 1973 these have not been used for comparison with private sector imports in 1972.
17. This lends empirical support for the general argument for co-operative

Prices and the International Pharmaceutical Industry 215

action on production and trade in pharmaceuticals between LDCs advanced in my (1975) study.
18. Figures on prices of purchases up to 1975.are, however, given in Bibile (1977), who also compares them to prices on bids submitted by some TNCs.

REFERENCES

Bibile, S. (1977), 'A Case Study of Pharmaceutical Policies in Sri Lanka', (Geneva: UNCTAD) TD/B/C.6/21.
Brooke, P. A. (1975), *Resistant Prices* (New York: Council on Economic Priorities).
Cooper, M. H. (1967), *Prices and Profits in the Pharmaceutical Industry* (Oxford: Pergamon Press).
Lall, S. (1975), 'Major issues in transfer of technology to developing countries: A case study of the pharmaceutical industry' (Geneva: UNCTAD) TD/B/C.6/4.
Monopolies Commission (1973), *Chlordiazepoxide and Diazepam* (London: HMSO).
OHE (1975), *The Canberra Hypothesis: The Economics of The Prescription Medicine Market* (London: Office of Health Economics).
OTA (1974), *Drug Bioequivalence – A Report of the OTA Bioequivalence Study Panel* (Washington DC: Office of Technology Assessment, US Government).
Reekie, W. D. (1975), *The Economics of the Pharmaceutical Industry* (London: Macmillan).
—— (1977a), *Pricing New Pharmaceutical Products* (London: Croom Helm).
—— (1977b), 'Price and quality competition in the United States drug industry', mimeo, *Journal of Industrial Economics* (Mar. 1978) pp 223–37.
Schwartzman, D. (1976), *Innovation in the Pharmaceutical Industry* (Baltimore: Johns Hopkins).
Slatter, S. St. P. (1977), *Competition and Marketing Strategies in the Pharmaceutical Industry* (London: Croom Helm).

9 The Political Economy of Controlling Transnationals: The Pharmaceutical Industry in Sri Lanka*

I INTRODUCTION

This paper attempts to analyse the experience of Sri Lanka in reforming the structure of production, importation and distribution of pharmaceuticals during the period 1972–76. Since the pharmaceutical industry is one of vital concern for every developing country, and since it is overwhelmingly dominated by transnational companies (TNCs) that possess considerable market power as well as proven ability to resist reform, such an analysis can serve two purposes.

First, it can help policy-makers in LDCs who wish to reform the industry by illustrating the sorts of difficulties, resistance and pressures they may expect to face, and the benefits that they may expect to achieve. The drug industry is one which has aroused considerable controversy in both the home and host countries of the TNCs which dominate it.[1] The US Senate, over about 18 intermittent years of hearings in various subcommittees, has produced volumes of criticism, evaluation and recommendation, on the basis of which the Food and Drug Administration (FDA) has set up a complex apparatus for controlling the introduction of new drugs, checking their effectiveness, regulating advertising and labelling and, most recently, reducing their cost to federally-financed health schemes (but not to the public). Other developed countries have also instituted controls of different degrees of intensity and comprehensiveness, though the dominant firms have, with the help of various groups, managed to thwart substantial reform. LDCs have not been able to successfully institute controls of the types used by advanced countries; and they have certainly not (with the exception of Sri Lanka) been able to achieve a complete rationalisation of the industry while retaining a basically capitalist system of production. A number of them have tried – Brazil, Pakistan, India, Turkey and others have undertaken or are proposing to undertake partial reforms – but have not yet achieved the desired result of providing effective and cheap medicines to meet the basic needs of their populations. We believe that the result is, with careful planning, achievable: the problem is *why* the effort is not undertaken. The Sri Lanka case throws light on this.

Second, it can further our understanding of the TNC phenomenon, in particular of the interaction between these giant firms and the various groups who are concerned with them in host LDCs. While a great deal has been written about the problems that TNCs raise and about the means that may be used to control them,[2] much of the discussion by 'conventional' economists has been conducted in a socio-political vacuum which abstracts from the conflict and compromise (or domination) between the interests involved. Many economists ignore the existence of rents arising from TNC operations about which bargaining can occur; even when they admit their existence, the game-theoretic approach generally used to analyse the process of distributing rents (with an enlightened government embodying a clearly defined 'national interest' on one side confronting a politically powerless TNC on the other) abstracts from crucial socio-political factors. It is mainly the 'political economists' who have tried to integrate economic, class, social and ideological factors in their analysis of TNC–LDC interplay. The attempts may not have always been successful – the theoretical constructs still need considerable refinement, and there is an unfortunate tendency to over-generalise from particular situations – but they have shown a much clearer grasp of the forces at work. The detailed analysis of one microcosm of the political economy of the TNC–host country conflict can certainly add to our limited knowledge of how such forces do work.

First, however, a word of caution: the experience of the drug industry in Sri Lanka should be generalised very carefully to other countries or other TNC-dominated industries. The small size of Sri Lanka's economy, its relative industrial backwardness coupled with relatively high degrees of literacy and political awareness, may, for instance, limit its relevance for large countries like Brazil, India or Pakistan or even small ones like Nepal. The peculiar nature of the drug industry, with its high technology and powerful promotional practices, its close relationship with the effective buyers (the medical profession) plus public and official sensitivity to its products, may similarly render it different from industries whose products are of less social importance and whose merits are more objectively assessable, or whose market power is easier to dilute. Despite this, however, we believe that some interesting and important lessons do emerge from the present case which are of general validity, especially as far as the formulation of health and pharmaceutical policies in LDCs is concerned.

Part II briefly gives the background to the reform of the pharmaceutical provision in Sri Lanka; Part III describes the main parties involved; Part IV deals with the actions of these various parties; Part V discusses the main achievements of the programme; and Part VI presents our conclusions. A postscript has been added later to describe developments in early 1977.

II THE BACKGROUND TO THE REFORM

Prior to the reforms undertaken in 1972, Sri Lanka had a structure of health delivery similar to that of most countries which do not have national health services or comprehensive insurance schemes.[3] There was a state sector, administered by the Department of Health, which ran hospitals and provided free medicines, and there was the rest, the private sector where drugs were provided by relatively unregulated local producers and importers. Although there were 14 firms which made drugs in the country, the bulk of their activity, which consisted of simple formulation and packaging of imported intermediate or finished pharmaceuticals, was concentrated on over-the-counter (OTC) or 'proprietary' drugs sold without prescription. The greatest part of 'ethical' or prescription drugs was directly imported into the country in finished form.

Imports for some 800 institutions in the state sector were handled by the Civil Medical Stores (CMS), while those for the private sector were undertaken by 134 local agents of foreign suppliers. The state sector was, till the end of the 1950s, subjected to the same exuberant promotion and product differentiation activity that the industry used in selling its products to the private sector,[4] and still uses in most LDCs where official control of promotion is relatively lax.[5] There were several thousand brands presented to the doctors, with the accompaniment of heavy advertising, distribution of samples and visits by detailmen. So great was the hold of promotion on information flows that prescribing doctors in Sri Lanka hospitals were often unaware of the generic names of the drugs they were using (and so of which drugs were equivalent in their effects)[6] and of the proper indications and contra-indications relevant to their use; certainly their practice showed an appalling lack of awareness of drug prices and the possibilities for economising on drug purchasing.

One of the present authors Dr Bibile, then Professor of Pharmacology at the University in Colombo, was asked to help the CMS rationalise drug prescribing. He advised the government to reduce the drugs used to the 500 (in 1000 presentations) that were actually needed and to publish a Hospitals' Formulary containing medicines by their proper generic names only, and with full and objective information on their use.[7] It was recommended that a Formulary Committee be appointed to prepare the Formulary and to review it every month, deleting obsolete or unnecessarily toxic drugs and introducing new drugs that had been proved effective. In 1959 the state sector was rationalised according to the advice given, but nothing was done about the private sector. Drugs were purchased and dispensed by generic names in the state system and the greatly reduced list proved over time not to have had any adverse effects on the hospitals' standards of medical care.

The 1960s witnessed a steady deterioration in Sri Lanka's balance-of-payments position. The government was compelled progressively to cut allocations of foreign exchange to both the CMS and the private sector. The CMS found, under this pressure, that it could economise on the purchase of the generic drugs in the Formulary by 'shopping around' on the world market and buying in bulk, rather than depending on the supplies and terms offered by its traditional TNC suppliers. The magnitude of savings was enormous, as we shall see later in the context of the rationalisation of the private sector; the experience gained by the CMS in this period was invaluable to the reforms that were to follow.

By 1963, the foreign exchange crisis had grown to such proportions that the Government decided to economise on the purchase of drugs in the private sector. Its first step was to reduce the number of drugs imported, a step taken in the belief that this would reduce the total cost of drugs purchased abroad. The 4000 drugs being used under a much larger number of brand names[8] were cut, on the recommendations of a Drugs Subcommittee headed by Dr N. D. W. Lionel, Associate Professor of Pharmacology, to 2100. No action was, however, taken to reduce the number of brands under which these could be sold and the proliferation of differentiated products continued as before. Thus, there were 23 brands of tetracycline capsules, 12 of chloramphenicol, 12 of tetracycline syrup, and 12 of prednisolone being imported: in every case there was a wide variation in the prices of generically identical medicines, *with the more expensive and more heavily promoted branded products dominating the market*.[9] Advertising continued unabated and the prices of imports remained unregulated: not surprisingly, savings on the total import of drugs turned out to be negligible.

From 1965 to 1970 the foreign exchange allocation for drugs was cut from a total of Rs. 33 million (Rs. 20m. for private and Rs. 13m. for CMS imports) to Rs. 24m. (Rs. 14m. and Rs. 10m. respectively). As population and medical needs had increased steadily, and prices had risen, over this period, the *per capita* supply of pharmaceuticals had declined drastically. The Prime Minister asked one of the present authors again to advise on the rationalisation of the structure, this time to encompass the entire country. A report entitled *The Management of Pharmaceuticals in Ceylon*[10] was produced in collaboration with a Member of Parliament. This report drew heavily upon the experience gained during the 12 years of operating a rationalised CMS list, and called on the expertise of a group of doctors, pharmacologists and clinical pharmacologists of the University of Sri Lanka. This expertise, drawn from an ambiance independent of the drug TNCs, proved to be of crucial significance in providing the complex of skills required to formulate and mount a comprehensive reform programme.

Before we come to the implementation, however, let us describe the main recommendations of the report:

First, it was recommended that all imports of processed pharmaceuticals and pharmaceutical chemicals be channelled through a state trading corporation. A comparison was made for prices of the 18 main categories of processed drugs (70 per cent of the c.i.f. value of private sector imports) with the prices that were being paid in 1969 for the same drugs by the CMS. It was found that the annual actual import bill of Rs. 11.7 million would have been merely Rs. 3.7 million,[11] *a saving of 68 per cent*, if the purchases had been made by a centralised agency taking advantage of the price differences in the international drug market and buying from economical sources in bulk. Prices of pharmaceutical chemicals were not compared, since the CMS did not deal with such imports, but it was assumed (rightly, as it turned out) that similar savings would be available here to a rational and informed buyer.

The second recommendation was to reduce the number of drugs imported and to amend patent laws (Sri Lanka offers strong patent protection in the form of product patents) in order to obtain newer drugs from the cheapest possible sources. It was noted that the University Departments of Pharmacology were already preparing both a rationalised list of drugs which would retain all the therapeutic properties of the previously imported drugs, as well as leaflets to inform prescribers of the proper use of the reduced list and to persuade them of the therapeutic efficacy and bio-equivalence of generic-named drugs.[12] The rationalisation and provision of objective information were to be extended to over-the-counter (OTC) drugs, where, it was noted, several ineffective, unnecessarily expensive, or 'irrationally' combined drugs were in common use.[13]

The third recommendation was to replace brand names by generic names in the sale and prescribing of medicines, and to stop the promotion of drugs by the manufacturers. The use of generic names would lead to better prescribing practices, while the provision of information on drugs from official sources only would remove the dangers and costs inherent in the extravagant promotional practices of the industry.[14] As there was already an official quarterly publication of the Formulary Committee, the *Formulary Notes*, in existence for precisely this purpose, it was recommended that it be upgraded, better financed and brought out more often.

Finally, the future development of local manufacture of pharmaceuticals was to be along lines laid down by the government. Local manufacturers would produce according to the rationalised drug list, use materials imported by the state trading corporation, and leave promotion and distribution to the state. If they proved recalcitrant, the government would have the power to nationalise them under the provisions of the Sri Lanka State Trading Corporation (Drugs) Act.

The report also contained a number of specific suggestions on where the older, commonly used drugs should be imported from (socialist countries of Eastern Europe), the training of pharmacists, improvement of quality-control procedures, and a restructuring of the CMS (which had suffered a drastic deterioration in their buying, storage and distribution procedures).

The Wickremasinghe and Bibile report set the stage for a complete overhaul of the system of drug provision in Sri Lanka. The government decided to establish the State Pharmaceuticals Corporation (SPC) of Sri Lanka, under the honorary chairmanship of one of the present authors, to enlarge the Formulary Committee and rename it the National Formulary Committee, and to hand over all drug importing and the bulk of distribution activities to the Corporation. Not all the recommendations noted above were implemented, and some proved more difficult to implement than had been envisaged. The industry protested strongly and made representations to the government, but by and large the rationalisation of the system was carried out; we shall come to its achievements and limitations later.

III THE MAIN ACTORS

We may identify six broad groups which were directly or indirectly concerned with drug provision in Sri Lanka, and which played a constructive or obstructive role in the implementation of the reform programme.

THE GOVERNMENT

Sri Lanka had at the time a government made up of a coalition of three left-wing parties. While certainly not unified in its objectives, the government had a strongly socialistic ideology. It had implemented land reforms, started several public sector industries, attempted to promote considerable equality of incomes and introduce welfare services, and was committed to a pattern of development of a primarily egalitarian nature. It was also a government in severe economic difficulties, which had two opposing effects: first, it made it much more willing to take measures to economise on pharmaceutical purchases along the lines described above; second, however, it made it more vulnerable to economic pressures from those opposed to the reform (in particular, the aid donor countries whose TNCs were threatened).

The government was, of course, neither monolithic in its structure nor fully consistent in its strategy. The very fact that it was a coalition meant that with the shifting fortunes of its constituent parties its ideological stand would shift, and so affect the political underpinnings of the entire policy. Since in any such policy a clear and strong political direction is absolutely vital, a change of direction could clearly weaken the implementation of difficult portions of the reform, leaving the lower sections of the government (the SPC at variance with the apex (the Prime Minister's office)). Until 1975, the Prime Minister fully supported her Minister of Industry and the SPC in their reform programmes, but with growing political problems and food shortages their paths diverged. The LSSP, the most radical party in the coalition, left the government; the PM moved, along with powerful sections of the government, distinctly

The Pharmaceutical Industry in Sri Lanka

to the right, accepted US food aid and backtracked slightly on her earlier strong stand on pharmaceutical reform. The Minister of Industry found it increasingly difficult to pursue his former strategy, and the SPC was obliged to compromise on some important elements of the programme as originally conceived (see below). Thus, the major achievements of the reform came in its early years; in later ones the momentum flagged perceptibly. The pace of reform had little to do with its objective merits — it was governed more by the course of power struggles at the apex.

LOCAL REFORMISTS OUTSIDE THE GOVERNMENT

These constituted the main intellectual, technical and organisational force behind the reform, and comprised a group of highly trained, well-placed, socialist academics and doctors, who could analyse the benefits of change, argue the case cogently and provide the technical expertise necessary to implement it. The combination of ideology and expertise with a socialist-minded government was, as long as government support was given, crucial. Many LDCs have the expertise and ideology but in disparate groups of people; others attempt reform at the wrong junctures. Then, depending on who is in power (or close to it), reform tends to be hasty and misconceived, or stalled by the machinery which is to implement it, or simply not undertaken (or reversed).[15]

THE DRUG INDUSTRY

It may be expected that the industry would be categorically opposed to reform. Not only would such rationalisation reduce the profitability of expensive branded products, it would set a bad example to other poor countries which were trying to get more medicines from very limited resources. It would, however, be misleading to consider the whole industry in this manner. There are several contradictory forces at work, and it is crucial to differentiate between them:

a. Local manufacturers

There are five large TNCs with subsidiaries operating formulation and packaging plants in Sri Lanka – Pfizer (USA), Glaxo (UK), Warner-Hudnut (USA), Unical (for Burroughs-Wellcome, UK) and Reckitt and Colman (UK) – which account for about 75 per cent of local drug production. Two local companies, producing under licence for TNCs, account for another 22 per cent. The remaining 7 producers are small local companies, generally producing preparations for skin application. It is clear that the TNC subsidiaries would be hostile both to the rationalisation of drug production and promotion (since over half their production consisted of elegantly packaged and heavily advertised minor remedies and vitamins of little therapeutic value to the majority of the population, who could not afford them), and to the channelling of imports of intermediate chemicals (which they previously imported from their principals at arbitrary prices) through the SPC. Clearly also, their hostility would be more virulent and effective the greater the support they could count on from their home government. The response of local firms would be more ambiguous. On the one hand, they would resent (especially the large firms operating under foreign licence) the interference of the SPC with their production and marketing decisions. On the other, they would welcome the cheapening of imports of intermediate chemicals, the provision of the technical expertise by the SPC, the protection given against foreign competition and the aid provided by the state to promote local enterprise. They may also be more susceptible to local ideological currents, and they may have a weaker base from which to resist any reform.

b. Foreign suppliers
Those TNCs which were previously selling high-priced patented and branded drugs would resent the reform, but they would not be able to apply anything but indirect pressure unless they found patent infringements and decided to risk a court action in Sri Lanka against a public corporation. Some TNCs are also competitive suppliers in generic markets, and in this context they would not lose from the change. (Some, like Roche, are both: Roche sells extremely expensive tranquillisers and very cheap vitamins). Smaller foreign companies in capitalist countries which sell by generic names, especially those which do not observe patent laws, would welcome the reform, as would the large public sector companies in socialist countries and developing countries like India and Egypt.

c. Local dealers
Those who, like detailmen, importers, and firm representatives, were dependent on the previous structure of the industry for a livelihood would be bitterly opposed to reform, unless they could be absorbed into the new structure or persuaded of its wider social benefits.

The Pharmaceutical Industry in Sri Lanka 225

LOCAL OPPONENTS OF REFORM

There are other interested groups, outside the industry itself, which would oppose reform. The most important of these would be the medical 'establishment' (the Sri Lanka Medical Association, SLMA) and the private medical profession, which received various direct (free samples and hospitality) and indirect (attractive advertising, easily digested information from detailmen) benefits from the drug companies' promotion, and which were convinced of the superior quality, efficacy and reliability of the branded products of the large manufacturers.[16] There are two, relatively minor, countervailing factors. First, a certain quantity of very common drugs are provided by doctors in Sri Lanka as part of the consultation fee, and doctors would welcome the lowering of cost for these drugs. Second, a few doctors would have a strong social conscience, or be aware of the criticisms of the industry voiced in the developed countries, to such an extent as to overcome the conditioning imposed by the industry's promotion.

Some opposition may also be expected from the consumers themselves, who have been used to brand names, or are persuaded by the advertising of OTC drugs, or are worried by the reduction in the number of medicines. Much of this opposition would tend to be concentrated in the ranks of the educated elite, who are conscious of branded and advertised drugs and who are able to afford them, but its effectiveness would, at least in the Sri Lanka case, be limited by the strength of the dominant ideology and the socialist commitment of the ruling sections of that elite. As the political climate changes, however, this factor may well prove to be of great significance: the next year or two will show the strength of the elite's resistance.

FOREIGN OPPONENTS OF REFORM

Since the TNCs as a group are likely to feel hurt and threatened by the reform and since they wield much more power than small firms, it is to be expected that their representative organisations and home governments will do what they can to oppose it. The power that they wield will depend on a number of factors: the extent of foreign investment (not just in the drug industry) already in the country, the expected inflow of direct investment and aid, and the involvement of the home country in the defense or support of the regime. The more is the LDC dependent upon the home country for aid, investment or military support, the more

226   *The Multinational Corporation*

pressure is the drug industry likely to be able to bring against drastic reform.

FOREIGN SUPPORTERS OF REFORM

These are, by their very nature, likely to be rather less powerful in most LDCs than the opponents. Those in the developed capitalist countries — reformist doctors or pharmacologists, charity organisations and even government bodies (like the FDA) — may give moral support and advice, but are unlikely to be able to influence their own governments if a real threat to foreign investments is perceived. Those in developed socialist countries can, of course, be more helpful in terms of selling drugs and providing technology, but they do not possess either the capital or the most advanced know-how of the TNCs, so that their support will be most valuable for countries in the first stages of pharmaceutical development and least for those with advanced pharmaceutical industries. For Sri Lanka, with hardly any local production, the socialist countries may be very useful; for India they may be less so. Thus, the former would be freer to implement reform than the latter.

These, then, are the various groups which have an interest in the pharmaceutical industry, and the reactions that we may plausibly expect them to have to a major reform. The outcome is clearly far from determinate. On the contrary, it depends upon a complex interplay of social, political and economic factors, and upon how these exercise their influence by means of ideology, persuasion, bargaining or straightforward domination. We can only scratch the surface of this complexity, but we do hope to illustrate something about the political economy of controlling TNCs in this area.

IV ACTIONS AND REACTIONS

Acting on the recommendations of the Wickremasinghe and Bibile report, the government set up the State Pharmaceuticals Corporation in 1971. It was initially empowered to import processed pharmaceuticals for the private sector, and later also for the CMS, but the patent law was not changed. The SPC was also permitted to import some intermediate chemicals for local manufacturers on a negotiated basis. The principle of changing from brand to generic names was accepted. The promotion of drugs by manufacturers ceased except for the relatively small proportion

The Pharmaceutical Industry in Sri Lanka

of the market for OTC drugs which were manufactured locally and sold through the existing retail network.

The process of reform may be best examined in terms of four major issues: the centralised purchase of a rationalised list of finished drugs; the purchase of intermediate chemicals for local manufacture; the non-observance of patents; and the change from brand to generic names, with the accompanying problems of quality control, bio-equivalence and provision of independent information.

CENTRALISED PURCHASE OF RATIONALISED LIST

The SPC was faced with two immediate major tasks. The first was to reduce the several thousand brands of the 2100 drugs being imported to a reasonable number without losing in therapeutic efficacy; the second was to undertake the task of buying drugs of adequate quality economically on world markets, replacing the 134 private importers which had previously done this.

The National Formulary Committee was entrusted with the task of rationalising the drug list for the private sector along the lines which had been used for the state sector in 1959. Three main criteria were used: (a) the deletion of imitative drugs which added nothing to the therapeutic value of particular drugs that were to be chosen on the basis of economy; (b) the deletion of a large number of 'irrational' fixed combination drugs (similar to the FDA's action in the USA) where good practice required the flexible use of single drugs; and (c) the deletion of drugs without clear therapeutic value or with high toxicity.[17] The number of drugs was reduced from 2100 to 600 (further reductions are being considered); since brand names were almost entirely (but not completely, as we shall see) abolished, the profusion of brands practically disappeared; drug prices (again, see below) were greatly reduced, and there is no evidence that health services were harmed in any way at all.

The main initiators of the rationalisation of the drug list were academic pharmacologists and clinicians. It was clear to them, from their study and experience, that such a reduced list was conducive to better prescribing and to economising on purchase. The main opponents of the reduction were the medical establishment, the local drug companies and their dependents, private importers and, in a few cases, the final consumers. Some doctors complained of interference with their professional judgement,[18] the drug companies and importers of the loss of therapeutically desirable drugs and the consumers of the loss of familiar brands. The tactics of the opposition ranged from publishing several adverse reports in the press and direct representations to the government to organising 'symposia' of opponents and the stirring up of popular resentment by rumour and insinuation (powerful weapons on a small island). There was little attempt to produce scientific evidence for opposing particular deletions (many went uncontested); but over the years a great deal of heat was generated by doctors and drug representatives about the restricted drug list and the activities of the SPC.

There were two ways of effecting a compromise on the rationalised list. The most important was to induct leading private practitioners into the National Formulary Committee and make them a responsible party to the decision-making process. In the Committee they could be exposed to scientific evidence based on clinical trials and the findings of other countries; the conflict would be localised and partly shorn of its emotional trappings; and the doctors outside would have a much weaker case to argue. The second was simply to give in on drugs where feeling ran exceptionally high,[19] in exchange for deleting drugs where this was more acceptable. As time passed and the doctors got used to working with the reduced list without obvious detriment to health care, the process of rationalisation became somewhat easier. However, with the departure of the LSSP from the government in 1975 and the weakening of government support for the SPC's reforms, criticism also grew more strident where vested interests were concerned. The local representatives of TNCs voiced more open protest in the newspapers, and doctors were able to force more concessions on the retention of particular branded drug imports from the Formulary Committee. The progress of rationalisation, while not reversed, was certainly slowed down in 1976; the battle is still being waged and the final outcome will depend on political developments in 1977 and thereafter. (see Postscript, p. 000).

The second immediate task of the SPC was to replace the private import system for finished pharmaceuticals. This clearly needed a great deal of careful planning, quality checks, inventory control, and so on, before implementation. The SPC studied the pattern of private sector imports for 6 months in 1972, and started by taking over the imports of about one-third of these imports. This proportion was increased as the SPC gained experience, and by the end of 1973 it had taken over total imports.

Since the purpose of the exercise was to economise without compromising on quality or therapeutic benefits, the SPC had to take the following factors into account: first, some drugs were so new that they were effectively monopolised by the innovator; on these, termed 'monopoly quotations' (about 26 per cent in terms of value in 1973 and 22 per cent in 1975) the SPC could only bargain for better terms – but from a weak position – until such time as a competitor (usually a non-patent observing firm) appeared and offered the drug more cheaply at satisfactory quality. Second, on older drugs price quotations could be obtained from a number of producers throughout the world. The maintenance of quality required that any small, generic drug producer considered seriously had to provide a certificate of quality plus an independent certificate of quality from a reliable laboratory (such as the Haffkine Institute in India), agent (such as the General Superintendence Company of Geneva for some East European purchases), or official body (such as the PARCOST programme in the province of Ontario in Canada). It was only after such certification that a low price bid would be accepted. The saving to the country of 'shopping around' and obtaining better information about market conditions was usually substantial, as we shall see in Section V. Third, in some cases, traditional TNC suppliers or other TNCs would themselves quote the best prices, substantially reducing the price they had charged before. There was, in other words, a distinct benefit to be gained from bargaining apart from simply 'shopping around'. This benefit also applied to some traditional East European suppliers, and not just TNCs; recourse to public sector firms clearly does not obviate the necessity of acting as a 'rational' consumer.

We shall not go into the detailed procedures for tendering, control of ordering and shipping, storage, and so on, which are fascinating but not relevant to the present discussion. Let us merely note two points of interest in passing. First, hardly any drugs were purchased from Italy, the best known source of cheap drugs (because it does not observe patents on drugs), simply because the SPC did not have information on the manufacturing practices of the cheaper generic producers who quoted on tender.[20] Second, the tendering system was far from ideal. Small manufacturers in the US for instance, never submitted bids, in part because they were not aware of the tenders, and in part because they prefer to bid anonymously for tenders channelled through their trade association (quite separate from the US Pharmaceutical Manufacturers' Association (PMA) which represents the TNCs) rather than openly under their own names, because of fear of commercial retaliation by the big TNCs which are also important customers.[21]

Resistance to the SPC buying procedures came from several sources. First, the TNCs themselves, finding the very basis of their oligopolistic pricing and profitability cut, mounted a campaign to persuade the government and the doctors to reject low-price drugs. In a letter to the Prime Minister, Joseph Stetler; President of the US PMA (the TNCs' association), argued forcefully against various aspects of the reform programme. The letter was delivered to the Sri Lanka ambassador in Washington and transmitted to the Prime Minister and to several Ministries concerned. We shall quote from this letter as the occasion arises; let us first see what Stetler has to say, with the full weight of authority of the US drug TNCs, about buying drugs economically in the world markets:

> The restraints and prohibitions placed on the industry, and particularly affecting the world-wide, research-based major producers, who not only inhibit the growth of an indigenous pharmaceutical manufacturing base in Sri Lanka, but would also have a number of corollary consequences. Some that might be anticipated are:
> 1. World-wide tender purchasing by SPC does not guarantee availability of drugs or raw materials, their availability at the time of pricing desired by SPC, or assurance that they would be, in fact, less expensive than those available to companies.
> 2. Those companies having high investments in research and development and quality control would be discouraged from bidding; sources without such expenses or quality control standards would more likely submit low bids . . .
> 3. Finally, the action calls in question the Government's position with respect to all foreign investment in Sri Lanka.[22]

The arguments sound persuasive, and the veiled threat of point 3 rather formidable. Yet events have proved the first two point completely wrong. World-wide tendering was shown to be amenable to strict quality, standards, inventory and forecasting control, and very much cheaper than the previous 'free' system. Research-based TNCs showed no aversion to bidding; many of them continued to submit high-cost bids up to 1976 in spite of never winning a tender for commonly available drugs. When they were asked to quote prices for the new drugs on which they had effective monopoly, they were as willing to supply the SPC as they had been to private importers. One is, then, left wondering at the veracity of Stetler's claim, in his concluding paragraph (p. 6) to be concerned with the effects 'not only on the pharmaceutical industry and on all private industry in Sri Lanka, but potentially for the health of all its citizens'.

There was, of course, very little 'muscle' to back up the PMA's threats, since the US had relatively few investments in Sri Lanka, and the TNCs themselves had no intention of boycotting the SPC. Other developed countries did not even raise an official murmur. However, the industry could wield more pressure *within* the country, through their importers and salesmen. A widespread and insidious campaign of denigrating low-cost suppliers was launched. And a second source of oppositon, the private practitioners, were drawn into the campaign. Reports were made of drugs being ineffective, substandard or toxic, but little hard evidence was produced. The SPC always checked on the quality of the drugs reported to be faulty, and in cases where such defects as unsatisfactory sugar coating, poor labelling, inappropriate ointment base, etc., were found the products were immediately recalled and replaced. In some, relatively rare, cases, where the manufacturing firm was thought to be negligent, it was 'blacklisted' and barred from tendering. The important point to note is that there is *always* a risk of particular batches of drugs being defective, even with the strict controls exercised in, say, the USA. The evidence from the US does not support claims that large manufacturers have a better record on drug 'recalls' than small generic manufacturers. To quote the FDA on its recalls in 1974 and 1975:

> The list [of 124 recalls] reveals the names of many large and small manufacturers, and the agency is unable to conclude from this list that there is any clear difference between these two groups based on recalls.[23]

In Sri Lanka also, recalls featured large firms (e.g. Roche's tetracycline or Burroughs-Wellcome's malt syrup) as well as small ones. The medical establishment, however, seized upon and publicised the latter, while keeping silent about the former. The distrust by doctors of lower-price, unbranded drugs is a universal phenomenon, and, indeed, is one of the main fruits of the expensive promotion undertaken by the big firms.[24] This is what accounts for the latter's products continuing to fetch far higher prices than those of small firms, even when there is no scientific basis to differentiate between them, or when, as in some cases, they are identical products with different labels. The reaction in Sri Lanka was, therefore, entirely to be expected. There is no easy way to counteract the hostility, and it still continues among sections of the medical profession. Some progress was, however, achieved by two methods. First, doctors were sent literature based on clinical and recall evidence to persuade them that cheaper drugs were not necessarily bad.

While such 're-education' was bound to be slow, it did show some success especially among younger doctors. Second, a few high price drugs were permitted to be sold alongside much cheaper equivalents, and patients were found to switch to the latter in the course of a year or so. When the cheap product was found equally effective, demand for the other gradually, disappeared, and it could be removed without protest.

LOCAL MANUFACTURE

The reform of finished drug imports proved far easier than that of buying pharmaceutical chemicals for local manufacturers. It had been one of the original purposes of setting up the SPC to economise on the cost of importing bulk chemicals as well as finished drugs. In April 1973 the SPC prepared a '34 drug programme' where a limited start would be made with 34 (of a total of 225) locally-formulated drugs where the chemicals would be imported on the basis of world-wide tenders by the Corporation. Where, however, the manufacturer was already buying materials at prices comparable to the best SPC tenders, it would be allowed to continue as before; for instance, one local firm was buying vitamin raw materials from Roche, the cheapest supplier, and carried on doing so; other producers were made to follow suit. The programme aimed:

a. to increase the local processing of drugs,
b. to reduce the cost of imported chemicals, saving an estimated Rs. 3 million out of Rs. 9 million on the 34 drugs, and
c. to work existing factories, which were running at well below capacity, at full capacity and in two shifts.[25]

The 7 small local producers responded favourably; the 5 TNC subsidiaries, however, showed resistance. Initially, they simply refused to respond, until in December 1973 the Director, Regulation of Industries, issued a stiff warning. Glaxo then accepted the Programme in principle, but the others did not. In may 1974, after further pressure and more warnings from the Ministers of Finance, Industries and Scientific Affairs, and Health, two other TNCs (Reckitt and Colman and Unical), agreed to cooperate. Pfizer held out a little longer, but then followed the others in agreeing to the programme in principle. Agreement in principle was, however, quite a different matter from cooperation in practice. Four of the TNCs started a further series of delaying manouevres, asking for further discussions, clarification and changes.

As a result, Unical tabletting capacity, which is 90 million a year in one shift, is lying idle; Reckitt and Colman, which has a 165 million tabletting capacity a year is making only 45 million tablets, and not making the 90 million tablets of Aspirin required in the SPC programme. Recently the SPC made an urgent appeal to Pfizer to make Tetracycline capsules required in the cholera epidemic and offered quality tested raw materials and capsules. Pfizer delayed, raising one query after another, as is usual with them. The urgency of the situation has not concerned them in the least.[26]

By 1975, only 14 of the 34 drugs were being produced according to the programme. The situation had improved slightly by the end of 1976, but *Pfizer was still refusing to use material imported by the SPC*, Glaxo had just agreed to start producing 7 drugs, and the other TNCs had not yet launched into actual manufacture with SPC materials. The final outcome of the battle, especially with Pfizer, is still unclear, but its refusal and stalling have enabled it to hold out for over three and a half years against a host government's clear intent and policy.

Two questions then arise: why did Pfizer hold out? And how did it manage to get away with it?

The 'why' is easily answered. Pfizer was buying tetracycline from its parent at a c.i.f. price of $99 per kilo, when raw material of equivalent quality was being offered by Hoechst (an even bigger transnational) to the SPC at $20 per kilo: a classic example of transfer-pricing behaviour, where the usual defense used by TNCs, in terms of quality (Hoechst could hardly be accused of poor quality products), or of reaping a return on R & D (the drug has long been out of patent and is technologically well-diffused) would not possibly be justified. Glaxo was engaged in an identical practice: its chlorpheniramine imports cost $411 per kilo from the parent firm and $53 from Halewood (a small British firm).

The 'how' is more complicated. The initial stalling and resistance of TNCs was to be expected in the nature of things. It may also have been expected that the UK firms would, in the absence of outside support, ultimately accede to the demands of the host government. The fact that the one large US TNC held out may be traced to two factors. The first and apparently determining one was pressure brought by the US government to protect Pfizer. By the end of 1974 the SPC, with the strong support of the Minister of Industries, was recommending nationalisation of Pfizer to ensure its compliance. The reaction of the US was swift, and, as it turns out, decisive in preventing such a measure. The US Ambassador personally intervened with the Prime Minister in the matter, and, while we can only speculate as to the nature of his intervention, the dependence of Sri Lanka on US aid (food aid had just become crucially important at the time) may have figured largely. The Chairman of the SPC was ordered to 'continue negotiating' with Pfizer; no further disciplinary action was taken. Pfizer is still holding out in the hope that the forthcoming elections (mid–1977) will bring a government which is more 'reasonable' about its pricing arrangements with its parent company. In the interim, of course, the government's move to the right has strengthened the TNC's resolve to minimise their compliance with the 34-drug programme, and there is a real danger that the whole plan may be emasculated by a leadership unwilling to take the necessary political measures to discipline TNCs.

The second factor, perhaps a minor one, affecting Pfizer's attitude may have been the tough line taken by the US PMA. In his letter to the Prime Minister, Stetler argued strongly against channelling raw materials through a state agency. To quote,

> We submit that it is entirely inconsistent with the drug manufacturer's responsibility [for quality] to withhold from it the right to select its source of supply for raw and partially finished materials (p. 3) [and later, point 3 of the list quoted above]. Inconsistency in source of raw material for any given drug would produce a wide range of medical and therapeutic problems, as well as production, sampling and testing difficulties (p. 5).

While the second point is valid if the raw materials were indeed of poor or variable quality, the stress laid on bio-availability – which we come to later – is almost certainly misleading. The familiar bogey-man of the drug TNCs' promotion – the poor quality, cheap, small supplier – keeps reappearing in different guises, and no amount of evidence to the contrary makes him go away. Pfizer and tetracycline provide a perfect example; the quality of materials was in fact one of the main delaying devices used by the firm in its refusal to use the Hoechst chemicals.

Stetler goes on to argue (point 4),

> With companies reduced to a service operation [i.e. not choosing their own raw materials], the flow of information concerning new technology and scientific development through the private sector would be impaired or cut off.

This deserves to be taken more seriously. While various TNCs have quoted for raw material tenders (see Section V), and this represents the sale of 'embodied' technology produced by pharmaceutical R & D, there may exist a distinct problem concerning the transfer of new technology to set up new plants for drug production. The problem is not, however, very pressing for Sri Lanka. The SPC is considering setting up a plant for formulating sterile products, and has received several offers for the supply of technology. Of these, one of the most attractive seems to be from Indian Drugs and Pharmaceuticals Limited, an enormous and highly sophisticated public sector manufacturer. No equity participation is demanded; the turn-key job will be done on a cost-and-commission basis. Whatever the merits of this offer, it certainly does not seem that the reform programme has set back the country's industrialisation process in the slightest.

But a word of caution: Sri Lanka is just starting on drug manufacture, and technology is relatively easily available at this stage. The cooperation of TNCs may be more of a constraint to countries at the level of, say, India or Mexico. These countries should consider Stetler's warning seriously, and explore alternative sources of technology from developed capitalist countries, socialist countries and other LDCs, before launching on a programme which antagonises TNCs. The solution to aim at would be not to accede to TNCs' desire for a 'free' market but to create conditions in which suitably regulated local enterprises could buy technology for appropriate fees from TNCs.

PATENTS

In spite of the recommendations of Wickremasinghe and Bibile, the government did nothing to amend the strong patent protection that it offers to drug processes and products. The SPC decided, however, to buy patented drugs from non-patent observing sources. Propranolol, patented by ICI, was available from Polfa (Poland) at $7.6 thousand instead of $27.3 thousand from the patent holder for the quantity needed by Sri Lanka, a saving of 72 per cent. Diazepam, patented by Roche, was available from Ranbaxy (India) for less than $200 when the TNC quoted $7760 a saving of 97 per cent (this was an extreme case, but savings were always substantial).

The patent holders (e.g. ICI and Roche) realised, of course, that patent laws were not being observed and have sent warning letters to the SPC which were forwarded to the Minister of Industries, but none of them has yet taken the SPC to court. TNCs are generally aggressive litigants when patents are threatened; however, the prospect of fighting a state corporation in a socialist-minded regime clearly did not appeal to them. If the regime changes, there may well be a spate of infringement cases. However, Argentina provides an interesting parallel. In 1970 a Supreme Court decision ruled that a local firm which imported a patented (Cyanamid) chemical from Italy was acting in the public interest.[27] The law in Argentina was not changed, but the precedent set allowed several other local firms to break the legal monopoly and import drugs at a fraction of the previous cost. The TNCs involved are dragging their feet about suing – a similar outcome is possible in Sri Lanka.

The patent issue is a highly sensitive one for the pharmaceutical industry. It is one of the few major industries which depends on patents for effectively guarding its technological innovations, and which is in the forefront of all battles to strengthen and extend patent monopolies. However, while it is clear that the TNCs need patents to reap and overall reward from their expensive and risky R & D, it is far from clear what benefit a small developing country receives from offering patent protection. It certainly pays much higher prices than it needs to: every new drug has effective competitors from non-patent observing bases in three to four years, and a world-wide buying service can save enormous sums by scouting and shopping around. What does it gain? Stetler answers forcefully:

> Such protections [on patents and trademarks] provide a major incentive for producers to make new medicines available to smaller markets, such as Sri Lanka, where product exclusivity is a compensation for low *per capita* income and a variety of business risks which otherwise would make the market unattractive. Patent protection is a strong inducement, not only for direct investment, but for the transfer of technology and know-how licenses. . . . The major international trend is to strengthen rather than weaken patents and industrial property protection (p. 4).

As with his other arguments, this is a mixture of half-truths and exaggerations. First, there is no evidence that Sri Lanka would be unable to get the latest medicines if it did not offer patent protection. Second, there is no evidence that non-observance of pharmaceutical patents inhibits the inflow of capital or technology: neither Brazil nor Italy have patents on drugs, yet in both cases the TNCs have been investing heavily, buying up local firms, and selling their latest products.[28] Third, there are several exceptions to the 'major international trend' Stetler describes: India has weakened drug patents considerably, as has

Argentina; Brazil has abolished them; UNCTAD is negotiating major revisions to the Paris Convention.

Stetler does not mention the main general reason for retaining drug patents: to promote innovation. But he clearly realises the futility of making this point to a country which constitutes a minuscule portion of world drug markets. It is doubtful, in fact, whether this argument would even apply to *all* LDCs taken together for a large part of drug innovation which is aimed at 'rich man's diseases' (like cancer, heart and psychotropic illnesses), and for which LDCs constitute less than 10–15 per cent of world sales. For innovation directed specifically at tropical diseases, of course, some form of guaranteed returns would be needed, but a system of universal patents for drugs does not seem to be the best from the LDCs' point of view.[29]

The increasing tendency in LDCs to weaken the application of patent laws on drugs has worried TNCs (even the Canadian government has loosened the laws somewhat). But it is not an issue, as opposed to a threat to direct investments, on which their home governments can act directly. Moreover, even TNCs are prepared to accept a few aberrations as long as they are allowed to operate freely in other ways, and so retain their market dominance and profitability. In the longer run, therefore, the counter-attack will probably concentrate on other elements of the reform, on the marketing side, rather than on the patent issue.

BRAND AND GENERIC NAMES, QUALITY, BIO-EQUIVALENCE AND INFORMATION

The mechanism of promotion and marketing in the drug industry is at the heart of the market power exercised by the large firms, and so must be the core of a programme to lower their prices. The profitability of the TNCs depends on their ability to introduce 'new' drugs – genuine innovations, duplicates or combinations – and to impress brand names upon doctors' consciousness and persuade them of the superior performance and quality of their products. So rapid has been the growth of introduction of 'new' drugs, so powerful the promotion system of the large companies, and so close the relationship built up with the medical profession that in most countries doctors are virtually dependent on the firms themselves for information about new therapies, are unaware of the economics of prescribing, and are convinced of the superiority of branded products. The situation is rather worse in LDCs than in developed countries. In the latter, consumerism, the growth of official concern and a better awareness on the part of doctors has provided a weak but growing contervailing force. In LDCs, belief in international brand names is stronger, official attempts to provide objective information weaker, and consumerism still nascent.

Reform of the marketing system requires tackling two distinct problems: first, ensuring that the cheaper generic products are of adequate quality and that they are biologically equivalent to the branded products of the TNCs; and, second, that the change from brand to generic names is accepted by prescribers, who are provided information on the proper use of drugs by means other than private brand promotion.

We have already commented on quality in an earlier section. Let us touch on it again briefly and illustrate how the bio-equivalence issue (see note 14) was used to hamper the SPC's programme. While the SPC undertook every feasible measure to ensure that drug imports were of adequate quality, the industry tried to prevent the acceptance of these drugs by claiming that cheap generic drugs were not 'bio-equivalent' with expensive branded products, i.e. that the generic producers' alleged lack of stringent quality control rendered their products therapeutically less effective or ineffective even if they met the chemical requirements laid down for the relevant drugs.[30] Doctors are, as we have noted, predisposed to believe this on the basis of the scantiest evidence, and the TNCs did their best to strengthen their belief: two examples will suffice to show the nature of the problem.

First, it was noted by late 1976 that:

> The prevailing impression among many doctors in Sri Lanka is that tetracycline supplied by the SPC is either ineffective or not as effective as it used to be when this drug was imported by the private sector. As a result some doctors even administer double the usual dose of this drug in an attempt to control bacterial infections. . . . [Locally capsulated tetracycline imported from Hoechst] was tested before it was capsulated and tested again after capsulating (by the Drugs Quality Control Laboratory of the Ministry of Health) before it was released on the market. Even so the SPC received complaints of clinical inefficacy of tetracycline although none of the complaints were accompanied by any evidence.[31]

A detailed examination by a bacteriologist at the General Hospital Colombo found that the problem lay not with the quality of the drug but with its serious over-use for minor ailments which had led to resistance to the drug. The bacteriologist commented that

The problem of drug resistant strains of staphylococci is a worldwide problem and develops because of the widespread use of antibiotics and the abuse of antibiotics. Our figures may be higher than in other countries since tetracycline is freely prescribed by all Government Medical Officers, by General Practitioners and Ayurvedic Practitioners.[32]

Doctors were placing the blame for their predilection to prescribe antibiotics freely, even for the common cold, on the buying policies of the SPC, despite the fact that in most developed countries such over-use had been widely recognised as a cause of the drug's reduced effectiveness.

Second, the industry resorted to more overt attacks on the SPC. One instance, of many similar ones, is as follows. On 11 September 1973, Mr C. Ponnalagan, a local representative of one of the drug TNCs, published a letter in the *Ceylon Daily News* arguing that, as the FDA in the United States had recalled a certain batch of generic oxytetracycline for not producing the desired blood levels, branded products of 'reputed manufacturers' were more reliable and should be purchased even if they were more expensive. He also asserted that 'most of the drugs imported [by the SPC] are not even tested for their chemical equivalency'.

The argument was misleading, and the assertion was simply wrong. As the Chairman of the SPC pointed out in the same paper the next day (and as we have noted above), drug recall data from the US did *not* support a claim that small generic producers were more prone to recalls than large brand-named producers. The SPC did not import any drugs that did not carry quality certificates from abroad, and also tested imports locally in the Ministry of Health's Quality Control Laboratory. Bio-equivalence *was* a problem, *but only for 25 drugs on the rationalised import list*. These were imported from traditional sources until bio-equivalence testing could establish the equivalence of cheaper suppliers. Despite these assurances and scientific evidence, however, *criticisms and distrust of generic drugs continue to this day*.

Bio-equivalence is a problem that plagues reform programmes everywhere, and TNCs constantly harp upon it to prevent a major change taking place. Stetler argued that:

It is now widely accepted, on the basis of chemical and other analytical tests, that the assumption of therapeutic equivalency in medicines is unsupportable.... The conclusion, we submit, is that 'generic equivalency' in medicines is a misconception which has now been refuted (p. 3).

If this were indeed so, a buyer would have no option but to continue to depend on large TNCs with products of proven efficacy. But is it? As with his other arguments, Stetler stretches the evidence to defend the *status quo*.

Where very careful and detailed tests are not utilised, it is true that for certain drugs chemically identical products may produce different bio-availability. Different bio-availability may or may not indicate therapeutic inequivalence – only trials can establish this. Moreover, the number of drugs where non-equivalence constitutes a therapeutic problem is small. The last test of the FDA (which can hardly be faulted for lack of exhaustive study – in fact, Stetler quotes a former FDA authority) have narrowed the list to 24, and the Office of Technology Assessment notes that here the methodology and experimental procedures required for bio-equivalence studies for these are available.[33] For other drugs, 'drug products meeting the standards and falling into categories for which evidence of equivalent bio-availability is not essential *can be considered as interchangeable and listed as such. . . .*'[34]

What Stetler and the industry are attempting to do is to confuse the government (and the medical profession) with half-truths conveyed in scientific jargon which no one but a trained pharmacologist could evaluate. Drug TNCs try very hard to establish generic inequivalence, and are sometimes not above manufacturing the evidence. To quote one example,

> In 1968, *JAMA* published an editorial critical of generic products. That same issue contained an article on the generic formulation of the antidiabetic drug tolbutamide. The generic product was compounded with less than the standard amount of agent and the article claimed that the generic formulation was far less effective than the tolbutamide marketed by Upjohn under the name Orinase. The paper, entitled 'The Generic Inequivalence of Drugs', was written by a member of the Upjohn staff. The inferior product had never been marketed, had never been proposed for clinical use, and had been developed for this article by the Upjohn laboratory.[35]

Bio-availability is a problem that requires expert understanding and exhaustive scientific testing, but it does *not* raise fundamental barriers to a rationalisation programme: What better evidence than that the FDA is launching (in the face of fierce opposition from the big drug firms) its Maximum Allowable Cost (MAC) programme to promote generic purchasing by government-financed health programmes in the US? In the Sri Lanka context, however, it is clear that the reform programme would have encountered insuperable difficulties if it had not been directed by experts with the relevant knowledge to counter the propaganda of the TNCs and the entrenched prejudice of the doctors. If bio-availability had not been checked for, and the results not made known, even on a few drugs, the whole programme may have been jeopardised. Doctors, being generally suspicious of the reform, would have raised much stronger protest than they did. Consumers would have joined them, and the TNCs would have been back in business.

The efforts of the FDA to establish drug interchangeability and reduce the cost of its own health programmes proved crucial in providing the example, techniques and findings necessary to the rationalisation in Sri Lanka. The 'openness' of the American system, with its detailed published accounts of the operations of the drug industry, and of the results FDA's exhaustive clinical and scientific tests, thus bore (unlikely) fruit in Sri Lanka. The FDA is by instinct sympathetic to attempts like this one, and potential reformers may do well to draw upon its experience. It would, however, be interesting to see whether it would be willing, and able, to provide positive and explicit support for reform in the face of opposition from US-based TNCs.

The change from brand to generic names faces other problems.[36] Patients have a strong belief in well-known brand names, not just for OTC drugs but also for prescription drugs with which they have become familiar. In a few cases, the demand for particular brands was so entrenched in Sri Lanka that the SPC had to give in, even when much cheaper generic substitutes were available. The strategy of the SPC was then, as noted previously, to sell both products at their respective prices, and let economic rationality win out over a period of time. This strategy seems to have been fairly successful.

Patients were the lesser problem. Doctors had become so used to prescribing by brand name that they were unaware of the generic names of several drugs. The change in their habits thus had to be gradual and had to be accompanied by a minor process of re-education. The SPC provided cross-reference lists of brand and generic names to doctors. For old drugs the changeover was relatively easy, since generic names had become more familiar as a number of competing brands had emerged. For newer drugs it took longer; in the interim the SPC permitted brand names on the packages but displayed less prominently (in half the size) than the generic names. As the traditional sources of supply were replaced, and as the prescribing habits changed, the majority of brand names were dropped. Some brand named products are still sold, mainly those which are new and still under the effective monopoly of some TNC.

While promotion was still allowed for OTC drugs made by local manufacturers, it virtually disappeared for drugs imported by the SPC. With the disappearance of promotion, distribution of free samples, hospitality and visits by representatives also practically stopped. The problem then arose, as Stetler put it, that:

> the information function on drug research and applicability now performed by companies through their medical and marketing representatives [was] eliminated. Doctors and pharmacists in remote locations, and even in urban areas, may be hard put to fill this information gap (p. 5).

Stetler was certainly right that an 'information gap' was created. The SPC has attempted to fill the gap by publishing and distributing two quarterlies: one edited by the Formulary Committee, called *The Prescriber*, and the other edited by the Independent Medical Practitioners' Association (private practitioners), called *The Sri Lanka Practitioner*. These publications carry the latest information on the rational use of drugs, drawing upon the state of the art and science internationally, and contain scientific findings on the indications, contra-indications and adverse reactions to drugs. While they are not as glossy or as seductive as the TNCs' promotional literature, the following points favour their use as a means of disseminating information:

(a) With the reduced list of drugs and the use of generic names, the need for information had also been greatly reduced . The flow of 'new' drugs is far less than under the free market system. The removal of the profusion of brand names makes the task of informing much easier.

(b) The information provided by TNCs is not renowned for its objectivity. It is intended to persuade as well as inform, and often contains exaggerated claims, suppression of adverse reactions, wrong indications and the implicit denigration of competitors' products. The potential for misinformation is much greater in LDCs, where authorities are relatively lax. Silverman (1976) has collected a horrifying compendium of data on the misinformation practised by US drug companies in Latin America, greatly extending and strengthening earlier findings by Ledogar (1975). He describes, for seven major categories of pharmaceuticals, the variety of labelling and promotional practices used in different Latin American countries as compared to the US. He concludes,

> It is abundantly clear that there are glaring differences in the ways in which the same multinational pharmaceutical companies describe essentially the same drug products to physicians in the United States and to their medical colleagues in Latin America. This holds not only for global corporations headquartered in the United States. It is true also for such companies based in Switzerland, France, West Germany and other nations. . . . With few exceptions, the indications included [in Latin America] in the reference books are far more extensive, but the listing of hazards are curtailed, glossed over, or totally omitted. In some cases, only trivial side effects are described, while serious or possibly fatal reactions are not mentioned.[37]

A strong case can, therefore, be made for official control of this 'information function' even in the absence of broader reform. In the context of a broad reform, of course, the case is overwhelming.

(c) Official information provision can be done far more cheaply than TNCs' promotion. As it is the consumer who pays in either case, there are certainly grounds for economising on this score. The SPC has decided to provide, in partnership with the Ministry of Health, the two 'official' publications free of charge to all medical practitioners.

The people in Sri Lanka who are unhappiest about the abolition of private drug promotion have been the local detailmen and importers, for whom it had provided a comfortable livelihood. Many private practitioners are not happy about the loss of free samples and glossy, easily-digestible literature on new drugs. However, it is not an issue which can be publicly aired – diverting their annoyance into complaints about drug quality – and a number of them accept the social desirability of channelling information through neutral publications. In fact, the SPC publishes such a journal on behalf of the private practitioners, spiking the guns of those who would argue for a return to the old system.

V THE ACHIEVEMENTS

We have already described the achievements of the reform in terms of reducing the number of drugs and abolishing brand names. This section will deal with some of the more tangible benefits.

Table 9.1 shows for a few selected drugs the savings achieved by the centralised purchase of finished pharmaceuticals. It shows the number of private sector suppliers before the SPC takeover and the number of tenders received for the drug after; the average weighted price paid before and the tender price after; the value of the SPC purchases for the second half of 1972 and the percentage savings achieved over what the same purchases would have cost under the old system. In 1972 the SPC took over the import of 52 drugs, and achieved an overall saving of over 40 per cent; some of the drugs shown in the table have been selected to show more dramatic savings.

It should be noted that the number of tenders received was always higher than the number of actual suppliers' pre-takeover. The SPC was able to introduce a much stronger competitive element into the market than had existed previously. The bulk of its savings resulted, however, simply from 'shopping around' and disregarding brand names and, where relevant, patent protection. In most cases, moreover, the lowest tender was *not* accepted. The very cheapest suppliers tended to be of dubious quality and manufacturing practice, and the SPC always got independent certification of quality before awarding a tender. Even so, the savings were considerable.

The benefit to the consumer showed up directly in price reductions. As distribution and retail margins have been determined for some time by the government, a reduction in c.i.f. prices led to a proportionate reduction in the final price to the patient.

A glance at Table 9.2 shows that similar savings were achieved in the import of pharmaceutical chemicals for local formulation. We remarked earlier on the fact that some of these imports were previously from the parent companies of the subsidiaries (Pfizer and Glaxo), and high prices were simply the clandestine transfer of profits abroad. However, it should be apparent that high prices reflect not so much the existence of transnational investments and intra-firm operations as that of a strong element of monopoly power in the final product market, based on the technological and marketing practices of the large firms. Thus, Beecham was able to charge an independent local firm extremely high prices for Cloxacillin and Ampicillin. Yet, when faced by the prospect of competition in a market where its brand name did not matter and where the buyer had information on alternatives, it was prepared to cut its prices by about 80 per cent in each case.

If bids submitted by the traditional TNC suppliers are an indication

TABLE 9.1 Savings achieved by the SPC takeover of finished drug imports (1972) (Ceylon rupees)

	Private Sector (First half 1972)			SPC (Second half 1972)			
	No. of Suppliers	Average Weighted Price	Unit	No. of tenders	Actual Price	Value of Purchase (Rs. 000)	Savings %
1. Tetracycline Capsules (250 mg)	23	74.26	1000s	44	40.77	531.5	45.1
2. Chloramphenicol Caps (250 mg)	12	64.88	1000s	41	46.26	208.2	28.7
3. Sulphadimidine tabs.	7	22.62	1000s	31	11.60	112.7	48.7
4. Neomycin tabs.	2	791.80	1000s	9	149.0	1.8	81.2
5. Phenylbutazone tabs. (100 mg)	5	43.09	1000s	36	7.48	7.7	82.6
6. Phenylbutazone (200 mg)	8	79.88	1000s	37	11.76	33.2	85.3
7. Chloroquine tabs.	6	41.68	1000s	34	28.23	14.1	32.3
8. Metronidazole tabs.	5	170.02	1000s	21	22.26	17.7	86.9
9. Aspirin tabs.	7	8.50	1000s	32	3.14	40.8	63.1
10. Chlorpromazine (25 mg) tabs.	2	48.86	1000s	29	6.30	3.1	87.1
11. Hydrochlorothiazide tabs.	1	139.40	1000s	3	10.98	3.3	92.2
12. Tolbutamide tabs.	1	55.80	1000s	19	16.00	4.0	71.3

NOTE
Rate of exchange (1972): US $ = Ceylon rupees 6.18

TABLE 9.2 Sri Lanka: imports of intermediate chemicals by the private sector, 1972 and by the SPC, 1973 comparison of costs per kilo and savings by SPC (US$)

Intermediate Chemical	Private Sector 1972		SPC 1973		Savings as % of Original Cost
	Supplier	CIF Cost per kilo	Supplier	CIF Cost per kilo	
1. Tolbutamide	Hoechst	40.62	Hoechst	19.24	52.6
2. Paracetamol	Sterling	3.24	Polfa	2.52	93.8
3. Chlorpropamide	Pfizer	126.21	Phone Poulenc	2.76	14.8
4. Aspirin	Glaxo	1.16	Pliva	9.46	92.5
5. Magnesium Hydroxide	Sterling	5.18	Polfa	0.99	14.7
6. Prednisolone	Organon	632.68	Nichiman	0.61	88.2
7. Chloramphenicol	Boehringer	25.24	Roussell	321.77	49.1
8. Cloxacillin	Beecham	606.47	Lepetit	15.46	38.7
9. Ampicillin	Beecham	569.90	Beecham	135.96	77.6
10. Tetracycline	Pfizer	98.87	Beecham	95.11	83.3
11. Chlorpheniranime	Glaxo	411.00	Hoechst	19.72	80.1
			Halewood	52.53	87.3

of what they would have continued to charge Sri Lanka, it appears that the SPC has continued to save considerable sums of foreign exchange year after year. In fact, as its tendering procedures have got more efficient and broad-based, the market it faces has become more competitive. Furthermore, as the organisation has grown (employment has risen from 103 in 1973 to 330 in 1976), it has become financially completely self-reliant. It pays market rates of interest, a 'contribution' to the government as well as taxes, and has made a healthy profit every period from the second year of its operation.

Let us say a few words on the benefits received by banning or restricting the use of particular drugs. Ledogar (1975) in his study of the drug TNCs in Latin America, names some drugs which were exceptionally toxic, but which were being promoted and sold without proper warning. Let us look at a few examples to see how the reform helped Sri Lanka.

a. Dithiazanine iodide
By the mid-1960s this drug had been banned in the US and France. Yet 'In the areas outside the jurisdiction of the FDA, Pfizer's marketing tactics have not been interfered with in the same way. Under brand names like NETOCYD and DILBRIN, the drug was being promoted in many countries of Latin America as late as 1974 as a broad-spectrum anti-parasitic agent'.[38] Pfizer was also promoting its extensive use in Sri Lanka up to 1972, when the National Formulary Committee banned it on the basis of US evidence.

b. Dipyrone
A painkiller with toxic side effects, which is severely restricted in its use in the US and banned in Australia. Yet it is sold by several TNCs in Latin America as a completely safe analgesic. In 1972, Winthrop's CONMEL was the twentieth most popular ethical drug in Colombia. Its use has been banned in Sri Lanka, except in the injectable form, rarely used, for bringing down high fever in patients who cannot take oral medication.

c. Long-acting sulfonamides
Again a drug which is banned or severely restricted in the US and many European countries, because of the associated fatal Stevens–Johnson syndrome and other severe allergic reactions, but heavily promoted and sold without adequate warning in Latin America. It was removed in Sri Lanka, but after a long battle with the drug companies, in which the

doctors, armed with literature provided by the detailmen, sided with the firms.

Other examples could be given, but we have made our point. Let us now conclude our discussion of the political economy of TNC reform.

VI CONCLUSIONS

What have we learnt from the Sri Lanka experience? And are the lessons valuable for other LDCs?

First, Sri Lanka has benefited in several significant ways from its reform of the international drug industry. Drugs are much cheaper. Undesirable and ineffective drugs have been excluded. Prescribing practice should show more rationality once the effects of the cumulative promotion of the firms have been counteracted.

Second, the process of reform is extremely complex and difficult. But it *can* be successfully implemented given an appropriate combination of technical skills, a strong and socialist-minded government, gradual, carefully planned and well-propagated change, and insistence on quality assurance.

Third, reform is much easier in terms of controlling imports of finished drugs than pharmaceutical chemicals, not because of the nature of the product but because of the attitudes of the TNCs concerned. They are willing to bid in world-wide tenders and occasionally sell cheap drugs, but they resent any attempt to channel their intra-firm trade through the state. It follows that the larger the direct investment of TNCs in a particular country, the more difficult it will be to implement reform of local production. Sri Lanka found it relatively easy to change the *status quo* simply because the structure was small and undeveloped.

Fourth, TNCs can bring several sorts of pressure to bear upon even the most committed government. They can use threats and persuasion from abroad; they can get their home government to support them in cases where nationalisation is threatened; they can restrict their future investments; and, most important, they can use their powerful alliance with doctors.

Fifth, even without pressure from TNCs, doctors are reluctant to accept a reformed drug delivery system. There are real problems posed by quality of cheap drugs and bio-equivalence which governments must face and overcome. Doctors must be persuaded that the new system is trustworthy, and their conversion needs time, education and determination. Furthermore, since they are used to a powerful promotion system, which has to be replaced by a less attractive, but cheaper and more objective, information-provision system, the change has to be gradual.

Sixth, locally-owned industry has proved amenable to reform in Sri Lanka, but this is no indication of how it would react in countries where it is larger, better established, and able to promote its own drugs effectively. It is likely that in a country where it is profitable and successful (as in Argentina), it would fight reform, especially of the marketing system, just as hard as TNCs do. This does not rule out the likelihood that local firms would support partial reforms which strengthened their position *vis-à-vis* foreign competitors. (The proposed Indian reforms clearly have this sort of flavour.)

Seventh, the local elite and the doctors accepted this and other radical reforms in Sri Lanka due largely to the mass pressure which had installed a socialist government in a land-slide electoral victory in 1970. The importance of political direction cannot be overemphasised: the SPC made its major achievements before 1975, when the government had a unified socialist ideology. From 1975 onwards the government shifted its course, succumbed to local and foreign vested interests and enabled the critics to slow down or halt the pace of reform, especially as far as local production was concerned. With the reemergence of right-wing forces, it is to be expected that the elite, and especially the medical establishment, will try to revert to the old system of TNC – dominated drug provision. The lessons of this are of vital significance: it is difficult to imagine a government in a developing country undertaking or implementing a genuine programme of reforming drug TNCs without a long-term and powerful socialistic base and ideology. The internal and external constellation of opposing forces would otherwise be too strong.

Finally, the development of domestic industry is not adversely affected by reform at early stages of development, since a great deal of the technology is widely available and there are few economies of scale (so capital requirements are low). At later stages, however, a cutting of TNC investment and technology may be more of a real threat, and has to be carefully considered. Economies of scale do become important in the production of intermediate chemicals, and the technology is often monopolistically held.

There are clearly all sorts of lessons to be learnt by other LDCs, by comparison and by contrast. Pakistan's generic name experiment failed, for instance, because sufficient attention was not given to factors such as quality control, the persuasion of doctors, the resistance of TNC subsidiaries and the attitudes of elite consumers. We may anticipate these very problems in India, where major reforms have been proposed by the Hathi Committee – plus those posed by a strong local private sector which would want to preserve brand names, and the need to find technology and capital abroad. We may draw all sorts of conclusions about why reform failed in Brazil, and will not even be undertaken in Mexico or Argentina. These remarks do not mean that we believe reform is not desirable in these areas. On the contrary, the present system is patently failing to meet the medicinal needs of their populations, and comprehensive reform seems to us to be the only solution. However, the process would be far more difficult than in Sri Lanka, and it is only wise to be aware of this. The political–economic climate at this time does not bode well.

POSTSCRIPT: DEVELOPMENTS IN 1977

The trends which became evident in late 1976 seem, unfortunately, to have strengthened in the first four months of this year. After the Sri Lanka Communist Party left the coalition government in protest over its handling of a general strike at the end of 1976, the swing to the right has become even more pronounced. By the end of February some Parliamentarians of the Sri Lanka Freedom Party had resigned from the government. More significantly, the Minister of Industries, a stalwart supporter of the SPC, also left on the issue of the right-wing policies of the Prime Minister; he specifically stated that, among other things, he had recommended the takeover of drug TNCs but the proposal had been shelved. Dr Bibile resigned from the chairmanship of the SPC, protesting over the lack of government support for SPC policies and the growing bitterness of the opposition from vested interests. He also remarked on the increase of disenchantment among the staff of the Corporation, and the danger that this may lead to a deterioration in its former levels of efficiency, honesty and dedication. The coming few months will decide whether or not Sri Lanka retains the valuable gains of the reform, and whether or not the TNCs and their supporters can re-establish their former hegemony.

NOTES

* The authors are grateful to the State Pharmaceuticals Corporation, Sri Lanka, for permission to publish the findings of their research into its operations and to T. Attapattu for collecting statistical material. They wish

to thank Ajit Singh for comments on an earlier draft. They retain full responsibility for the contents of this paper.

1. For critiques see Lall (1975), Klass (1975), Ledogar (1975) and Silverman (1976), and for the defense see Reekie (1975). A balanced and concise exposition of the US situation is provided by Measday (1971).
2. For a discussion and references see Lall and Streeten (1977).
3. See Bibile (1977) for a detailed description.
4. And had used in the developed countries in the years of early excess. Furthermore, various US Senate hearings, especially those under Kennedy in 1974, show that many of these excesses still continue today. On the UK see the Sainsbury Committee (1967), Coleman (1975); on Canada see Klass (1975); on Germany see Möbius et al. (1976). The evidence suggests that the US is subjected to the greatest amount of high pressure promotion; the UK has experienced a fairly sharp fall in promotion expenditures recently, as has West Germany, as a result of strict official control. These expenditures are, however, still quite large (12–15 per cent of sales in the UK) and the governments concerned are trying to reduce them further.
5. See Ledogar (1975) and Silverman (1976) on Latin America and the Hathi Committee (1975) on India. For a more general discussion see Lall (1975 and 1978) and the Haslemere Group (1976).
6. This often led to the situation that when particular prescribed brands were not available patients were deprived of that drug, or had to engage in long searches, when hospital dispensaries and private pharmacies had stocks of identical medicines under different brand names. In some cases doctors unwittingly substituted one brand of a drug for another, which had identical effects, in the belief that they were changing the treatment. See Bibile (1977).
7. Most hospitals in developed countries use such Formularies and try to encourage prescribing by generic names, but they have to wage a constant battle against the promotion of the companies. Given that such promotion costs are between 15–30 per cent of sales, it is easy to imagine the difficulties that hospitals face in mounting a counter-education programme. In Sri Lanka, there was considerable opposition to the rationalisation of any purchasing and dispensing from drug companies and doctors, which reappeared in more violent form later.
8. We have no record of the number of brands then on the Sri Lanka market, but it may have ranged between 10,000–15,000. India had some 15,000 drugs in the early 1970s (see Hathi Committee, 1975), Brazil and Spain between 20,000 and 30,000, the US even more.
9. Information taken from data on private sector purchasing collected by the State Pharmaceuticals Corporation for early 1972. For a study of the antibiotic market in the US, where for well-established and out-of-patent drugs the more expensive branded products invariably dominate the market, see Brooke (1975). So strong is this trend that Brook finds a statistically significant relationship between the price of a product and its market share: the higher the drug price, the larger the market share, with *no therapeutic or quality difference* between the different products. Such 'pure' examples of product differentiation must be extremely rare, with price differences of up to 1000 per cent for scientifically-proven identical products being sustained over many years.

10. Wickremasinghe and Bibile (1971).
11. Wickremasinghe and Bibile (1971), table II Of the 4 most important categories of drugs examined, the cost of analgesics and antirheumatics (Rs. 4.9m.) would have been cut by 88 per cent, antimicrobials (Rs. 3.7m.) by 52 per cent, antidiabetics (Rs. 0.8m.) by 87 per cent and antihistamines (Rs. 0.5m.) by 79 per cent.
12. The problem of 'bio-equivalence' or 'bio-availability', i.e. of whether different drugs which are generically equivalent have the identical therapeutic effects, is one of the major difficulties in rationalising drugs and using cheap generic sources. We shall return to this below, but we should note here that proof of bio-equivalence, and convincing doctors of its validity, is crucial to the launching of a reform programme.
13. Studies by the US Food and Drug Administration, based on exhaustive reviews of the literature and clinical trials, have found that up to 60 per cent of prescription drugs and (based on a smaller sample) up to 75 per cent of OTC drugs lacked evidence of effectiveness (see references in Rucker (1973)). Many of these drugs have been withdrawn from the US market, but continue to be sold in markets with less strict supervision, not only in LDCs, but also in the UK. See Lall (1975).
14. These dangers and costs are: over-prescribing of drugs, inappropriate use of drugs, lack of awareness of adverse effects of particular drugs, and prescribing of drugs regardless of economic considerations. For further discussion, evidence and references see Lall (1975), Silverman (1976), Rucker (1973) and Speight (1975).
15. We have examples of each of these possibilities. In Pakistan, the abolition of brand names in 1973 was undertaken by a left-wing minister; it was introduced too suddenly, the requisite tests, quality control and re-education of doctors were not undertaken, the public was not properly informed, and the experiment failed. In the UK, Labour Minister of Health sought to implement the Sainsbury proposals, and the government/civil service certainly had the requisite expertise, but the opposition of the industry and the civil service led to a weak compromise solution (see Lang (1974)). In Brazil, a nationalist military group abolished drug patents in 1969 and set up the Central de Medicamentos (CEME) in 1971 to provide cheap, basic drugs to the poor; a change of government and an ideological reversal considerably emasculated its original aims (see Ledogar (1975) and Evans (1976)).
16. The 'symbiotic' relationship between the drug manufacturers and pre-scribers is an obstacle to reform which has been widely noted in developed as well as less-developed countries. In Pakistan, doctors and elite consumers were vociferously opposed to the generic scheme; in India, several doctors have attacked the Hathi Committee's proposals to introduce generic names (for a typical reaction, see Datey (1975)).
17. Some of these deletions are described, and the pharmological justification explained, in Bibile (1977).
18. This is one of the most common arguments used in the US by the drug industry to oppose the FDA's efforts to rationalise prescribing practices and achieve economies in government drug purchases: a profitable line of defence, since it permits the drug firms to indulge in heavy brand-name

promotion of expensive drugs when this constitutes the primary source of doctors' information on new medicines. (See Lall (1975), Coleman (1975) and Klass (1975) as well as the various US Senate Hearings). The objectivity and scientific basis of the knowledge on which 'professional judgement' as regards the therapeutic value of alternative drugs is based is open to question, especially in LDCs where official control is far less stringent than in developed countries. The very fact that such control had to be imposed in the latter testifies to the risks inherent in situations where the drug companies have a relatively free hand: some of the risks are mentioned below.

19. This was the case with soluble aspirin, which has no therapeutic advantage over ordinary aspirin but costs three times more. The detailmen for local TNC subsidiaries concerned mounted an intensive campaign, via the private practitioners, to have the drug retained. So powerful was this campaign that the National Formulary Committee was forced to retain the drug, which, backed by persuasive but misleading advertising to the public, continues to dominate the private aspirin market.

20. By 1975 the market shares of various supplying countries had changed dramatically as compared to pre-SPC days in early 1973: the UK supplied 16 per cent of imports (47 per cent in 1973), the US 2 per cent (16 per cent); India 17 per cent (7 per cent); Hong Kong 6 per cent (0.5 per cent); Japan 7 per cent (0.2 per cent); and Poland, Hungary and Czechoslovakia together 10 per cent (0.4 per cent). Switzerland and West Germany proved themselves to be competitive and maintained their former shares of 7–9 per cent, though of course some former TNC suppliers were replaced by small generic manufacturers from these countries.

21. An important fact noted by Brooke (1975) about the US antibiotic market is that many large firms buy finished drugs from small manufacturers but sell them under their own brands at much higher prices than their suppliers. It is not surprising, therefore, that these suppliers would not want to openly undercut 'big brothers' in the world market.

22. Page 5 of Mr C. J. Stetler's letter, dated 10 May 1973, to the Prime Minister of Sri Lanka. Points 3–5 of the letter are quoted later in appropriate places.

23. FDA, *Federal Register* (1975) vol. 40, no. 120, p. 26147. Brooke (1975) shows for antibiotics how a few firms manufacture the pharmaceutical chemical for others, who then formulate and package it to sell under their own brands. The name itself cannot be taken to establish the quality of the real manufacturer.

24. The cost of promotion per doctor in the US came to about $5000 per annum around 1970 (see Measday (1971) p. 176), the bulk of it on detailmen. There are about 10 doctors per detailman in the US, as compared to 5 in Colombia and only 3 in Mexico, Guatemala and Brazil (Silverman (1976) p. 122) – a striking illustration of the relative intensity of promotion and image-building in LDCs. Figures for promotion in Sri Lanka prior to 1972 are not available, but on a very rough estimate the value of free samples alone may have approached Rs. 1000 per doctor per month in busy urban areas. This sum represents about half the value of the monthly salary of a medium-level civil servant.

25. The SPC found that the installed capacity (single-shift) of the seven large

producers could manufacture 750 million tablets annually but was only producing 300 million; the total tablet requirements of Sri Lanka were 1000 million. Similarly, installed capacity for capsules was 40 million, actual production was 6 million and total requirements were 120 million. Thus, the entire requirements of tablets and capsules could have been met by increasing the number of shifts to two or three without adding further capacity; Sri Lanka would have saved considerable foreign exchange by formulating and packaging pharmaceuticals domestically.

26. '34 Drug Programme: A Summary of Negotiations with Local Manufacturers', S. M. Edirimanasinghe, Managing Director, SPC (23 Nov. 1974). The outcome of Pfizer refusing to encapsulate SPC imported material (from Hoechst of West Germany) during the epidemic was that the tetracycline lay unused in SPC stores and Pfizer equipment lay idle, while tetracycline capsules had to be airlifted to the country at enormous expense.
27. Ledogar (1975) pp. 63–4.
28. However, the unrestricted marketing and pricing activities of the TNCs in spite of patent abolition, leads, in these countries, to internal drug prices being relatively high. The real advantages of patent abolition only show up when, as in Sri Lanka, the importing and marketing function is also rationalised.
29. This is discussed at greater length in Lall (1978).
30. For a summary discussion of bio-equivalence see Brooke (1975), and for an exhaustive study of the US see the OTA (1974).
31. Bibile (1976).
32. Mahendra (1976).
33. OTA (1974).
34. ibid., emphasis added.
35. Brooke (1975) p. 42.
36. Because of the gradual pace of change and the retention of brand names on some locally manufactured drugs, the SPC avoided an all-out battle with local firms. In Pakistan, however, the local subsidiaries of TNCs opposed the generic scheme bitterly; Ciba-Geigy even sold out its local operations in 1973 in protest, and 'pressure from other firms led to extended permission of the use of brand-named products for 18 months after the implementation of the Act' (Heller (1977) p. 59). Thus, hasty and inadequate planning was compounded by poor political strategy.
37. Silverman (1976) p. 106. He also reports on several fatalities which have resulted from these practices; and notes that they are common throughout the world.
38. Ledogar (1975) pp. 30–1.

REFERENCES

Bibile, S. (1976), 'Tetracyclines in Sri Lanka', *The Prescriber* (Dec.).
—— (1977), *Pharmaceutical Policies in Sri Lanka* (Geneva: UNCTAD) TD/B/C.6/21.
Brooke, P. A. (1975), *Resistant Prices: A Study of Competitive Strains in the Antibiotic Markets* (New York: Council on Economic Priorities).
Coleman, V. (1975), *The Medicine Men* (London: Temple Smith).

Datey, K. K. (1975), 'A doctor diagnoses dangers of brand abolition', *Eastern Economist* (20 June) pp. 1298–301.
Evans, P. B. (1976), 'Foreign investment and industrial transformation: a Brazilian case study', *Journal of Development Economics*, pp. 119–39.
Haslemere Group (1976), *Who Needs the Drug Companies?* (London: Haslemere Group).
Hathi Committee (1975), *Report of the Committee on Drugs and Pharmaceutical Industry* (New Delhi: Ministry of Petroleum and Chemicals).
Heller, T. (1977), *Poor Health, Rich Profits: Multinational Drug Companies and the Third World* (London: Spokesman Books).
Klass, A. (1975), *There's Gold in Them Thar Pills* (Harmondsworth: Penguin).
Lall, S. (1975), *Major Issues in Transfer of Technology to Developing Countries: A Case Study of the Pharmaceutical Industry* (Geneva: UNCTAD) TD/B/C.6/4.
—— (1978), *The Growth of the Pharmaceutical Industry in Developing Countries: Problems and Prospects* (UN Industrial Development Organisation, Vienna) ID/204.
Lall, S. and Streeten, P. P. (1977), *Foreign Investment, Transnationals and Development Countries* (London: Macmillan).
Lang, R. W. (1974), *The Politics of Drugs: A Comparative Study of the British and Canadian Pharmaceutical Industries, 1930–73* (London: Saxon House).
Ledogar, R. J. (1975), *Hungry for Profits: The US Food and Drug Multinationals in Latin America* (New York: IDOC/North America).
Mahendra, M. (1976), 'Resistance to tetracycline', *The Sri Lanka Practitioner*, no. 37.
Measday, W. (1971), 'The pharmaceutical industry', in W. Adams (ed.), *The Structure of American Industry* (New York: Macmillan).
Möbius, K., Seusing, E. and Ahnefeld, A. (1976), *Die Pharmazeutiche Industrie in der Bundesrepublik Deutchland* (Tübingen: J. C. B. Mohr).
OTA (1974), *Drug Bioequivalence – A Report of the OTA Bioequivalence Study Panel* (Washington DC: Office of Technology Assessment, Government Printing Office).
Reekie, W. D. (1975), *The Economics of the Pharmaceutical Industry* (London: Macmillan).
Rucker, T. D. (1973), 'Economic aspects of drug overuse', *Medical Annals of the District of Columbia* (Dec.) pp. 609–14.
Sainsbury Committee (1967), *Report of the Committee of Enquiry into the Relationship of the Pharmaceutical Industry with the NHS, 1965–67* (London: HMSO).
Segall, M. (1975), 'Pharmaceuticals and health planning in developing countries' (Univ. of Sussex, Institute of Development Studies, Communication 119).
Silverman, M. (1976), *The Drugging of the Americas* (Berkeley: University of California Press).
Speight, N., 'Cost effectiveness and drug therapy', *Tropical Doctor* (Apr. 1975) pp. 89–92.
Wickremasinghe, S. A. and Bibile, S. (1971), *The Management of Pharmaceuticals in Ceylon* (Colombo: Industrial Development Board of Ceylon). Summary published in the *British Medical Journal* (1971) no. 3.

Author Index

N.B. 'n' indicates that author is mentioned in a note. The page number refers to the main text.

Adam, G., 33n, 34n, 57
Adams, J. D. R., 154n, 156
Adams, W. J., 44n, 57
Adelman, M. A., 96n, 108
Agmon, T., 70n, 88
Agrawal, J. P., 50, 57
Agrawal, P. S., 180n, 182n, 183n, 184n, 196
Allen, T. W., 49, 57
Arpan J. S., 145n, 156
Arrow, K. J. 97n, 108

Baerresen, D. W., 35n, 57
Bailey, E. L., 24n, 27
Bain, J. S., 37n, 57
Balasubramanyam, U. N., 46, 50, 57
Baranson, J., 32, 32n, 48, 57
Barker, B. L., 135
Barnet, R. J., 40n, 57
Barrett, M. E., 145n, 157
Baumann, H. G., 4n, 27, 50n, 57
Bell, R., 47n, 49, 58
Bergsten, C. F., 3n, 27
Bhagwati, J., 111n, 113n, 115, 135
Bhalla, A. S., 44n, 47n, 57
Bibile, S., 206n, 210n, 218n–20n, 227n, 236n, 254
Blair, J. M., 96n, 108
Board of Trade Journal, 123n, 135
Booth, E. J. R., 148n, 157
Borghey, M., 31n, 58
Bradshaw, M. T., 94n, 95n, 108, 121n, 135

Brooke, M. Z., 110, 113, 114, 135
Brooke, P. A., 204–5n, 215, 220n, 229n, 231n, 236n, 240n, 254
Buckley, P. J., 6, 27, 97n, 104n, 108, 142, 157
Business Week 148n, 157

Cain, J. C., 167n, 196
Casson, M., 97n, 108
Caves, R. E., 4n, 10, 11n, 13n, 27, 38n, 43n, 58, 65–7, 71–3, 88–9
Chang, Y. S., 34n, 58
Chudnovsky, D., 39n–40n, 58
Cohen, B., 49, 58
Coleman, V., 218n, 227n, 254
Comanor, W. S., 10n, 24n, 27, 107, 109, 165n, 166, 196
Connor, J. M., 65n, 78n, 89
Cooper, C., 47n, 49, 58
Cooper, M. H., 167n, 171n, 177n, 196, 201n, 215
Copithorne, Z. W., 112n, 113, 135
Corden, W. M., 7n, 27
Courtney, W. H., 48, 58
Ceyhun, F., 3n, 6n, 10, 18, 27

Daftary, F., 31n, 58
DANE, 124n, 135
Datey, K. K., 225n, 255
De Groot, G., 35, 35n, 58
De Jong, F. J., 38n, 40n, 58
De Jong, H. W., 58, 97n, 109, 139n, 157

Author Index

De La Torre, J., 34n, 58
Duerr, M. G., 112n, 116n, 119n, 135, 145n, 157
Dunning, J. H., 3n, 4n, 6–7n, 8n, 11n, 27, 43n, 58, 65n, 89, 97n, 105n, 109, 110, 135
Dyas, G. P., 37n, 58

Economist, The, 166n, 168n, 175n, 196
El Tiempo, 179n, 196
Evans, P. B., 39n, 58, 65n, 67n, 89, 223n, 255
Evers, B., 35, 35n, 58

Fajnzylber, F., 39n, 45, 50, 59
Ferguson, D. G., 7n, 27
Fernandez, R. A., 35n, 59
Finan, N., 34n, 35n, 59
Financial Times, 164n, 168n, 196
Finger, J. M., 34n, 59, 140n, 157
Forsyth, D. J. C., 39, 45, 45n, 47, 51, 59
Foster, S. B., 120, 136

Gaude, J., 47n, 49n, 59
George, K. D., 66n, 78n, 89
Gershenberg, I. 42, 44, 51, 59
Ghosh, A. 37, 37n, 59, 66n, 75n, 89
Golemis, C. P. 137n, 157
Goodman, B., 3n, 6n, 10, 18, 27
Graham, P., 147n, 157
Greene, J., 112n, 116n, 136, 145n, 157
Grubel, H. G., 6n, 27
Gruber, W. H., 8n, 10n, 27
Guardian 170n, 172n, 174n, 196
Gupta, A., 184n, 196
Gupta, V. E., 37n, 59

Harris, S. E., 163, 196
Haslemere Group, 218n, 255
Hathi Committee, 218n–19n, 255
Hazari, R. K., 37n, 59
Helleiner, G. K., 33n–5n, 43n, 48n–9n, 51n, 59, 99n, 109, 124, 136, 140n, 157

Heller, T., 241n, 255
Hellinger, D., 48n, 59
Hellinger, S., 48n, 59
Henning, J. A., 66n, 89
Hewett, E. A., 35n, 59
Hirsch, S., 5n–7n, 7, 11n, 28, 34n, 59, 97n, 104n, 109
Hirschman, A. O., 29n–30n, 30n, 59
Hone, A., 34n, 59
Horowitz, I., 37n, 60
Horst, T., 3n, 4n, 6, 10, 15, 18, 28, 37n–8n, 43n, 60, 65n, 67n, 78n, 89, 113, 136
Howe, W. S., 97n, 109
Hufbauer, G. C., 6n, 28, 31n, 60, 110, 128n, 136
Hymer, S., 4, 43n, 60

Intriligator, M. D., 5n, 10n, 13n, 66n, 71n, 75n, 90

Jacquemin, A. P., 97n, 109, 139n, 157
Jo, Sung-Hwan, 31n, 40n, 46, 50, 60
Johnson, H. G., 110, 128, 136, 167n, 196
Jones, R. W., 7n, 11, 28

Kaplinsky, R., 47n, 49, 58
Katz, J., 39n, 60
Keegan, W. J., 116n, 119n, 136
Kefauver, E., 162n, 169n, 171, 196
Kidron, M., 40n, 60, 182n, 185n, 197
Kindleberger, C. P., 4n, 28, 97n, 109, 110, 128, 136
Klass, A., 216n, 218n, 227n, 255
Knickerbocker, F. T., 8n, 28, 67n, 89
König, W., 35n, 36n, 65
Kopits, G. F., 42n, 60, 137n, 148n, 157

Lake, A., 60
Lall, S., 29n, 31n, 32n, 34n, 35n, 40n, 42n, 42–4, 43n, 46, 47n, 50, 60, 144n, 147n, 152n, 157, 199n, 200n, 209n, 215, 216n–18n, 221n, 235n, 255

Author Index

Lang, R. W., 173n, 193, 223n, 255
Lecraw, D., 70n, 89
Ledogar, R., 216n, 218n, 223n, 234n, 243, 247, 247n, 255
Leftwich, R. B., 42n, 60
Leipziger, D. M., 48, 50, 60-1
Leroy, G., 21n, 28
Lim, D., 44n, 47n, 61
Lim, L., 34n-5n, 36, 42n, 61
Little, I. M. D., 33n, 61
Lloyd, P. J., 6n 27

McBain, N. S., 47n
McLinden, J. E., 61
Magee, S. P., 7n, 28, 97n, 104n, 109
Mahendra, M., 234n, 240n, 255
Mann, H. M., 66n, 89
Mason, R. H., 31n, 49, 61
Measday, W., 216n, 231n, 255
Mehta, D., 8n, 10n, 28
Meller, P., 37n, 44n, 46n, 61
Merrett, S., 44n, 61
Michalet, C. A., 33n-4n, 61
Ministry of Foreign Trade (GOI), 180n, 182n, 197
Mobius, K., 218n, 255
Monopolies Commission, 119n, 125, 163n, 165n, 169n-71n, 173n, 175n, 179n, 197, 199n, 215
Moran, T., 3n, 27
Morawetz, D., 47n, 61
Morley, S. A., 49, 61
Morrison, T. K., 34n, 61
Mote, V. L., 180n, 184n, 197
Mueller, W. F., 38-41, 62, 65n, 78n, 90
Müller, R., 40n, 61

Nam, W. H., 66n, 89
National Science Foundation, 24, 107
NEDO, 163n, 173n, 197
Needham, D., 38n, 61
Negandhi, A., 43n, 62
Newfarmer, R. S., 38-41, 62, 65n, 67n, 68, 90

New Scientist, 170n, 172n, 197

OECD, 44n, 62, 162n-4n, 169n, 180n, 197
OHE, 201n-2n, 215
O'Herlihy, C.St.J., 47n, 49n, 62
Oi, W. Y., 96n, 109
Ornstein, S. I., 5n, 10n, 13n, 28, 66n, 71n, 72n, 75n, 78n, 90
OTA, 205n, 236n, 255
Ottuketkal, 183n, 197

Pack, H., 47n-9n, 51n, 62
Panic, M., 37n, 62
Parker, R. C., 173n-4n, 197
Pathak, H. N., 180n, 184n
Pearce, R. D., 6, 104n, 142, 197
Penrose, E. T., 177n, 178, 178n, 183n, 197
Petras, J., 37n, 62
Phillips, A., 38n, 62
Pickett, J., 47n, 49n, 62
Porter, M. E., 89, 96n-7n, 109
Prasad, B., 43n, 62
Pryor, F., 37n, 62

Ramachandran, P. K., 180n, 182n-4n, 196
Reddaway, W. B., 100, 136
Reekie, W. D., 199n, 201n-3n, 202, 215, 216n, 255
Reidel, J., 35n, 50, 62
Remmers, H. L., 110, 113, 114, 135
Reserve Bank of India, 46n, 62, 180n, 182n, 186n, 197
Reuber, G. L., 31-2, 41n-2n, 48, 61
Robbins, S. M., 42n, 62, 145n-6n, 157
Rose, W. D., 150n, 150, 157
Rosenbluth, G., 65n, 67n, 90
Rosenthal, G., 44, 62
Roumeliotis, P. V., 137n, 157
Rowthorn, R., 38n, 62
Rucker, T. D., 221n, 255

Sabolo, Y., 42n, 62

Author Index

Sahagun, V. M., 35n, 39n, 62–3
Sainsbury Committee, 173n, 197, 218n, 255
Satyarakwit, W., 47n, 49, 58
Sawhney, B. L., 37n, 63
Sawhney, P. K., 37n, 63
Scherer, F. M., 167n–8n, 197
Schifrin, L. G., 163n–4n, 166n–7n, 169n, 173n–5n, 197
Schmalensee, R., 38n, 63
Schwartzman, D., 199n, 215
Scitovsky, T., 30n, 33n, 61
Scrip, 151n, 157
Segall, M., 255
Seusing, E., 218n, 255
Sharpston, M., 33n–5n, 63
Sharwani, K., 37n, 63
Shrieves, R. E., 5n, 10n, 13n, 28, 66n, 72n, 75n, 90
Silverman, M., 216n, 218n, 221n, 231n, 242, 243n, 255
Singh, A., 40n, 63
Slatter, S.St.P., 201n, 215
Smith, G. W., 49, 61
Solomon, R. F., 51, 63
Sourrouille, J. V., 39, 45, 45n, 51, 63
Speight, N., 221n, 255
Steele, H., 164, 167n–72n, 197
Steuer, M., 65n, 67n, 90
Stewart, F., 47n, 48, 63
Stigler, G. J., 96n, 109
Stobaugh, R. B., 42n, 62, 145n–6n, 157
Stopford, J. M., 146n, 157
Strobl, J., 151n, 157
Sunday Times 171n, 197

Thanheiser, H. T., 37n, 58
Thoburn, J. T., 31n, 63
Times, The 171n, 173n, 197
Trade and Industry 164n, 198
Trajtenberg, R., 42n, 62
Tron, J. M., 147n, 157

Tugendhat, C., 113, 118n, 136
UN, 178n, 198
UNCTAD, 34n, 63, 125, 136, 137, 144n, 158
US Tariff Commission, 3n, 12, 24n, 28, 34n, 41, 63, 93n, 94, 94n, 96n, 99n, 109, 140n, 157

Vaitsos, C. V., 31n, 40n, 42n, 45, 49n, 50, 63, 110n, 113, 116, 119, 124n, 125n, 136, 137n, 140n, 144n, 158, 177n–9n, 198
Van Houten, J. F., 35n, 63
Vanlommel, E., 70n, 90
Vernon, R., 7, 7n, 8n, 10n, 11n, 28, 41, 43n, 63, 104n, 109, 110, 136
Verlage, H. C., 137n, 154n, 158

Walker, H. D., 163, 163n, 165n, 169n, 171n, 198
Walker, H. O., 35n, 64
Ward, T. S., 66n, 78n, 89
Watanabe, S., 32, 32n, 33n, 35n, 64
Wells, L. T., 51, 64, 118, 123, 136, 146n, 157
Weston, J. F., 5n, 10n, 13n, 28, 66n, 71n, 72n, 75n, 90
Whalley, J., 154n, 156
White, L. J., 37n, 47n, 51n, 64
Wickremasinghe, S. A., 220n, 255
Wilder, R. P., 169n, 198
Williamson, O. E., 118, 136
Willmore, L., 39, 43, 46, 64
Wilson, T. A., 10n, 24n, 27
Winston, G. C., 111n, 113n, 136
Wolf, B. M., 5, 5n, 15, 21n, 28, 43n, 64, 67n, 90
Wortzel, L. H., 164n, 176n, 177n, 198

Yamey, B. S., 66n, 75n, 90

Zeitlin, M., 37n, 40n, 64

Subject Index

Advertising expenditure
  intensity of, 72–4
  and intra-firm trade by MNCS, 101, 104–5
  and market control, 170–7, 237–43
  in pharmaceutical industry, 169–73
  in Sri Lanka, 218–20, 237, 242
  Transnational Corporation, 18–22
Argentina
  foreign control of manufacturing output, 39
  pharmaceutical patents, 236
  transnational corporations, 39, 45

Barriers to entry
  and advertising expenditure, 153
  and foreign investment, 5, 5n, 7, 22
Brazil
  market concentration in, 39, 65n, 68
  multinational corporation in, 39, 41, 49, 65n, 68
  pharmaceutical industry in, 176–7, 236, 249

Canberra Hypothesis, 201–4
capital intensity, 5, 11, 22, 44–7, 81, 85
Central America
  foreign control of industry in, 39, 46
Chile
  transnational corporations in, 37, 125, 177

Choice of technology
  in LDCs, 47n
  and role of TNCs, 47–51
Colombia
  TNCs in, 31n, 43–4, 247
  transfer-pricing, 119, 124–7
Costa Rica
  TNCs in, 44

Direct foreign investment
  and industrial organisation, 3–4
  and monopolistic advantages, 4–8
  by US MNCs, 3–23

Exchange rates
  and transfer-pricing, 113–14
Exports of manufactures
  from LDCs, 33–7, 43n

Factor mobility
  and pure trade theory, 7–8
Firm size
  and diversification, 5n
Fixed capital assets
  and market size, 75
  as measure of capital intensity, 72
  and US foreign investment, 18–20

Ghana
  TNCs in, 51
GSP privileges, 36
Guatemala
  TNCs in, 39, 44

261

Hoffman La Roche
  advertising practices, 171–2
  in Colombia, 179
  in India, 181, 182–3
  R & D expenditure by, 164–5
  in Sri Lanka, 224, 231–2, 235
  in UK, 164, 168, 175
Hong Kong
  TNC and exports, 35, 35n
Host government policy towards TNCs
  and intra-firm trade, 99, 105
  in Less Developed Countries, 30–7, 150–2
  (i) in India, 184–6
  (ii) lessons from Sri Lanka, 210
  and MNCs, 44, 68, 147–50
  and transfer-pricing, 111–12, 130–2, 143–4, 146, 150–2

India
  capital intensity in industry, 46, 50
  import dependence of industry, 44
  pharmaceutical industry in, 180–6, 188–9, 248
  TNC activity in, 31–5, 40n, 42–3, 115
Industrial market concentration
  determinants of, 4, 66, 73, 77, 81, 84
  in LDCs, 37–9
  in Malaysia, 73–86
  and TNCs, 3, 37–8, 66–9, 77–8, 145
Intra-firm trade
  and conventional trade theory, 93, 105, 128–9
  determinants of, 96–103, 139
  and LDCs, 95–6, 102n, 123, 137–43
  and TNCs, 93–106, 140–3, 232–4, 248
  and transfer-pricing, 93, 110, 118, 120–3
  and UK exports, 123
  and US exports, 121

Iran
  TNCs in, 31n
Jamaica
  TNCs in, 31n
Kenya
  TNCs in, 31n, 49, 51
Malaysia
  industrial concentration in, 73–8, 80–1, 84–6
  TNCs in, 31n, 65–87, 147, 149–50
Market imperfections
  and intra-firm trade, 97
Market size
  and capital intensity, 75
  definition of, 72
Mexico
  TNCs in, 31n, 35n, 38–9, 41, 45, 50, 148
Minimum capital requirement, 72, 75
Minimum Efficient Plant Scale, 71, 74
Monopolistic advantage
  and foreign investment, 7–8, 18–19
  and intra-firm trade, 139–40
  transferability of, 8–12, 22, 138–40
  and US MNCs, 7–28, 67

Pakistan
  drug industry in, 186–7, 249
Patents
  and pharmaceutical industry, 166–9, 176–8, 203, 237
  protection and advertising, 169–71
  in Sri Lanka, 235–7
Peru
  industrial productivity in, 45
  TNCs in, 31n, 50
Pfizer, 223, 232–4, 244, 247
Pharmaceutical industry in LDCs, 176–99, 208–9, 237, 242–3, 247

Subject Index

bioequivalence, 221n, 237–40
  in Sri Lanka, 205–9, 216–49
Political conditions
  and TNC activity, 34, 47–8, 249
  and transfer-pricing, 115, 147–8
Price competition
  in pharmaceutical industry, 200–13
Productivity
  gains and TNCs, 44–7
  measurement of, 44–5
Product Cycle Model, 7–8, 8n, 104, 128
Product differentiation
  and international competitiveness, 5, 6, 11
  and monopolistic control, 5, 10, 22
  in pharmaceutical industry, 169–73, 203–5, 219–20
  and TNCs, 10, 18–23, 31–4

Research and Development (R&D) Expenditure
  and intra-firm trade, 101, 104–5, 139
  in pharmaceutical industry, 152–3, 164–9
  and transfer-pricing, 118–19, 139, 150–2
  and US foreign investment, 14, 18–19

Scale economies
  and foreign investment, 11, 15, 19, 22
  and intra-firm trade, 98, 105
  measures of, 71–2
  in pharmaceutical industry, 164, 249
  and TNCs, 47, 71–3
Singapore
  TNCs in, 35n, 36
South Korea
  TNCs in, 31n, 46, 50

Sri Lanka
  pharmaceutical industry in, 216–55
  TNCs in, 206–7, 209–10, 217–19, 224–30, 242–3

Taiwan
  TNCs in, 35n, 50
Takeovers
  by TNCs, 40–2
Tanzania
  TNCs in, 49
Taxes and tariffs
  and TNCs, 113n, 114n, 119, 148
  and transfer-pricing, 113, 140, 145, 153
Technology
  choice of, 47–51
  intensity and intra-firm trade, 104–6, 138, 140, 144
  and monopolistic advantage, 9–10
  used by TNCs in LDCs, 22–3, 48–50
  transfer of, 34, 234–5
Transfer-pricing
  determinants of, 111–20, 146, 152–4
  implication for LDCs, 127–32
  and intra-firm trade, 93, 100, 137–43, 145
  in LDCs, 116, 137–55, 179
  and maximising profits, 112–14, 117
  in pharmaceutical industry, 144–6, 153–5, 175, 178, 181, 233
  by TNCs, 43, 100, 110, 117–20, 138, 143–6

Uganda
  TNCs in, 42, 44
United Kingdom
  pharmaceutical industry in, 162–71
  TNCs in, 123, 145, 161–2, 171–3
  transfer-pricing by TNCs, 148

United States
  Food and Drug Administration, 172, 199, 205, 216, 227, 230, 239–41
  foreign direct investment in, 120
  foreign involvement by, 3–28
  intra-firm exports by TNCs, 93–109
  pharmaceutical industry in, 161–71, 204–6
  Pharmaceutical Manufacturers Association, 229–30, 230, 234–6, 239–42

Transfer-pricing by TNCs, 148–51

Value-added
  and advertising intensity, 104
  per employee and intra-firm trade, 101, 104–5

Vertical integration
  determinants of, 98–100
  and intra-firm trade, 93, 96–100, 105

Wages
  in LDCs and TNCs, 34

The manufacturer's authorised representative in the EU is Springer Nature Customer Service Centre GmbH, Europaplatz 3, 69115 Heidelberg, Germany. If you have any concerns regarding our products, please contact ProductSafety@springernature.com

Printed and bound by CPI Group (UK) Ltd, Croydon, CR0 4YY

23/03/2026

02076673-0015